ASSEMBLING RELIGION

Assembling Religion

The Ford Motor Company and the
Transformation of Religion in America

Kati Curts

NEW YORK UNIVERSITY PRESS
New York

NEW YORK UNIVERSITY PRESS
New York
www.nyupress.org

Please contact the Library of Congress for Cataloging-in-Publication data.

ISBN: 9781479831586 (hardback)
ISBN: 9781479831616 (library ebook)
ISBN: 9781479831609 (consumer ebook)

This book is printed on acid-free paper, and its binding materials are chosen for strength and durability. We strive to use environmentally responsible suppliers and materials to the greatest extent possible in publishing our books.

The manufacturer's authorized representative in the EU for product safety is Mare Nostrum Group B.V., Mauritskade 21D, 1091 GC Amsterdam, The Netherlands. Email: gpsr@mare-nostrum.co.uk.

Manufactured in the United States of America

10 9 8 7 6 5 4 3 2 1

Also available as an ebook

for my parents *and* for Eme

CONTENTS

Totemic Fording

In the spring of 1947, Henry Ford died. Later retellings of his death would repeat that it was a dark and stormy night. Early April rains had moved in swiftly and aggressively, resulting in a deluge that persisted for several days. Much of Dearborn, Michigan, was under water by Easter weekend, as the Rouge River spilled over its embankments. Electrical lines snapped and trees bit nearby windowpanes. Like their Dearborn neighbors, the Fords had eaten dinner by candlelight. The couple retired around nine o'clock, but the industrialist had been ill for some time and was, that night, as restive as the weather. Ford suffered serious coughing fits and woke in the middle of the night, complaining of a headache. He seemed to want to leave the bed, but he could not stand. His throat was dry, and he was having difficulty catching his breath. In the candlelight, Clara propped her husband up with pillows, resting his head on her shoulder and offering him sips of water. Just after midnight, when Ford's doctor arrived with the industrialist's grandson and namesake, it was too late. Henry Ford was dead.

Three days later, mourners gathered at St. Paul's Cathedral in Detroit. Hundreds of invited guests and dignitaries paid their respects, as nearly 30,000 grieving spectators and curious onlookers crowded surrounding streets. Offices and factories closed, and at 2:30 pm when Ford's funeral commenced, church bells tolled across the Motor City. The day prior, Ford lay in repose at Greenfield Village. Accounts of that event reported, in carefully quantified terms, a mile-long line of more than 100,000 people filing past the open casket. In the weeks to come, obituaries, tributes, sermons, editorials, and Company press releases eulogized the so-called Sage of Dearborn. Even some who had boldly critiqued Ford during his lifetime softened their tone before the fallen Motor King.[1]

Why begin with a view of Ford's death? To recognize at the outset how much this book is and is not about Henry Ford. It is about him insofar as his ideas and endeavors, and narratives about his life and work, infuse the industrial system that occupied his era. It is not about him because he fought hard for it not to be: so that Ford would supersede himself and his time. Any study of Ford must necessarily account for this "economy of death," through which the personal and commercial are bargained. "We are each of us celebrating some funeral," Charles Baudelaire observed in his ruminations on the heroism of modern life. Though Baudelaire coined the term "modernity" and described its fashioning, there may be no other man, machine, organization, or economic system that has been more closely associated with it than Ford—as both industrial hero and capital villain. Simultaneously deemed the "Businessman of the Century" and the "Mussolini of Highland Park," Ford is a contested character and a controversial icon of American modernity.[2]

Among the features of modernity's making, the impulse to narrative experimentation and interpretive subjectivity is one to which Ford is less often connected. Yet, in the forms, structures, and surrounds of Ford's storied self, the "auto" was mobilized both biographically and bureaucratically in the twentieth century. One of the ways interpreters have sought to recount and explain the kind of narrative surplus glimpsed in Ford is through recourse to the mythic. Mythic in the sense Roland Barthes suggested: "a material which has *already* been worked on." Ford is then mythic not because of some inherent or essential aspect of his capitalized persona or corporate product, but rather because of "the way it utters"—because of its methods of making and remarking. You will notice I have switched from calling Ford a *he* to an *it*. This is to emphasize how Ford transfigures from person. Human and machine, myth and method, historical period and political economy, Ford is no mere passing subject. Intimately connected to the assembly line and its consequences, Ford's modern and its quickening discontents have long conveyed more than the cars tumbling off its moving line. That "more," and the mass production of it, was central to Ford's emergence as a household name and recognizable brand. So, too, the "more" of Ford's spiraling surplus—its incorporative power and capital accumulation— are central to this book and to the narratives of Ford that are redescribed and analyzed within it.[3]

Ford did not just mass-produce cars. This book shows how Ford engineered and assembled new religious forms and administered powerful new economies of religion. Tracing Ford's capital scale from human to brand to political economy, it examines the corporate formation of Ford as totemic assemblage. It historicizes and theorizes the religious workings of Ford's mass-produced brand of secular modernity, demonstrating that, while Ford Motor Company and its founder may seem to some readers strange subjects for scholarship on religion, by paying attention to Ford's prosperity gospel, ritual practice, metaphysical relations, and material reliquaries, we gain important insights into relationships between theology and technology, bureaucracy and social organization, concepts of work and concepts of ritual, histories of media and histories of antisemitism, and theories of history and theories of religion.

* * *

Narratives of the eponymous founder of Ford Motor Company often begin by recounting his birth in Dearbornville, a rural farming region outside of Detroit, Michigan, to an Irish immigrant farmer-father and an orphaned Dutch mother who died in childbirth when the young man was only thirteen. Much chronicled, Ford's life (1863–1947) is regularly framed by national and global unrest—from a nation severed in civil war to a planet reeling in the wake of nuclear destruction. Positioned amid tumultuous times, Ford has often been described as a fractured and turbulent sort, a volatile mix of populism and progressivism. The industrialist is recognized for commissioning cutting-edge, glass and reinforced concrete factories, designed by modernist architect Albert Kahn, that were also among the first to offer Ford's largely immigrant workforce increased cleanliness, light, and ventilation, and he's remembered for implementing a living wage for all Ford factory workers early in the century. Yet he also gained a well-deserved reputation for union busting as the "Flivver King" and was a prominent supporter and one-time executive board member of the America First Committee. Garnering a name early in the twentieth century for hiring and paying equal wages to Black workers, Ford also routinely and systematically placed those same workers in the most dangerous and difficult jobs. Heralded in the press for his efficient systematicity and willingness to hire men often shunned by other manufacturers, including disabled workers along with the formerly incarcerated, Ford institutionalized a surveillance system to monitor workers and enforced a rigid code of conduct for employees. Cited as the impetus behind the Model T as "the people's car" and known for implementing and popularizing the moving assembly line in heavy industry, Ford likewise garnered notoriety for the antisemitic writings published in his newspaper, the *Dearborn Independent* and, later, for accepting the Grand Cross of the Supreme Order of the German Eagle, one of the highest medals of commendation given to foreigners by the Third Reich.

In recounting these aspects of Ford's life, we can not only notice historical complexity and contingency but also recognize claims of biographical paradox as tropes in such tellings. According to Samuel Simpson Marquis, a former Ford executive and one-time confidant—who was an early and influential biographer of the manufacturer and Dean of the Episcopal Cathedral attended by the Ford family—the auto-industrialist was a mysterious figure, one never easily or wholly revealed, but instead best expressed as a "rapidly changing," shifty kind of portrait characterized by a constant play of shadow and light. According to Marquis, ever-adept in his sideways compliments, Ford remained ever just out of focus: "There are in him lights so high and shadows so deep that I cannot get the whole of him in proper focus at the same time." Unlike the relentlessly systematic form of factory assembly in Ford's plants, Marquis rendered Ford as a muddled and never-entirely-enlightened entity, one in which "there is something deep within . . . so complex, so contradictory, so elusive as to defy description." Ford's many biographers have since followed Marquis's critical lead, echoing his early rendering of Ford as a mysterious figure—simultaneously so brilliant and so dim—in whom such defiant elusions manage to tease and entice new generations of interpreters.[4]

* * *

Ford's emblematic assemblage is something that the field of religious studies is uniquely positioned to interrogate. Not because it is designed to demystify the mysterious or debunk the diviner but because it is charged with the study of relational power and examinations of the forces of difference wielded and incorporated in its gathering. Just four years after Ford introduced the Model T, Émile Durkhiem described assemblage as central to the totemic principle, the *mana* of mythology and magic, the religious force of seemingly secular symbols. "The very fact of assembling is an exceptionally powerful stimulant," Durkheim wrote. The totem, in Durkheim's telling, collects and materializes the stimulating power of social assemblage—a clan's collective effervescence—and serves as an emblem of its consummate relational making. While students of religion often look to the dancing bears of Grateful Dead concerts, school mascots leading cheers at sporting events, or the flag-waving photo-ops of political rallies to glimpse the exuberant carousing, intoxicating effects, and patterned insignia of Durkheimian effervescence, I turn to the totem as a way to reapproach Ford as an emblem of religious forces wrought in the relational assembly of humans and machines, corporate form and corporeal self. It is in looking to the assemblage of a totem, Durkheim contends, that "we can understand the source of the ambiguous picture religious forces present when they appear in history, how they are both physical and human, moral and material." As totemic traces, Henry Ford and the Ford Motor Company are pictured in the following pages as ambiguous religious forces. Henry Ford's lifetime (1863–1947) serves as a rough chronological frame for this book, though I pay particular attention to the first four decades of the twentieth century, the period of time during which the Company's contributions to the nascent automotive industry and its impact on American culture assembled increasingly formidable power—physical and human, moral and material. An examination of Ford reveals the relational dynamics and processes of incorporation that helped constitute religion in the automobile age.[5]

If the relations forged in social assemblage are, as Durkheim argues, "the soul of religion," in the early twentieth century its historical force was, I contend, increasingly *forded*. I propose this language of fording as a gesture toward the common usage of the verb "to ford": to cross, to move across, or to otherwise traverse unstable or fluid plots—of land and rivers usually—but more so here, of fields and methods, sources and stories. As a verb, to ford suggests something of the work of the bricoleur, who pieces together whatever is at hand to create, to conceive, and to conjure anew. Yet, as a verbalization of Ford, the terminology of fording suggests the wholeness of the Engineer, one who constructs, in Jacques Derrida's telling, "the totality of his language, syntax, and lexicon," creating and systematizing the very terms of modernity. As inventor, Ford is "a subject who would supposedly be the absolute origin of his own discourse and would supposedly construct it 'out of nothing,' 'out of whole cloth'." He is, in this engineered articulation, "the creator of the *verbe*, the *verbe* itself." In such an inaugural story, Ford is proverbial actor and verbal predicate—creating, manufacturing, engineering, *fording*.[6]

Yet, this origin story can only be recognized as momentous, as an Event, when its "structurality of structure" has been thought; once it has been repeated—repeatedly. In popular histories, television documentaries, and educational posters, we see it repeated. Ford as the Great Man. The Transformative Technology he made. We recognize these characters—man and machine. We understand their plots as inaugural moderns. Yet, we know too that they emerged only in opposition to that which apparently was not so. Calling each other into being, systemic totality is named, is thought, is (mis)recognized just as and only when struggled against, when scandalized—and as such, it is never complete, never whole, never total. But this is to repeat what we have already, almost, come to know. The odds are, Derrida reminds us, the Engineer is a myth, a theological idea produced by discourse—by the bricoleur, by the tinkerer who emerges from the workshop out back, borrowing concept and idiom, composition and vocabulary, scraps from inherited resources, congealed fragments of a textual and contextual heritage. But then, so too, the bricoleur, whose difference took on meaning only in contrast to its intellectual and mythopoetic product. "Fording" suggests the wholeness of the Engineer, a verb becoming a gerund, an interpretive process transposed onto the imposing mythopoetic product circulating in our stories and assumptions today. Rather than resist this engineered presence or debunk again stories of entrepreneurial exceptionalism, I use this language of fording to analyze the means and mechanisms, the metaphysics and mediations, by which Ford was fabricated as a commanding brand of modernity. In the following chapters, I linger in Ford's language and pause in Ford's promotions in order to describe and understand the particularity of that modern making.[7]

In the process, I endeavor to name a specific brand of world transforming power and religious reformation in the early twentieth century. This nominating endeavor is meant to be an analytically descriptive one—descriptive insofar as I want to observe Ford's efforts to organize and announce such epic aims for itself, as itself. Ford's was a hubristic project if there ever was one. To transform the world? To reform religion? Scholars have swaggered into descriptions of discursive formations and world-altering paradigms in the past, naming those projects modernization, rationalization, Christianization, secularization. But efforts to name and narrate cannot be easily divorced from the descriptions they offer. This is a risk here, too. Given the immanent intensity of these analytic frames, then, how to proceed without yielding critical perspective? Scholars have usefully urged humility in such undertakings, rightly cautioning the recognition of how any attempt to describe and, especially, to label inevitably falls short. The referent somehow always exceeds the capacity to name it. "What is this logic? What is this totem? This divinity? This categorical imperative?" John Modern implored students and scholars to ask in his own rumination on and review of attempts to name epochal historical events. "But call it Christianity. Or original sin. Or big science. Or imperialism, capitalism, or secularism. Does it matter, really, given how much blood has been shed?" How can anyone satisfactorily respond to the inhuman enormity of such encompassing interrogative trials? In the face of such gaping demands and never-quite-knowing leaps, Modern suggests something more like a dubbing—a self-addressed placeholder, an evocation, an unassuming aside. "Call it Christianity," for one. "Call me Ishmael," an/other.[8]

I share Modern's concern about the weighty immensity of categorical confinements that never quite register the looming atmospherics of it all. Nevertheless, I remain unsatisfied with what can seem like an apparent throwing up of hands that such a reply can suggest to some of its readers. Though I am convinced that Modern's own writing ultimately belies such dispirited interpretations, his cautionary reply risks whispering an apathy I have sometimes heard from students new to the study of religion, particularly when the category is wrest open discursively at the same time as we begin to glimpse anew the ordinary cruelties of American history. ("Does it matter, really?") It is partially for this reason that I risk a naming. I do so not for the sake of presumptuous name-calling, but to begin a descriptive analysis of Ford's discursive fo(u)nt. To identify the particular ways Ford worked to absorb its looming excess, claiming its own atmospheric escape as capital gain. How he sought to incorporate all difference into his own pioneering strut. Indeed, Ford has been repeatedly invoked as the personification of precisely that kind of powerful pretense. To invoke the religious in connection with formal change and commanding reform, and to name that reformation process through recourse to Ford is an effort on my part to describe and, yes, to name more precisely the surplus of Ford's discursive formation, historical cast, and capital brand. It is to pursue a study of the forms and the formulations of his ostensible overdetermination. Call it fording. Does it matter? I think so, yes. Not least because Ford insisted that it did and set about to make it so.

To invoke Ford as a religious corporation in connection with the language of "reform" is also to gesture toward the distinctly Protestant genealogy of historical categorization. Nevertheless, it also finds something different there—a form that is also a transformation. Naming something religious is already to perform an act of discursive incorporation, insofar as this marker ("religious") invariably identifies the corporal and corporate qualities of something—it acknowledges its corpus, the bibliographic and human bodies it draws upon and into itself, and simultaneously those it dissociates from. The term *incorporation* has an etymological history with religious consequence. Its early usage suggests relations between bodies—conceived differently over time as a union simultaneously human, legal, social, institutional, and educational, as well as both material and immaterial, linguistic and affective, religious and secular. Incorporation is then, too, a process of being with and bringing into another body, or an othered body. This is to say that to incorporate is at once to merge and to determine that one and another are separate and thus in need of merging. It is an articulation of difference and, in the same moment, dissolution of that very distinction. This book shows that Ford's system was so powerfully and particularly incorporating that it authorizes a gerund of its own. Ford's corporation—that is, the products and processes of Ford's incorporation, its *fording*—is among the most crucial modes of differentiation and distinction in the twentieth century. To this we must not be indifferent.

Even as I play with the personification of Ford, I am, generally speaking, more concerned with tracing the associations by which Ford, the man, is always-already Ford, the brand. We should not, Durkheim advised, define religion "in terms of mythic personalities, gods or spirits . . .

not particular and distinct objects or beings that possess a sacred character in themselves." Instead, he argued that definitional focus should be directed toward something decidedly less singular, orienting instead on "vague powers, anonymous forces." Religion "always preserves a halo of impersonality that enables it to enter into new combinations . . . because religious forces are by nature incapable of complete individualization." Durkheim reminds us that Ford is never fully or finally resolved in the man, Henry Ford. While I play with the individuated persona, the "he" of Henry Ford, and dig into documents and stories that characterize Ford as a human subject in and of corporate archival holding, I also ask after the extra of Ford's being and doing. I look to the making of Ford's surplus. Tarrying between the personal and impersonal—"he" and "it"—I consider the ways in which the personal gets caught up in, gets incorporated into, the impersonal. As human casting and formal script, Ford is an emblem around which to interrogate the ways in which processes and products, things and concepts—artifacts, images, bodies, affects, ideas, and ideals—have been assembled, incorporated, and mass-produced together in the twentieth century.[9]

The archive of this book thereby focuses on Henry Ford and the Ford Motor Company. In so doing, I aim to offer a glimpse into how the impersonal gets personified and the incorporeal made into corporate personhood. Ford's archival trace simultaneously appears and is deferred in the surplus of the industrialist and his empire, a trace glimpsed in Ford's ghostwritten autobiographies and in the manifold published interviews that made his name recognizable around the globe, interviews that were inevitably routed through the corporate offices of Ford's personal secretaries to correct and sign off on. The making of living person into historic subject is part historiographical effect. Similar to how some biographers and commentators have approached the automaker, Ford was made to be a public persona, one cultivated for and crafted by Ford Motor Company's marketing and administrative efforts. Likewise, I am influenced by and hope to contribute to scholarship that has begun to explore, examine, and assess the making of celebrity. From itinerant ministers like George Whitfield and Sister Aimee Semple McPherson converting the masses or in the mass-mediated celebrity of Britney Spears and Stephen Colbert, scholars of religion have explored iconic figurations and mediated personas as central to religious formation in

America. As a discursively constructed subject in and of history, Ford was sometimes cast as the naïve Midwesterner or provincial purveyor of an "aw-shucks" sensibility. At other times, he was characterized as an international diplomat advocating for world peace, or a scientific manager calculating and recalibrating machinery. Variously too he was industrious educator, shrewd entrepreneur, or rustic yeoman, among other representations. Ford was a series of narrative products and celebrity promotions, as much an assembled article as the Model T's rolling off his factory floors.[10]

While drawing on Durkheim's totem as emblematic materialization of relational assembly, I supplement his approach with one that considers relations across more varied entities, including the assemblage of animate and inanimate, human and non-human, that together produce this flattened form of Ford—from bureaucratic reports and employee testimonials, wage scales and shift times, factory buildings, newspaper accounts, safety bulletins, cafeteria food, political cartoons, neighborhood maps, graduation ceremonies, time and motion studies, libel laws, stopwatches, encyclopedia entries, museum displays, ghostwritten accounts, filmstrips, and printing presses, among others. Ford is here figured as totemic trace through these never-quite-complete associations. Yet, even as I begin here with the totem as a way to redescribe and consider anew the force of Ford's assemblage, the last chapter closes with a reflection on the effigy. Routed through Michael Taussig's examination of mimesis, I consider how my own rendering of Ford harkens toward the "magically effective copy" of the effigy as a way to reckon the historical conjure of Ford's modern making. In the pages that follow, I trace Ford's associations and representations amid the enormity of Ford's making, finding there not only a new stage in a history of capitalism but also a different set of forms in a history of religions.[11]

Introduction

Slanting toward the Religious

Samuel Simpson Marquis, Ford's parish minister and one-time employee, offered one of the first portraits of the industrialist's religious formation. Recording his impressions in a series of magazine articles, later compiled into a book-length biography of Ford, Marquis described his years as an executive at Ford Motor Company as a kind of religious mission, a new vocation, and second calling for the Episcopal minister. In his interpretation of the industrialist, Marquis recounted and responded to sets of questions often posed to him about his former boss and parish member, including inquiries into Ford's religiosity: "Is he a churchman? Is he a Christian? What are his religious views? Is he a religious man?" The answers he offered read as a kind of catechism. On first glance, the minister acknowledged, this set of questions may initially seem to be versions of one single, larger inquiry but, Marquis said rightly, they are not. Demonstrating careful attention to subtle discursive differences, Marquis explained that "the information sought in each case is far from the same." Instead, the executive-pastor argued, "each question reveals, all unconsciously, a peculiar religious 'slant' in the mind of the person asking it."[1]

Many scholars and students of religion are familiar with this kind of interrogative "slant." To address questions like those posed to Marquis requires us to recognize the ways that both academic interlocutors and colloquial questioners often slip from *church* to *Christian* to *religious* and back again. There is a history to that discursive gradient and its slippage—one routed through Latin roots, Protestant rifts, and racial imperialism, among other avenues of conquering misrecognition and classificatory misadventure. To enter into the study of religion is to find yourself clambering with a category that holds within it an array of complicated and never-innocent translational leaps, colonial histories, anthropological distinctions, and philosophical queries. The Christonormative contours and imperial frames of the category have long "slanted" the angles of perception that brought many to its study and that continue to help carve the topography of the field. Marquis recognized the "peculiar" pitch of such queries even as, in the face of such tiltings, he remained ever-inclined toward his own Christian ecclesiology. I redescribe Marquis's responses below to examine some of the earliest critical analyses of Ford's religiosity from the auto-industrialist's archive. I also do so because the questions asked of Marquis are familiar to me. As I researched Ford and presented preliminary findings, I found myself in conversations that echoed those Marquis intimated in his text. I learned much from studying his responses, but mine are not his. In what follows I move through multiple registers of reply, including Marquis's responses as detailed in his published interpretation, the ways that the study of religion often returns to the kinds of questions asked of Marquis, how materials from Ford's archive speak in support of Marquis's reply or help nuance, extend, or contrast with the minister's accounts, and how my own arguments interact with this set of materials.

"Is he a churchman?"

In his writing, Marquis unpacked each question and addressed it in turn. The first prompt was an interrogation into Ford's status as a "churchman," and its brevity, closed frame, and polar structure seemed to insist upon a binary (yes-no) reply to be substantiated through a marshalling of empirical data. Marquis is attuned to those formal demands, even as he aimed to eventually disrupt them. Beginning with the facts of Ford's church membership, he answered: "If to the one who asks the first question you state the fact that Mr. Ford was baptized and confirmed in the Episcopal Church, he is quite satisfied. He has gotten all the information concerning Mr. Ford's religion he wants. He belongs to a church. Then he is all right." Having affirmed his questioner's empirical interest in Ford's church affiliation, Marquis supplements his response with a citation of relevant ecclesiastical heritage and rites of passage. "His father was a vestryman in the little Episcopal church in Dearborn. It was in this church that Mr. Ford was baptized and confirmed." In a separately reported interview, the auto-industrialist verified his relationship to churchly matters in similarly succinct terms: "I was brought up in the Church. I belong to the Church. I attend church." Empirical data effectively marshalled, Marquis imagined his questioner "quite satisfied" with these facts. Or rather, Marquis set himself up as the careful disruptor of the too easily satisfied. Better, he goes on to suggest, would be to understand the interpretive limits of such quick or easy answers. Discerning "Mr. Ford's religion" was more complicated than flattened statements or factual rehearsal about church membership could attest.[2]

Complication and interrogative disruption are impulses scholars of religion recognize. Historians and theorists of religion in America have long insisted upon the importance of looking beyond membership rolls. Echoing internecine concerns and foundational claims about right relations to church authority voiced since at least the Half-Way Covenant of seventeenth-century New England Congregationalists, questions about the relationship between church membership and ecclesiastical significance have for some time been up for debate in American religious history. Studies of popular and lived religion have also showcased the import and creative capacities of people outside both pulpit and pew and have looked to the converting mechanisms of religious belonging far beyond baptism and confirmation. Religion is never just what happens in churches or among the leaders and members of them. More complicated still, some scholars say, "there is no data for religion," save the naming of it as such. Indeed, to decide that "church" or "baptism" are data for the study of religion is never merely some outside observation of an already-"religious" datum from some Archimedean point, however anthropologically or terrestrially positioned. It is rather to make and re-make it so. It is to construct, manufacture, and assemble it thus. Who does the making and remaking matters, then, and as emic blurs etic, the slant of us/them opens anew, becoming questionable. Who decides— questions of authority and community—are thereby enjoined to queries of empirical data as evidence for further interpretation.[3]

Part of the complication Marquis wanted his interlocutor to understand in assessing Ford's status as "churchman" was about organizational support, not simple membership. Showing up and putting up mattered to Marquis. Merely documenting Ford's family history or acknowledging his baptism and confirmation was not enough. Ford, Marquis acknowledged, was "not a churchman in the sense that he attends any church with regularity." More important, though, in Marquis's calculation, was Ford's failure to help sustain the work of his church "in a manner commensurate with his means." Marquis called his readers' attention to the way that Ford's "churchman" status must necessarily falter if one took into account the industrialist's history of (not) putting his money where his mouth was, so to speak. Issued from the perspective of a celebrated church builder concerned with securing funds for the maintenance of his institution, this lamentation from the Dean of the Episcopal Cathedral might also be considered an expression of pastoral concern or ministerial guidance on the tithing practices of Ford, who once was, after all, a member of Marquis's flock. At this point, perhaps Marquis's reader would glean the minister's answer to the question of Ford as churchmen. But not yet. Marquis continues complicating what initially seemed such a simple query.

If his reader really wanted to understand "Mr. Ford's religion," Marquis suggested that more important than church membership, attendance, or financial support was to properly account for Ford's capacity for efficient organization and driving care. Marquis speculated that if Ford "were to accept the authority and responsibility for the reorganization of the church," the auto-industrialist's work "would go down in ecclesiastical history." With an ironic slant of his own, the clergyman imagined how Ford's organizational prowess could have put the church in such a unique position that ecclesiastical leaders would convene annually "to devise ways and means for using a surplus, instead of assembling, as at present, for the purpose of working out some plan for meeting the deficit in last year's missionary budget." Though, Marquis drolly conceded, Ford might very well "take care" of the clergy "by giving them a job six days of the week in the foundry; with the understanding that they preach gratis on the seventh." The minister's wry lament was a sardonic critique in the spirit of sectarian rivalry. "I cannot conceive of [Ford] working contentedly and enthusiastically in any organization in which he is not the dominating spirit and majority shareholder," Marquis continued. Although Ford failed to maintain the kinds of close church contact and parish commitment that the pastor thought he should, there was a place where Ford readily served as "dominating spirit and majority shareholder": Ford Motor Company. In fact, during the time Marquis worked at Ford, the great organizer engineered a corporate takeover of all outside shareholders, solidifying his controlling interest and formidable power over the Company. Marquis's tongue-in-cheek remark about Ford's potential to reorganize the church suggests that the auto-industrialist's ecclesiastical affiliation and sectarian belonging might be more importantly and consequently seen in Ford's corporate command.[4]

One of the avenues of argumentation I pursue in this book is that the "church" of the automobile age may well resemble something closer to Ford's manufacturing plant than to Marquis's Episcopal Cathedral, where Ford occasionally attended services and over which Marquis presided. The emphatic edge of this contention—that in the early twentieth century Ford is more like what we have historically understood religion to be than almost anything else—may seem surprising to some, but among those steeped in the knotted histories of religion and economy it likely will not, much. Whether in the aesthetic displays and ritual purchase of American department stores, the mercantile trust and sacralized solidarities of franchise models in the bazaars of Banaras, the crafty legality and godly services of US big box retailers, the holistic medicines, charms, and candles used among "spiritual merchants" in the polyvalent "work of possession(s)," or in the discourse of detox and purging rituals of boutique postindustrial purchase in online venues and influencer platforms, the "heavenly merchandizing" of commerce has been a central site of observation and critique for many in the study of religion. Scholars have questioned the national mythologies of corporate conglomerates from the United States to Japan in order to probe the genealogies of religion, corporation, state, family, and other durable collective commitments. Attending to both for- and not-for-profit entities, a burgeoning line of scholarship has turned toward "business" as a way of observing religious institutionalization. Other scholars have homed in on techniques and technologies of consumption and communication to reckon with the relational dynamics of capital. From studies of the printing press to the telegraph, the phonograph to the photograph, in examinations of media and its missions, this line of scholarship has shown how vehicles of religious selfhood and social-making transact with national economies and corporate interests. Studies into the industries of transportation and transformation—from oil extraction, steel manufacturing, and coal mining to canal-building, railroading, and road construction—have furthered explorations into the enterprises and infrastructures of religion and industry. And recent work in the field has begun delving into analyses of the proliferating categories and characters of capital and political economy.[5]

This book joins this significant and ever-growing area of scholarship in the study of religion. Examining the products and practices of Ford Motor Company—including efficiency standards, wage and labor policies, mediating technologies, and historical projects—reveals the institutional forms and sectarian belongings that Ford authorized, organized, and incorporated. Bringing stories from Ford's archive together with historiographical narratives and analytical categories that may seem to some readers rather disparate, this study of Ford seeks to demonstrate how—even as scholars ask after new forms of data to think through changing conceptions of religion, no matter how unexpected the product—the matter of religion cannot be understood outside its modes of processing. The religious cannot be reckoned as separate from its patterns of production or severed from idiomatic suggestion. Looking to Ford, I find that assemblage matters. It mattered on the factory floor as much as in congregational gathering. It matters in historiographical rendering, and it matters in theorizing the religious. Yet Marquis reminds us that the dominating spirits of assemblage also make a difference. In popularizing and mobilizing new mechanisms of manufacture, I contend that Ford authorized and reassembled the very terms and conditions of religion in the twentieth century.

In the coming pages, readers will find description and interpretation of specific documents of Ford's archive. Reading into Ford's personal papers, corporate records, and published accounts, I connect Ford to interpretive tropes from the historiography of American religion, including those of Puritan industry, metaphysical experimentation, Christian primitivism, and antisemitism. Enjoining these redescriptions to analytical rubrics that have structured the study of comparative religion (e.g., myth, ritual, relic, and magic) and economy (e.g., efficiency, labor, profit, accumulation), this study of Ford reapproaches and confirms their dynamic historical relations. The point is not only to reveal or unmask the churchly qualities, religious forms, or Christian contours of Ford Motor Company. While Marquis's observation of organizational competition offers a starting point to recognize the ecclesiastical conventions, sectarian belongings, and organizational spirits of Ford and his Company, this is not my argumentative end. My aim is more expansive. It is to further a study of how critical examination of the programs and projects organized and incorporated by Ford can allow us not only to recognize religion and economy as discursively embedded, historical concepts but to engage the study of religion as a way into a renewed and sustained analysis of our time—into a persistent critique of a present that is never-entirely-post-Fordist. The conceit is that the study of religion is a way into a critique of how Ford has organized our behaviors and directed our ideas, how capital optimistically fashions our desires, attaches them to its cruelties, and forecloses our imaginings otherwise. It might also be a way to find in the study of religion the histories and vocabularies to describe and define our own prophetic visions, metaphysical labors, pioneering vernaculars, and secular futures in order to delimit Ford's organizational directions—opening a gap for other imaginings, other desires, and other attachments.[6]

"Is he a Christian?"

In the second query of Marquis's catechistic account, the clergyman commented on questions about Ford's "Christian" credentials. While for some of Marquis's readers, the industrialist's Christian commitments may have been gleaned in family history, church membership, and denominational affiliation, Marquis understood those who asked him this question to really be wondering about something else. In questioning if Ford is a Christian, what they actually wanted to know, Marquis interpreted, is "something about the individual moral standards of Mr. Ford and the character of his private life." In response, the preacher rehearsed crisply "that Mr. Ford's private life is clean, his tastes are simple, his pleasures are wholesome, and that he loves and enjoys his home." Notably terse in his description of Ford's "Christian" character, Marquis curtly affirmed the industrialist's ethical proclivities and domestic commitments as part of his Christian commission while also subtly hurrying past those concerns in order to press into questions of the "religious."[7]

To hasten from Christian designation to moral appellation and back is a familiar scurry. Since at least Kant's Enlightenment-era critiques in service of a naturalized and universalized religiosity, Protestant Christian conceptions of rightly privatized faith and moral uprightness have been historically harnessed together in expressions of bourgeois values. Protestant practices of interiority, individualized faith, and appeals to domestic virtue also have long histories in the annals of American religion as concerns about religious (dis)establishment and familial capital engendered new economies of virtue and taste. Marquis succinctly deployed and extended these tropes of middle-class respectability in his reply to questions of Ford's "Christian" status. These tropes—cleanliness, simplicity, wholesome pleasures, domestic commitment—also recur throughout the biographical and promotional materials of Ford's personal papers and corporate records. Set up as an agent of bourgeois moral reform and middle-class manners, Ford was a public proponent of Prohibition, spoke often on subjects of health and diet, reprinted materials from the Christian physical culture movement, and published his own anti-cigarette pamphlet entitled *The Case Against the Little White Slaver*. The auto-industrialist claimed that he read the Bible daily, kept Christian scriptures in every room of his home, and publicly confessed his belief "in God and in Jesus Christ." It was also reportedly Ford's commitment to Christian moral reform that initially brought Marquis to Ford Motor Company. In October 1915, as the Episcopalian minister turned corporate administrator, Ford reportedly directed Marquis to "put Jesus Christ in my factory." Just what Ford might have meant by that directive requires additional interrogation and explanation, particularly in the context of Ford's metaphysical views and the social gospel–inspired projects he institutionalized, both of which are explored in coming chapters. For his part, Marquis seemed to think Ford was on the right track. Writing to a ministerial colleague, the clergyman insisted, "I know of no man living who is doing more for his fellow men in the spirit of christian religion than Henry Ford." Setting christian in lowercase helped Marquis affirm Ford's belonging and situated the auto-industrialist in the spirited relation of fraternal fellowship that Marquis would come to avow in terms of the religious.[8]

Documents from Ford's archive attest to the industrialist's engagement with and commitment to a form of Christianity that he confessed "in the broadest sense." In Ford's telling, the "broad" kind of Christianity he was interested in "carries no sectarian meaning with it." The auto-industrialist used this disavowal of sectarianism as an opportunity to claim comprehensiveness on behalf of his Christian form, even as it was also component to Ford's particular project of industrial enterprise. Ford's way of manufacturing the universal from the particular was part of what made his mass production a standardizing feature across the twentieth-century United States and beyond. Following the industrialist's nonsectarian concerns into fraternal affiliations, financial disputes, legal decisions, and corporate structures, we will observe how Ford touted capital service, white nationalism, and broadly Christian primacy, and to what effects. Despite the fact that many people think of Ford as a secular subject, the auto-industrialist's concern for industrious subjectivity in modernity was conveyed in broadly Christian and specifically antisemitic terms. An examination of Ford's system of production reveals the particular idioms and values, techniques and technologies, that Ford mobilized as component to his industrial enterprise. Ford sloganized in notorious and highly publicized antisemitic headlines about "international Jews." In legal disputes about corporate governance and "non-working stockholders," he boldly proclaimed his firm's profitable exception to those he deemed parasitic profiteers. And in romanticized and relentlessly sentimentalizing appeals, he propagated the pioneer as the properly industrious subject in and for American history. Contextualizing Ford in histories of Puritan industry, muscular Christianity, Social Darwinist metaphysics, prosperity gospels, and Christian primitivism, I propose the concept of supersessionary secularism to articulate and explain the system of racial capital and religious distinction that Ford reassembled and mass-produced in and through his media empire.[9]

Ford did not refer to himself or his work as secular, nor did his firm pronounce the system of political economy popularized in its name as a kind of secularism. To some readers it may then seem strange or even incendiary that I am referring to Ford's broadly Christian confession as a specific kind of secularism. I do so to acknowledge the disciplinary work Ford's confessional claim did. With a foothold in contemporary scholarship in religion that has examined the study of the secular and secularism as ways to make sense of and to manage the sensemaking of what is and is not "religion," I name and describe Ford's supersessionary secularism to mark not only that he made sense of the rightly religious (the broadly Christian, industrious, and properly waged pioneer) alongside that which he deemed wrong (the "international Jew" and the parasitic, "non-working stockholder") but the conditions and processes Ford used to systematize his sensemaking, including the disciplinary regimens and media products of his corporation. Joining scholarship that approaches secularism and the secular as "constantly drawing each other into existence," I find in Marquis's observation—that inquiry into Ford's "Christian" status embeds questions about the moral economy of the industrialist—an entry into how he deployed the broadly Christian and the nonsectarian as supersessionary wager. Administered as a massively mediated project of articulating, regulating, and assessing the religious from the not-religion, Ford governed and disciplined his public in right and wrong religion.[10]

Following decades-long critiques of classical secularization theses, which assumed the secular as a kind of epistemic remainder in the wake of religious declension, scholarship in secular studies has shown that the secular is not what is left over after the religious has been subtracted. Observing the dominant deployment of religion and the secular as differentiating distinctions in modernity and questioning the shape and scope of their authorizing configuration, scholars have examined these tense, and sometimes contradictory, twinned productions. My aim is less to worry their differentiation than to mark their mutual making and remarking. More than debunking secularization theses of religion/secular separation, this examination of Ford aims to demonstrate how stories of subtraction and inclusion are standardized in Ford's spiraling genealogical power and capital interest. Ford made this historical speculation central to the "pioneering" religio-racial identity he sought to mass-produce and historically incorporate as component to American history and values. At Ford, broadly Christian concerns and claims of American exceptionalism were put to work in service of nationalist projects and material histories rooted in antisemitic assertions and racial capitalism. Part of the enormity of that power was Ford's ability to systematically reassemble, discipline, and mass-produce both (secular and religion) at scale.[11]

"What are his religious views?"

Concerns about the church and Christ, institutionalization and valuation, rose to prominence in Marquis's previous replies, but the pastor also knew well the pluralisms promised in modern America. The minister's response to the third question suggested his sensitivity to the often-exoticizing idioms in which developing attention to comparative religions were uttered. His response acknowledged directly the unorthodoxy of Ford's religious views. "He is disposed to do his own thinking in matters of religion as in other matters," Marquis summarized. "Theology interests him, but it is not the kind that is found in the seminaries." Even still, the minister understood that this was not quite what his questioner most wanted to know. "The man who asks the third question is just burning up to know if Mr. Ford is a Theosophist, a Spiritualist, or a New Thoughter," Marquis explained, rehearsing the kinds of inquiries that underwrote questions about Ford's "religious views." "Does he believe in transmigration of the soul, or in reincarnation? What does he think of Confucius and Buddha? Would it be possible to have a talk with him on the esoteric teachings of the ancient mystics, or the doctrine of the Stoics?" Marquis addressed these implicit questions by acknowledging that Ford "entertains some very original ideas on everything under the sun concerning which he speaks." Surely, the minister acknowledged, it was understandable to presume that Ford must also "have some very original and interesting views on religion."[12]

There was certainly reason enough for the burning desires Marquis interpreted in his questioners' attempts to understand any of the more esoteric affiliations of the auto-industrialist. The "alchemical logic" of American industry was a familiar enough trope by the time Ford founded his motor company in 1903. From electrical wizardry to spiritualized machinery, the metaphysical imaginary of industrialists and their contemporaries had long garnered public attention. Ford joined many of these inventors and engineers in linking mechanical pursuits and metaphysical enterprises. Like many before him and harkening those yet to come, Ford insisted on an experimental approach to distinctions of matter and spirit, the engineer and the prophet.[13]

Marquis understood this well and quickly affirmed his imagined interlocutor's presumptions about Ford's unconventional "religious views." "For the satisfaction of this man," Marquis continued, "permit me to say that Mr. Ford believes, or did once believe, in reincarnation." Yet, the clergyman's response gestured obliquely to hearsay, and he refused to speculate further on his former boss's belief in reincarnation. "I have never gone into the subject with him," Marquis explained, "so I do not know to what extent the belief has taken hold of him." How can anyone know the "extent" of another's beliefs or how much "hold" something has on someone? These are questions that scholars and students of religion have also asked. Marquis averred no proprietary insight or specialized discernment on the subject, reporting instead on the discursive practices of his former employer. "I have heard him say," Marquis attested, "that he has a knowledge of some things with which it seems to him he was born. It comes to him as out of the experience of a former life." Other documents from Ford's archive support Marquis's testimony. Indeed, if news reports and published interviews are to be believed, Ford spoke often and eagerly on the subject, describing at some length "the gospel of reincarnation," as he understood it. The industrialist also initiated corporate-led inquiries into reports of reincarnation on the Indian subcontinent, read books on the subject, and was convinced that a young girl in his extended family was the reincarnated personage of his mother.[14]

Unlike Marquis, who evaded his interlocutor's interest in Ford's possible New Thought, Theosophical, or Spiritualist proclivities, we can look simultaneously into Ford's personal papers, family bookshelves, and corporate archives and find considerable documentation to support those popular curiosities. Marquis's interlocutor's burning desires were much more than simple news fodder. Personal correspondence and Company imprints point to a deep engagement the industrialist had with a variety of metaphysical pursuits, including, for example, the Unity School of Christianity, an organization founded by Charles and Myrtle Fillmore and rooted in the nineteenth-century New Thought movement. A historical heuristic in the study of American religion, New Thought names what one scholar described as a "restyled mind-over-matter worldview." As we will see, Ford's institutional network of metaphysical concerns extended well beyond Unity, including the industrialist's rustic rituals, his friendly connections to Transcendentalism, and a personal pledge and family heritage of Freemasonry. Ford's combination of naturalist tradition and fraternal association offers a way into questions about romanticism and ritual in twentieth-century America, extending scholarship that has begun to interrogate the crucial incorporation of "sovereign ritual," civic leadership, and corporate fellowship in American history. That conjunction—of rites, governance, and belonging—aided industrial enterprises like Ford's in authorizing, communicating, and enlarging their power and making it feel real. I expand upon these affiliations and affinities in order to understand the religious techniques and ritual realizations of sovereign comportment and racial underwriting that were affected through Ford's corporate governance.[15]

Even as Marquis's readers pressed him to acknowledge the esoteric religious ideas of the automaker and despite Ford himself publicly commenting on his "unorthodox" religious ideas, most historians have tended to overlook or hurry past what Marquis regards as Ford's "very original and interesting views on religion." When mentioned at all, most scholars have been inclined to cast them as a kind of eccentricity—what one biographer called Ford's "oddly radical ragbag of beliefs and allegiances" and another termed "his rather outlandish religious ideas." Among the challenges in approaching Ford as a subject for the study of religion and in doing so at this particular genealogical moment in the study of religion (and, so too, the secular) is recognizing and explaining, rather than uncritically reproducing or reducing, categorical instability and incoherence. What I mean is that to take up Ford in the study of religion today is to further open up what can be considered within the category of "religion." Empirical study of Ford's archive reminds us that to do so is also archivally correct. It is a way to track Ford's own expansive approach to the category. "I believe it is possible for us to experiment in the special field we call religion," Ford urged. "Not that I think religion is a field off by itself, separate. No, it includes everything, and everything includes it." Experimentally possible and imperially inclusive, Ford fielded religion.[16]

Yet the categorical prying that this book contributes to is not meant to be merely additive, nor is my study intended to simply reproduce Ford's archived allegiances. We need not further his massive production. Rather, I consider how Ford experimented and fielded religion in order to interrogate the study of religion as a field of critical possibility, to trace its prospects in order to glimpse its limits. Drawing upon and contextualizing Ford's "religious views," I contend that we can better see the metaphysics of his prevailing brand of mass production. With a more profound understanding of how he harnessed a metaphysics to his mechanics, we can also confront the ways Ford worked to reassemble time—in carefully calibrated machinery and working hours on the production line, as reincarnated lives progressively reborn, in debunked histories pioneered through his industrial museum, and in a future that

Ford prophesied as the coming Machine Age. To gain critical purchase on the making of our modern times, I thereby redescribe the Janus-faced modernity of industrial proportion that Ford quickened.

"Is he a religious man?"

Given Ford's expansively experimental relation to the category of the religious and how scholarship in the study of religion has begun to recognize the category's complicated histories, any reply to this closing question requires something significantly more sophisticated than a simple "yes" or "no" answer. Marquis understood this, too. More complex and critically inclined than the question may seem in its initial appearance, the apparent flatness of such a query—asking if someone or something is religious—quickly gives way to a depth of inquiry discursively embedded in the question's frame. For his part, Marquis says that this last question was typically posed by those who wanted "to draw out a statement as to Henry Ford's ideals, his social theories, his doctrines of industrial relations." To ask if Ford was "a religious man" was really, in Marquis's interpretation, a way for the questioner to find out more about the ideas and ideals of sociality industrialized by Ford. Marquis's reply reminds us that to ask if someone or something is "religious" shuttles all involved once again into the kinds of definitional challenges and categorical contests that have long animated the study of religion. Structured around enduring and evolving deliberations—among them, essence and identity, origin and etymology, translation and form, occupation and image, story and source—the study of religion and the academic (inter) discipline of Religious Studies unfurl amid distinctions like these that are exhorted in their very asking. Rather than signaling some kind of inquisitive naiveté or analytical pedantry, to question the category of the "religious" and its study can serve as an interrogative springboard into demanding aporias of thought—of interpretation and explanation, description and prescription, comparison and authority.[17]

Marquis's interpretive focus on social relations and industrial ideals in Ford's plants was not unexpected, particularly given the crucial role the minister played at the Company. Marquis led Ford's Sociological Department, the bureaucratic entity created alongside Ford's much-acclaimed Five Dollar Day, a wage and labor policy initiated one year before Marquis's hire, which promised up to $5 per day for all eligible Ford workers regardless of skill or experience. As we will see, the methods and aims of the Sociological Department included elaborate survey practices and surprise home visits, systems of financial auditing and advising, and the compulsory education program it organized, which combined language training, citizenship instruction, and tutelage in middle-class etiquette. What this history reveals are well-established tensions between corporate welfare and surveilling governance, paternal enterprise and industrial goodwill. For Marquis, the strain of that ambivalence resolved in the mission of benevolent industry, the practices of which, the minister insisted, were "as sound economically as they were humane." Marquis understood his work at Ford as "part of a great experiment in applied Christianity in industry." Framing Ford as a Christian manufactory for the making of men as much as motor cars, Marquis insisted that part of Ford's "religious" work was "to get the men in the way of right living." At Ford, the executive minister pronounced religious significance in the vitality of industrial application, Christian practicality, and an active pedagogy of American industry, middle-class manners, and capital goodwill.[18]

That Marquis aligned a Christian mission with claims of humane capital and privately funded pedagogical programming is not particularly surprising. When he detailed Ford's commitment to "making men in this factory as well as automobiles," or pronounced that "before everything else" Ford's interest was "the education of his employees," or when he insisted that a Ford factory should really be understood as a school not only of vocational training but also to "develop a man's mind and soul in the training of his hand," the clergyman was showcasing the ways that Ford had joined a great many others in connecting humanist endeavors, Christian commission, and educational avowals of corporate enterprise. Historians of American religion have examined the manifold claims capital has made about its humanitarian appeals and pedagogical consequences alongside a Christian errand of reform. From oil and steel tycoons to department store magnates, scholars have described the bold assertions of nineteenth-century social betterment through prosperity gospel promises of baron philanthropy, Gilded Age commerce, retail pricing, and privately funded educational institutions. Around a century later, in chain store businesses, caffeinated commodities, and global celebrity ambassadors, idioms of spirituality and service have routinely advanced neoliberal projects of consumptive subjectivity and devotionally mortgaged credit economies. Positioned between these late nineteenth- and late twentieth-century moments, Ford Motor Company has been held up historiographically as an exemplar of early twentieth-century welfare capitalism's version of humanitarian social reform. In this scholarship, the "religious" reforms understood as central to Ford's welfare capitalism orient on the social gospel—a capacious category that organizes within it a wide array of Christian concerns meant to address and aright the social ills of modern life.[19]

This historiographical emphasis on the social gospel at Ford is in large part due to the important role Marquis played there. The clergyman insisted that those who asked if Ford was "a religious man" were actually angling to understand Ford's commitment to the social gospel—what Marquis defended as a form of Christianity that "places an emphasis on social rather than individual righteousness." Scholars have spilled considerable ink on the social gospel. Notable attention has been paid to the capital infrastructures, movement of peoples, patterns of city living, and new forms of racialized violence that compelled many of the "applied" projects promoted by the wide swath of Christians who, like Marquis, have been variously categorized as part of the movement. Who has and has not been included within the social gospel and the ambivalent politics and legacies ascribed to it continues to be debated among scholars. What is clear is that for liberal clergymen like Marquis, the pursuit of social salvation meant addressing the role of industrial enterprises like Ford's and reforming the social relations organized around those corporate concerns. Supplementing missionary emphases on individual conversion as foremost to one's Christian duty, social gospelers like Marquis sought to effect conversion on a more massive scale. Proclaiming his interest "in the fruits of religion more than in its theological and ecclesiastical roots," Marquis sought to direct the formation and incorporation of social gospel principles and practices at Ford Motor Company. This is why, according to the minister, to rightly recognize Ford's religious status meant understanding how Ford confronted, enriched, and later impaired relations among capital and labor.[20]

Notice that Marquis's answer to this final question—"Is he a religious man?"—redirects readers from concerns about Ford's church membership or ethical living, and likewise turns away from the auto-industrialist's views on "the religious," pressing instead into Marquis's own definition of religion as a marker of social relation, Christian application, and humane industry. In the minister's estimation, Ford's professed "religious views" were ill-defined. Yet, Marquis reasoned, "there is in [Ford] something bigger than his ideas, something of a practical nature that is far better than his nebulous theories." In Marquis's interpretive description we find embedded prescription; amid the minister's careful parsing of his interlocutor's "peculiar religious 'slant'" we find the social gospeller's own normative inclination. This is not a singular failing. There is no disinterested, neutral perspective in the study of religion. Historically wrought and discursively in flux, the category of the religious is not some empirically singular datum to be observed, defined, or compared; it is reassembled anew in each articulation. Notice my own tilt. This is one of the argumentative contentions of this book: that Ford reassembled the religious through the relations incorporated, metaphysics manufactured, services reworked, and histories pioneered there. Marquis was, for a time, part of that industry and contributed to the religion-making that Ford mass-produced in the twentieth century. Yet, if Marquis articulated the religious in the pitched intonations of the social gospel, the minister's was but one component in Ford's larger religious production.[21]

Redeemer Myths and Free Enterprise Jeremiads

While Marquis sought to advance the "humane policies" of Ford Motor Company, the minister soon found himself disillusioned, his tenure cut short. If he initially found "a deep and genuine interest in the well-being of Ford employees," by the time he left the Company to return to regular ministry in the Episcopal Church, he was warning of countervailing forces at Ford. In just five years' time, Marquis resigned. Or, rather more accurately, he was one of the men forced out of the Company as part of the great executive exodus of 1920–1921. Newly ascendant, the minister explained, were powerful but cruel men—those Marquis called "industrial scavengers"—who delighted in "brutal methods" in order to "put the fear of God into labor" and who "were always thinking of themselves as the little gods who were to be feared." The era of industrial fellowship had given way, Marquis lamented, to a period in which Ford's relentless drive system took vicious hold over the corporation, initiating what one scholar referred to as a "reign of terror and despotism."²²

In the years after Marquis left Ford's employ, the Company did become a site of increasingly intense (and increasingly publicized) combat between management and labor. Personnel matters and labor relations were folded into the work of the Service Department, Ford's internal plant security and private police force, and as the nation began to contend with economic depression and large-scale unemployment, the Company found itself increasingly and more publicly at odds with labor leaders. Inflationary surges in the cost of living and wartime intensification of the pace of work fueled worker discontent. Deploying now-notorious methods of industrial espionage, serious physical violence, and personal intimidation, Ford battled unionization in its factories with increased vehemence amid what some have termed a transition "from welfare to warfare capitalism." No scholar can then rightly doubt the prescience of Marquis's cautionary tale. Harsh and erratic treatment and a persistent speed-up culture were part of Ford labor policy in the following two decades. Some of the more nostalgic employees lamented "the passing of the 'Ford Spirit' and the coming of the new attitude toward the employee." Worker complaints about production demands increased, and telling new health issues and "industrial neuroses"— including a nervous condition that laborers referred to as "Forditis"— emerged alongside the bureaucratic changes Marquis grieved, while at the same time new forms of resistance—including the "Ford whisper," a covert form of worker communication used without taking one's eyes off the assembly line—emerged as Service Department forces cracked down on all talking, laughing, whistling, smoking, or even sitting during lunch breaks. Alongside workers' accounts of these years, the minister's critique is an important historical source, offering a valuable perspective not only on changes at Ford Motor Company but also on a transition from sociological to service work, a notable discursive transformation and inflection point that has begun to be narrated in other genealogies of religion and American capitalism.²³

The redescriptions of capital relations that I trace in this book can be located along the curvature of this broader historiographical consensus. Yet I also remain distinctly wary of the arc of redemption to which Marquis's lamentation harkens. The clergyman insisted that, though

Ford had "lost faith," the corporate apostate could yet be redeemed, calling epideictically, for a return to and fulfillment of Ford's earlier, more righteous form of capital fellowship—one Marquis located and sought to advance in the industrialist's "early idealism" about the consecrated role of corporate enterprise and humanitarian industrial relations. In the minister's telling, Ford's corporate redeemer was to be Edsel Ford, the founder's only son, who Marquis said had "the kind of spirit that guides private wealth in channels that makes for social and industrial betterment." In this, Marquis's aspirations for his former employer were again largely dashed. Despite bestowing upon Edsel the title of President of Ford Motor Company, the founder almost entirely sidelined his son's leadership. When Edsel died rather unexpectedly in 1943, Marquis's hopes were officially thwarted. By then, though, other critics and commenters had begun to look elsewhere for their figure of capital redemption, and they found deliverance in a familiar name: Henry Ford II, the founder's eldest grandson and namesake, who officially took over the Company in 1945. Less than five years after the elder Ford reluctantly signed an agreement with the UAW-CIO, the second Henry Ford was quickly gaining in popularity, not least for his reinvigorated commitment to confront and address "the human problems inherent in mass-production" and for publicly vowing to foster more congenial labor relations with Ford's new union.[24]

Told this way, Marquis's jeremiad sets up the salvific resolution of American capitalism in Ford's mid-century corporate succession and the negotiations it made with unionized labor. Yet, there are many and good reasons to be cautious about the consequences of such redemptive calls for more conscientious capitalism. Sacvan Bercovitch's influential study of the tradition of the American jeremiad rightly describes this strain of redemptive rhetoric as a "free enterprise vision." Bercovitch details the way "US history is a story of conflict resolved in an increasingly comprehensive capitalist culture." There is little reason to doubt that Ford has long stood as a primary protagonist of such sweeping forms of twentieth-century capitalism. The effect of Marquis's dissent—in which he castigated Ford's failure to live up to its ambitious intention to mass-produce an "industrial paradise"— enabled the minister both to commemorate and to confirm an abidingly virtuous nature to American capitalism, "simultaneously lamenting a declension and celebrating a national dream." If done right, Marquis suggested, the hallowed fellow-feeling he had once directed at Ford could be reclaimed from the violent forces that had eclipsed his work there. Such a redemption would, Marquis hoped, return the Company once more to that righteous form of capital relation he envisioned.[25]

This book interrogates the workings of those capital relations. The result of Marquis's adversarial celebration of Ford's system of political economy was to simultaneously and successfully confine and conserve capital and its dissent, turning transgression into continuity. My aim therefore is not only to contextualize and question the social gospel contours of Ford's welfare capitalism as it was ministered and administered by Marquis. I also introduce Ford's rite-to-work religion, a concept I propose to help mark Ford's advancement and institutionalization of a ritual theory of labor in which to work is to right oneself and one's social world through the corporate form of sociality and proper industry mass-produced at Ford. "You preach one gospel and I another," Ford once told Marquis, insisting on a difference in the clergyman's commitments and his own. "My gospel is work. If a man is down and out, the only thing that will save him is work—work that will give him something to live on and to live for." Ford's driving emphasis on the value of work powered the projects of both socialization and service at the automobile firm. Ford presented this gospel of work as his idea of philanthropy and proffered the labor he waged as a salvific force for social change in the twentieth century. In addition to redeemer myths of social gospel–inspired programs for humane labor relations and alongside his regime of driving service, Ford conveyed this ritual theory of labor through the mass-produced economy christened in his name.[26]

* * *

There are inevitably many routes through this book. Each of the chapters examines particular aspects of Ford's makings in order to glimpse new insights not only into the figure and font of Ford, but also into how the study of religion can help make sense of, and why it needs to theorize, the transformations wrought by commerce and industry, historical renderings, and corporate relations. Structured roughly chronologically, the history traced in the following pages is not strictly linear. Spiraling outward from Ford's metaphysics, to his articulation of the human and visions of social reform, and into his mediations of history in service of these projects, the first and last chapters frame the study through attention to the ways Ford engineered time in metaphysical enterprises of a divined future and through harrowing histories of past-making. The central chapters consider Ford's assemblage and mobilization of religion and secular forms as corporate enterprise and business relation.

I endeavor to show how Ford engineered and assembled new religious forms and machined powerful new economies of religion in an age managed and marketed as secular. My point is not simply to advocate that scholars reach for new and different entities and call them "religious," however expansively theorized the category certainly can be. Rather, I am more concerned with how to understand and explain the ways religion has been powerfully reworked, and how that reworking continues to do work. If Ford's means of production have tended to be prescribed secular, Ford's mass production of that mean prescription—its spiraling promises, labored rites, harrowed reliquaries, religio-racial infrastructures, and serving spirit—has been central to the making of a modernity engineered to matter as such. The study of religion offers a way to theorize that process and provides a view into the fording of American life and labor—how days are ordered, how relations and differences are conceived and managed, how histories are made and contested, how futures are imagined and foreclosed. These are best gleaned not in some linear historical fashion or as component to the teleological machinery of progress but as a dash—a movement of categorical quickening and discursive trace, one that spans subjects, intersecting analytics, crossing stories, and traversing sources.

If we have never been modern, this book seeks to demonstrate how Ford sought urgently and relentlessly to make us so. Modernity, Michel Foucault explained in his reading of Baudelaire, "is the attitude that makes it possible to grasp the 'heroic' aspect of the present moment . . . the will to 'heroize' the present . . . a desperate eagerness to imagine it, to imagine it otherwise than it is, and to transform it not by destroying it but by grasping it in what it is." Not mere spectatorship, this heroization is, Foucault reminds, a labor of irony—an exercise of "extreme attention to what is real," one that "simultaneously respects this reality and violates it." My critique of the industrialist and his auto-production recognizes that any critical insight offered here occurs amid the historical manufacture Ford engineered, even while it also necessitates reflection upon its limits. Accordingly, I seek the conceptual forms, logics, scripts, and assumptions that he pressed into the organized livelihoods and historical makings of twentieth-century America. An epoch and an abstraction, a method and an obsession, Ford's modern was an invention, an industry of auto-production. In an era that regularly positions itself as post-Fordist, I prefaced this book with the death of Ford to broach questions of how his time has and has not passed away. This book thereby offers a critique of Ford as a critique of the ways Ford defined and delimited us. The ambition is that it might also enable a dash toward possibilities of transgressing, of violating, those defining limitations.[27]

1

A Metaphysics of Mass Production and Ford's "Gospel of Efficiency"

It was Christmas Eve, 1893. Family would soon be gathered in the small Detroit home where preparations were well underway for tomorrow's holiday dinner. Henry Ford, a lanky, mustachioed man of thirty years, was invading his wife Clara's domain, lugging an odd machine from his backyard shop inside the new brick duplex. Edsel, the couple's seven-week-old son, was swaddled and asleep in a nearby room, as Henry positioned the contraption on a board and clamped it to a carefully scrubbed kitchen sink. The contrivance was pieced together from scraps of metal, salvaged from a local electrical company, where Henry worked when he was not out tinkering with clocks and watches and spare parts in his shop. After Henry solicited Clara's assistance, the Fords worked in tandem to splash petroleum into a tiny metal cup, twist a screw that opened an intake valve, and spin a wheel made from an old lathe. The kitchen light flickered when the house's electrical current helped deliver a spark to the device. The couple looked expectantly at the precariously melded machine, but nothing happened. Making slight adjustments, they tried again. This time something sputtered. The sink shook. The machine coughed. Flames jumped, and the room filled with black smoke. Ford's apparatus had seized to life, if only for a few seconds.

So begins the myth of Ford's Christmas Eve engine, a figure and a device whose force would, in coming years, not only multiply the driving mechanisms of automotive travel but also power Ford's corporate command. In this account, Ford is both Engineer and Tinkerer, inspired inventor, master maker, and patriarchal creator—a mythic figuration. "There is an immense amount to be learned simply by tinkering with things," Ford proclaimed in his first ghostwritten autobiography. "It is not possible to learn from books how everything is made—and a real mechanic ought to know how nearly everything is made. Machines are to a mechanic what books are to a writer. He gets ideas from them, and if he has any brains he will apply those ideas." If the Christmas Eve engine was Ford's first engineered triumph, timepieces were his earliest form of mechanical training. According to the stories Ford and others told, the industrialist demonstrated an early curiosity about clocks and watches. Neighbors described how "every clock in the Ford home shuddered when Henry approached the house." Friends said he was able to reassemble even the most scattered pieces surprisingly quickly, managing to create "a timepiece that ran perfectly." By the time he was seventeen, the young mechanic was already applying himself as an apprentice in Detroit's machine shops, while moonlighting in a local jewelry shop to repair watches. Yet, the industrialist remembered, he ultimately found little affinity for "ordinary jewellery and watchmaking work excepting where the job was hard to do." Ford recalled his early engagement with watchmaking and timekeeping primarily as a primer in mechanical engineering, which operated as object lessons and ideal types for future pursuits. "A good machine of any kind," Ford asserted, "ought to last as long as a good watch."[1]

Ford's concerns for the mechanics of time were never simply biographical amusement, nor were they merely the idiosyncratic interests of a chronometrically obsessed industrialist. The disciplinary time of industry, centered in the factory but extending to social and domestic life, has been ripe fodder for historical analysis. Historians position Ford as the apogee of American industrial time consciousness. To understand how Ford came to be considered so central to time discipline we must consider Ford's broader production process—including not only what has been presumed a kind of "secular" manufacture (his machinery, use of interchangeable parts, deskilling and division of labor, conveyance assemblage, etc.) but also what, in another idiom, would be understood as Ford's "religious" production. Looking simultaneously to the mechanics and metaphysics of Ford's method—at his endeavors to reengineer time and reassemble notions of matter and mind, motorized engines, and energetic human movement—helps us better reckon with Ford's time-altering impact on American modernity and to see how his religious ideas influenced the way work time has been subsequently structured and systematized.[2]

Always seeking shuddering perfection, to machine the good and watch its lasting was, for Ford, not only mechanical virtue. It was also an enterprise of divination. This descriptive trade of the prophetic and the commercial is a transposition Ford regularly and publicly insisted upon. "There is no reason why a prophet should not be an engineer instead of a preacher," Ford told the Reverend William Stidger in an interview with the controversial media crusader for *Good Housekeeping*. "Would Isaiah be writing more Bibles if he were here today?" Ford brazenly continued, prodding the Methodist minister. "He would probably be working over a set of blueprints; remaking the world rather than writing about it." Figuring himself a latter-day Isaiah, Ford contended that engineering was, or could be, prophecy.[3]

One way to glean the divining fabrication of Ford—engineer and prophet—and the "world-shaking" power of his modern-making is to consider his endeavors to tinker with and systematize time. He did that in two distinct registers. First, through the mechanization of automotive engines and assembly line conveyance made famous in his factories. Second, through his theorization of reincarnation and his millennialist aspirations about messianic machines. Importantly, though, what I describe here as differentiated analytic registers were not, for Ford, distinct nor dual. They were instead one corporate component of a prophesied Machine Age yet on the industrial horizon. To wrestle with Ford's treatment of time is not only to follow the archive of Ford's industry. It is also to join scholars who have increasingly described religion as an apparatus through which to negotiate ways of being in and across time. Historical questions of temporality have often been translated into projects of distinguishing an ostensibly religious history of time from a seemingly secular one. In Ford's temporal tinkering and prophetic engineering, we can begin again to see relations of the religious and the secular in early twentieth-century US history. This chapter urges us to see how Ford refuses to fit neatly into stereotypes of "the secular" partly because he ascribed metaphysical significance to a material ordering of time that rejected any separation between secular and sacred, a temporal distinction that many theories of modernity rely upon.[4]

Like any good prophet, Ford proclaimed the extra of his being. Prophecy, in the roughly Ford-contemporaneous words of Max Weber, is denoted through "an effort to systematize all the manifestations of life." The work of the assembly line was never just mechanical; mass production at Ford was always more than that. "The ultimate question of all metaphysics has always been something like this," Weber summarized in the conclusion of his study of the prophetic character: "[I]f the world as a whole and life in particular were to have a meaning, what might it be, and how would the world have to look in order to correspond to it?" This chapter details Ford's answer as it was proffered both in the "magic methods" of his automotive assembly and in the material and mental magic of the American metaphysical traditions with which Ford so productively traded.[5]

I contend that Ford mechanized a new temporal regime and incorporated new means of production as central to the modern system he sought to advance—one he understood to be at once spiritual and material. In Ford's archive, I glimpse a metaphysics in his mechanics and study the mechanics of his metaphysics in order to better understand the modern time Ford mass-produced. I examine how Ford reengineered experience and automobilized industry alongside an understanding of (re)incarnational progress and the power of the human mind. In his assemblage of the industrial and the religious, Ford located existential ease, systemic order, past progress, and millennial promise. This was not because he somehow found something he could finally believe in. Rather, these economies offered the automaker a way to organize the doing of life. Throughout this chapter I refer to "progressive reincarnation" and "scientific management." The latter was an industrial term of art, the former a marker of what I discern as Ford's metaphysics. Together, these two categories summarize systems he incorporated to manage the material inequities of his modernity. Reassembling the machinery of modern lives and livelihoods, the auto-industrialist set about to perfect modernity's problems as he understood them and to ford "all the manifestations of life" in correspondence with the systems his corporation manufactured. In structures of matter and mind, system and spirit, Ford mechanized time.

Machining the Gospel of Efficiency

Ford's modern was one in which everybody seemed to be engaged in some kind of temporal engineering. Progressive reformers pressed for better times to come. Ragtime pianists and jazz musicians improvised with polyrhythmic syncopation, and Einstein sought precise calculation in special relativity. Photography snapped time short, and films moved pictures quickly. Sundays and daylight time were "saved"; working hours reduced. Electricity cast shadows in the shade of nighttime. Post offices, telegraphs, and telephones reduced communication time. Refrigerators extended nonperishable time. Lunchtime divided labor time. Cocktail hours raised spirits and signaled leisure time. Painters rendered simultaneity in multiple perspective and imaged the melted persistence of dreamtime in surrealist depiction. Science fiction writers traveled through time. Geologists gauged Earth's time in lengthening years, while Creationists recalculated its age in biblical consultation and premillenialists charted apocalyptic return.[6]

Among so many powerful forms of temporal engineering, the work of railroads proved central to time's increasingly standardized allotment and apportionment into zones. By the 1880s, railroad time was not only the prevailing way that clock-time was ordered. Drawing lessons from military organizations, railroad companies also began to centralize their managerial systems to control this newly popular and carefully engineered temporality, even as workers boldly agitated in protest. In the wake of confrontations with labor organizations, including strikes organized by the Knights of Labor in the Great Southwest Railroad Strike of 1886 and the Pullman Strike of 1894 organized by Eugene Debs and the American Railway Union, railroad carriers began employing mechanical engineers and other leaders in the shop management movement as "efficiency" experts. This newly professionalizing class of consultants was brought in to advise railroad executives about how to increase output without substantially increasing costs.[7]

From the beginning these efficiency consultants professed an expertise extending far beyond the mechanical, offering a basis for a new moral economy. Their work was, in the words of one such consultant, "a gospel of efficiency" that would establish new grounds for "a higher and more universal morality than that afforded by either ancient religions or modern philosophies." As railroad companies sought to implement their guidance, the movement gained further currency through the moniker: "scientific management." The most famous of the many emerging proponents for this new managerial science was Frederick Winslow Taylor, whose *Principles of Scientific Management* (1911) has been referred to as "the Summa Theologica of . . . faith that sound, fact-based management could improve productivity." The scientific manager's correct use and proper direction of material resources—including workers' bodies—along with the reduction of all "waste" would, Taylor argued, yield measurable results in shop efficiency. Yet, like his predecessors, Taylor was quick to insist that scientific management was never only about industrial productivity. It was also, he said, an advanced system for more scientifically sound practices of social reform. The worker and the factory served as models in Taylor's telling for how to organize and manage "all kinds of human activities"—in homes and on farms, in businesses, churches, charities, universities, and government programs—"from our simplest individual acts to the work of our great corporations," scientific management would facilitate the meritocratic rise of "the best man," someone able to rightly oversee a more efficient world order. Modern institutions did not need charismatic leaders, he said; they needed capable scientific managers—a class of specialists and technically trained decision-makers soon designated "the technocrat." Taylor's principles of scientific management found a ready audience among businessmen and entrepreneurs around the globe. Within two years, the book was being translated into at least eight different languages. Workers, Taylor insisted, did not need to be inspired by "some unusual or extraordinary man" but would instead fall in line through proper financial incentives, including higher piece-rate and bonus pay, alongside right industrial discipline. "A high-priced man," in Taylor's telling, "does just what he's told to do, and no back talk."[8]

Taylor's "magic of scientific management" proved less popular among those being told what to do. Authorities in the scientific management movement increasingly pressed workers to relinquish what managers understood to be more time-consuming skills, along with the traditional tools that had historically characterized workers' crafts. The long-held experience and on-the-job knowledge of craftsmen conflicted with the newly heralded expertise of scientific managers and their deskilling demands. Conflict was significant. In 1911, for example, a worker in the foundry of the Watertown Arsenal in Massachusetts refused to participate in a time and motion study organized by the company's scientific management consultants. The worker's refusal helped initiate a walkout at the Watertown plant, which quickly garnered attention and provoked early critiques of the so-called Taylor system of management. The Watertown walkout also sparked a US congressional review of the company's practices and ultimately resulted in a federal ban of time studies in government arsenals. In such a context, competition among production engineers and efficiency consultants grew, with many promising more humane practices of scientifically managed efficiency measures. There were differences between, for example, Taylor's stopwatch science and the motion studies of Frank and Lillian Gilbreth. Contemporary observers and later historians have spilled considerable ink trying to name and analyze these and other distinctions as they were manufactured within the larger efficiency movement. Yet, at least in terms of their assertions of humane industry, such distinctions often resulted in little more than a narcissism of minor differences.[9]

Popularizing yet another newly coined expression, *mass production*, Ford Motor Company promoted a self-celebratory version of its own brand of efficiency in a ghostwritten entry for the 1926 *Encyclopedia Britannica* published under Henry Ford's byline. In it, Ford suggested that, while efficiency experts rightly directed attention to previously neglected principles of "scientific manufacturing," the time-and-motion studies of the larger efficiency movement still failed to recognize that "a wholly new method was possible which would simply abolish the problems of the old method." Ford credited the automotive industry with bringing this new method to "experimental success." Crucially, the Motor King wrote, Ford Motor Company was the recognized pioneer of this new method, so much so that to "simplify the history of mass production and the description of its principles," it was sufficient to simply use Ford's experience "as a basis" for the concept. It was an audacious assertion given the much broader history of the efficiency movement and related practices of scientific management, of which Ford's brand of mass production was but one. Yet it largely solidified the historiographical record. As one interpreter rightly observed, "there is little doubt that . . . the article signed by Ford endowed the expression *mass production* with a certain universality." Ford's manufacture of the universal from the particular was crucial to the firm's broader practices of standardization. The company that created the Model T and sloganized it as "the universal car" also wrote itself in as the basis from which all principles of mass production were to be understood.[10]

"Mass production," Ford theorized in the abstract, "is the focusing upon a manufacturing project of the principles of power, accuracy, economy, system, continuity, and speed." More colloquially, mass production was tied to a particular kind of method and a specific technological form: the mechanized and continuously flowing assembly line. Even as the encyclopedic distinction Ford made between mass production and the broader efficiency movement was at least partly a publicity project on behalf of the Company, it was also accepted as a serious difference by many commentators and consumers. In the words of one contemporary, Taylorism seemed excessively and repressively centered on labor efficiency, whereas Ford "developed American rationalization of labour . . . into the larger rhythm of the flowing production process." To these observers, what Ford offered was a more fully incorporated manufacturing project—one whose temporal measure promised a more focused and principled project for their dynamic era of industry. Although the planning and design stages of mass production still required a careful breakdown of work processes and division of labor and materials, the Ford plants themselves appeared to many observers as one "great productive machine," an enormous metaphysical entity operating in sync and with harmonious accord.[11]

If the efficiency consultant and his stopwatch characterized Taylor's scientific management, the central discursive idiom and operative force at Ford was its machinery. Notably, the machinery that mattered at Ford was more than the finished automobile sold to its buying public. In the Ford plant, machines moved machinery that would ultimately come to move themselves automotively. One visitor to Ford's Highland Park plant described the dazzling effect of Ford's productive machinery, walking beside cars that were themselves being mechanically moved toward final completion. As the final parts were assembled, the visitor observed how each car rolled off the line, its motor pumping while "the little Ford moved out into the wide, wide world, a completed thing, propelled by its own power." As commodities were assembled and made to move as "a completed thing," Ford's "flowing production process" seemed to many such visitors to move with its own propulsive power. What the assembly line offered was, as the same visitor put it, a way to "perceive the system." To glimpse Ford's mass-production processes was, then, to glimpse its conveyance of a new industrial order.[12]

For many industrial observers what was key was not Ford's powerful machinery but how the Company seemed to master time. Studying the massive gains in production efficiency wrought through Ford's machine-driven chassis assembly, technical reporters Horace Lucien Arnold and Fay Leone Faurote noted that, in September 1913, it took fourteen hours per worker to assemble one chassis standing still in one place. At the end of April 1914, after implementing chain-driven assemblage, workers were able to assemble one chassis for every ninety-three minutes of labor. Similarly, comparing the assembly of Ford Motor engines, Arnold and Faurote cited a 250 percent increase between October 1913 and May 1914. If Ford was reengineering time, mass production seemed to simultaneously split it into ever-more-miniscule increments while also speeding it up and spreading it around. The result was a kind of temporal quickening. Amid the enormous quantities of cars assembled, Ford's was fast becoming a gospel of efficiency manufactured for the masses.[13]

"The term mass production," Ford's encyclopedia entry reiterated, "is used to describe the modern method by which great quantities of a single standardised commodity are manufactured." But, it claimed, quantity was decidedly *not* the primary factor in mass production. As with so many things for Ford, what mattered most was method. "As commonly employed [mass production] is made to refer to the quantity produced, but," Ford clarified, "its primary reference is to method." For Ford, as for its modernist contemporaries, product and process were intimately related. If Taylor and other efficiency consultants propounded "one best way," Ford insisted that it heralded no such static certainty, arguing instead for scientific management as a kind of perpetual motion, a method of persistent progress and ceaseless advancement.[14]

Machinery was "a new messiah," Ford proclaimed; it would accomplish "in the world what man has failed to do by preaching, propaganda, or the written word . . . binding the world together in a way no other system can." Ford set about to engineer a new world system of machine-made machinery, engineered and automobilized for advancement. The point was not only to increase manufacturing productivity. Like so many others in the efficiency movement, his claims to the power of mechanical engineering were always more than assertions of industrial exertion. Mechanical advancement would, Ford said, cast machines as "the best servant man has ever had . . . perform[ing] still greater tasks for him, making life more comfortable, refined and humane, more worth the living."[15]

The final element that set mass production apart from other methods of manufacture was, Ford insisted, the "capacity, latent or developed, of mass consumption, the ability to absorb large production." As product and process were harnessed together in Ford's "magic methods," so too were production and consumption. He declared, "The two go together, and in the latter may be traced the reasons for the former." Dialectically derived, mass consumption was understood to be the raison d'être of mass production. Consequently, it too must be conceived, engineered, and rightly ordered. "Mass production begins," Ford explained, "in the conception of a public need of which the public may not as yet be conscious and proceeds on the principle that use-convenience must be matched by price-convenience." Although Ford wavered slightly when pressed to prioritize "which precedes the other, consumption or production," the industrialist ultimately reminded the encyclopedia-reading public that his own "pioneering" company was the basis for any solid understanding of the principles of mass production. "The experience of Ford Motor Co. has been that mass production precedes mass consumption and makes it possible," Ford concluded. Amid its churning machinery and alongside the conveyors of its line assembly, the mechanics of Ford's metaphysics were increasingly driven through the harnessing together of production method and massive consumption increases. Ford's definitive example of mass production insisted that conceiving "public need" was central to its developing manufacturing processes.[16]

The aim of supplying a consuming public was not—should not be—about profit, Ford said. "Engineers constantly discard the old and replace it with the newer and better without waiting for the old actually to wear out," he explained, "their ideal is product, not profit." The point was instead to proactively replace the old before it could wear out. "With engineer management a business is constantly replenished with the best methods regardless of cost and the public gets a better product," Ford explained. And the result, he insisted, would be to usher in a more abundant era. In fact, so great would the value of this industrial engineering be that Ford suggested we might yet find time to make and have it all. Ford's metaphysics of mass production promised All, and its Company would order the way to it: "What we call spirit and what we call matter are one, and the All," he explained: "I don't like to talk about 'spiritual' and 'material' as if they are different or opposed. They are all one, part of All that is." Ford argued on behalf of a monist philosophy, identifying one and all, the mass and the monadic. "It is all here; everything is here and we simply acknowledge that it is here—the essence and substance of all there is," he declared. Both spiritual and material, Ford's capital command was a way to do, have, and be it All in the here and now. "It is all here now—we don't have to think of it as mysteriously distant and separate—all there is; everything is right here among us, and we can appropriate and use it." Ford's engineering was never simply focused on scientifically managed labor time or its carefully calibrated machinery; it was about conceiving, valuing, and appropriating public need. And then selling it back to that public en masse, for their spiritual benefit.[17]

The price of the Ford car was low precisely to target more people than any other automobile manufacturer had ever sought to, transforming the lived experiences of the masses. Ford boasted, "every time I reduce the charge for our car by one dollar, I get a thousand new buyers." The Model T was "a motor car for the great multitude," Ford proclaimed, and so he continually reduced its price—from $950 to $780 in 1910, down to $690 in 1911, $600 in 1912, $550 in 1913, $490 in 1914, and on and on until it reached its lowest price at $290 in 1924. Billboards pronounced the car a great populist product: "Even You Can Afford a Ford." Before the Model T, motorcars were luxury goods. Ford meant to make them durable commodities, as attainable for the worker laboring on its own factory lines as for the man presiding over the country from the Oval Office. For this mechanically inclined, price-engineering populist, to buy was to benefit. "I do not consider the machines which bear my name simply as machines," Ford explained. "I take them as concrete evidence of the working out of a theory of business which I hope is more than a theory of business—a theory that looks toward making this world a better place in which to live. The fact that the commercial success of the Ford Motor Company has been most unusual is important only because it serves to demonstrate, in a way which no one can fail to understand, that the theory to date is right." Like other entrepreneurs and engineers throughout history, Ford insisted he was not just making better machines in a better way but was making the world a better place.[18]

In its mechanics and metaphysics, Ford worked to reassemble the new and the now—in factories and philosophies, as products of temporal engineering, commercial success, and world betterment. Heralding the messianic machine in advance of a better era, the Machine Age, he positioned himself in contrast to other advocates for scientific management, contending that he was no mere technocrat. Others in the efficiency movement too readily saw stability and permanent prosperity in a tech-now that, according to Ford, was incomplete. Such a perspective "forgets the fluid and progressive elements in life," he explained, and "life," the auto-industrialist breezily assured, "has a funny way of pushing out where we least expect it. It breaks up all our diagrams." Claiming his brand of efficiency's gospel truth was centered less in ideal figurations or in a carefully calculated state but in process—in a relentlessly improving method of mechanical betterment—Ford proposed that in mass production the best was always being bested. As engineer-prophet, his blueprints for a mechanized modern proved crucial to the brand of scientific management it popularized. Yet, Ford likewise insisted that all diagrams of managerial expertise would be disrupted by "the fluid and progressive elements of life." Efficiency experts and technocratic managers might diagram right action but, Ford insisted, mass production promised something more—something active and lively, something urgent and, like those conveyors increasingly spiraling around Ford's plant, ceaselessly advancing. As we will see, the formal qualities of such a vision—all those winding, continuously progressive assembly lines pressing endlessly onward—proved compelling, not only in how Ford theorized right manufacturing but also in his understanding of what the auto-industrialist referred to as "the riddle of life," which is also to say: death.[19]

Reassembling the Gospel of Reincarnation

As much as Ford aimed to engineer millennial futures in the mass-produced improvement of a coming Machine Age, he also sought metaphysical pasts in reincarnated lives. Part of a long history of progressive reincarnationists in America, he engaged with and reproduced many of the tropes and traditions identified by scholars of religion. This includes practices of past-making, which as Courtney Bender has shown, often supplement the genealogies that scholars have used to historically locate and interpret American reincarnationists. Ford's practices of past-making were many, including the production and popularization of antisemitic and white nationalist narratives, debunking of textualist historiography, and construction of material reliquaries, each to be detailed in subsequent chapters. Among these, the auto-industrialist also joined his fellow reincarnationists in seeking out knowledge of past lives. In the process, Ford theorized experience, connected reincarnation to Christian scriptures and scientific practices, and drew upon these ideas as interpretive techniques to understand and explain his capital place in history and society.[20]

When asked about his views of the afterlife, Ford twice told a reporter, "I belong with the Buddhist crowd." Yet, the industrialist's introduction to reincarnation did not come through a specific Buddhist community or tradition. Ford learned about reincarnation through the work of Orlando Jay Smith, a former cotton planter and Civil War general from Mississippi, who also helped name and edit William Jennings Bryan's *Commoner*. On September 17, 1901, the day that the nation was mourning its fallen President, William McKinley, and collectively pondering what kind of successor the young Rough Rider Theodore Roosevelt would be, one of Ford's fellow workers shared Smith's book, *A Short View of Great Questions* (1899). The two men reportedly talked for some time about the text, and Ford later cited it as his entrance into philosophies of reincarnation. In the book, the war general—he was still addressed more than three decades later as "Major" Smith—presents a theory of reincarnation, centered on the idea "that man has an immortal soul which existed before his birth and survives the death of his body." Refusing all notions of creation and annihilation as fatalistic misinterpretations by both materialists and reformed theologians, Smith argues that all existence is eternal and unending, including the human "soul" or "vital spark." This is what it means to speak of a philosophy of "complete immortality." "Life here is only one short act in an existence that has had no beginning, and will have no end," Smith wrote. Drawing on an array of poetic references from American romanticism alongside Herbert Spencer's Social Darwinist ideas and European conceptions of vitalism, Smith's book presents his theory of reincarnation as the most logical, most scientific solution to the "Eternal Problem" of human temporality—what Smith referred to as the "origin and destiny" of humanity.[21]

If Smith's book was Ford's early introduction to reincarnation, it was not, as we shall see, the only influence. Nevertheless, reading Smith's book offers a useful perspective into reasons Ford would have found reincarnation so appealing: namely that Smith rendered reincarnation a commitment not only to the responsibility and freedom of man and to the dignity of one's soul but also to a concept of justice as eternal and exact, at once a mathematical calculation and a cosmically ordered movement. "It knows only Justice," Smith argued, "Justice to the finest degree, as exact as arithmetic, as the movements of the stars, as the order of the Universe." Presented by Smith as an "Eternal Law," reincarnation was likewise understood to "afford a powerful stimulus to the practice of morality, and to the study of exact definitions of right and wrong in the affairs of individuals, of society, of the state, and between nations." In Smith's formulation, Ford seems to have glimpsed a pathway to universal order and exacting justice amid existing inequities.[22]

As Ford explained it, "the gospel of reincarnation" was "the essence of all knowledge." What he meant by this was that reincarnation enabled a "long view of life," in which one's understanding is carried over into another mortal life and then another and another. "I believe we are reincarnated. You, I, we reincarnate over and over," Ford declared. "We go on. We don't stop. The further we go the better it becomes, I think." Humans are entities of progressive accumulation, he opined, gathering experiences, acquiring understanding, and improving themselves over the course of many lives. "We live many lives, and store up much experience. Some are older souls than others and so they know more. It seems to be an intuitive 'gift.' It is really hard-won experience." Ford was overt about the connection between spiritual concept and industrial innovation. As the assembly line promised to systematize the mechanical mayhem of modern industry, reincarnation brought structure and unity to the lived reality of his concerns—material, social, metaphysical—through the progressive processes of lived accumulation:

> Until I discovered this theory I was unsettled and dissatisfied—without a compass, so to speak. Religion offered nothing to the point—at least, I was unable to discover it. Even work could not give me complete satisfaction. Work is futile if we cannot utilize the experience we collect in one life in the next. When I discovered reincarnation it was as if I

had found a universal plan. I realized that there was a chance to work out my ideas. Time was no longer limited. I was no longer a slave to the hands of the clock. I was 40 when I went into business, 40 when I began to evolve the Ford plant. But all the time I was getting ready. That is one thing the larger view does for you, it enables you to take time to get ready. Most of my life has been spent in preparation, for I know that the vista before me is endless. The discovery of reincarnation put my mind at ease. I was settled. I felt that order and progress were present in the mystery of life. I no longer looked elsewhere for a solution to the riddle of life.[23]

In reincarnation Ford found organization and direction—a larger order to orient the mysteries of human being, working, and knowing. Reincarnation eased the urgency of ideation that otherwise seemed to preclude, for Ford, the necessary discernment and preparatory working out of one's coming-to-consciousness. "It offers an explanation for so many things that otherwise remain unexplained," he emphasized, "and it answers the rule that experience is the purpose of life." Progressive reincarnation systematized life and labor into a grand scheme, sorting and standardizing what he otherwise found to be unsettling and dissatisfying. "It is merely one phase of the world-wide and ancient belief . . . that life is continuous, that we go on and on." From one view Ford's first forty years might be seen through the lens of failed corporate ventures and other seemingly plodding preludes to business success. From the vantage of reincarnation his early stumbles were no lamentable arrested development; they were a necessary component in his longer evolution. "I had to stop for ten years and get ready," Ford explained, "I made my first car in 1893, but it was 1903 before I had it ready to sell." No futile practice, work took on added valence, becoming a way to prepare and to amass experience amid life's endless expanse. "I expect to go on and gather more experience," the industrialist said. "I expect to have opportunities to use my experience. I expect to retain this central cell, or whatever it is, that is now the core of my personality. I expect to find conditions of life further on, just as I found conditions of life here, and adapt myself to them, just as I adapted myself to these." Reincarnation proffered Ford a past that was progressively present, and it promised a future in cosmic alignment with the industrialist's expectations.[24]

Knowledge, even that which seemed instinctual, was not some kind of divine favor or natural endowment, Ford said. It was an inheritance, the epistemic winnings of former lives stockpiled as one's very soul. "A man comes into this world, I believe, with accumulated experiences," Ford wrote, "which make his mind into a certain sort of career." So it was that some men already held within them a kind of occupational, epistemological, and ontological surplus. "Geniuses are old experienced souls," the industrialist philosophized. In the longue durée of reincarnated life, experiential surplus could be quite extensive. "Life on earth, as scientists recently assured us, is twenty-three thousand million years old," Ford stated, "in twenty-three thousand million years the soul goes through many experiences." Across such a vast span, reincarnation offered Ford "an explanation for so many things that otherwise remain unexplained," including the reality of human inequality. The unevenness and variation of human ability, understanding, and disparity was merely a marker of differential experience. Reincarnation, Ford reasoned, "offers an intelligent explanation of the inequalities in life, of the differences in wisdom and maturity of people born into the world." In his formulation, those with more simply had accumulated more life experience upon which to draw. "After all, that's all life is—experience," Ford explained, "the world is only a clearing-house in which we gain experience." The "winning" power driving the auto-industrialist was, he claimed, his own experiential surplus. "We are here to work out something, and we go on from where we leave off. That's my religion, though I was brought up an Episcopalian," he explained. "For myself, I'm certain that I have lived before, that I stored up considerable experience before the present stage, and that I will proceed to the next stage when it is finished." Working, getting ready, winning, and going on. As the "clearing-house" of the world validated the auto-industrialist's abundance, Ford claimed these experiences as more central to his religious understanding than his church upbringing or sectarian identification.[25]

The "power that wins" might be difficult to name or fully define, Ford acknowledged. Like Socrates's daimon, he explained, it "may be an allegory or it may be a name for certain institutions which man acquires in the course of a long series of incarnations." The industrialist credited his own "career" and the "institutions" he amassed as having been guided by an invisible force or unseen power. How to name this powerful force?

Ford suggested many options, seemingly preferring no one in particular: "There is a great spirit. Call it creative evolution or world mind. Call it collective intelligence or call it God." "Somewhere," he further theorized, "there is a Master Mind which sends brain waves or messages to us—the Brain of Mankind, the Brain of the Earth . . . the Brain of the Universe." As we will soon see, Ford's theory of mind and his language of a "Master Mind"—a phrasing coined in works by Theron Q. Dumont, one of the many pen names of William Walker Atkinson—was central not only to his understanding of progressive reincarnation but also to a history that closely connects the auto-industrialist to a religious development dubbed by historians as "New Thought," a movement that Kate Bowler described as "a cluster of thinkers and metaphysical ideas that emerged in the 1880s as the era's most powerful vehicle of mind power." What Ford's understanding of a Master Mind or Brain of the Universe contributed to his theory of reincarnation was the way it helped him source processes of guided, experiential accumulation. Ford used such monikers as a discursive fount to identify and explain his particular modernity among a broader sweep of history, while connecting it to a Social Darwinist anthropology of those "old souls" that Ford so admired. "No doubt this phase is an essential part of human evolution," he said, when asked about his take on the twentieth century. "The world was ready for the motor age. Hence, the world brain sent men like Edison . . . to work it out." As humans gather up lives and experience, Ford continued, "We too may be but a part of the Brain of the Universe."[26]

Alongside other reincarnationists in the United States, Ford was sometimes at pains to reconcile his regenerative metaphysics with more mainstream conceptions of Christianity. "The trouble with you preachers is that you keep insisting upon calling the Bible the 'sacred book' all the time," Ford openly lamented to Reverend Stidger. At the outbreak of the world war, the industrialist had publicly pledged to read a little of the Bible each day, a practice he claimed he still maintained years later. More people would join him in such practices, the industrialist told Stidger, if the so-called Good Book was removed from all pedestals of sacrality, which only served to intimidate the average reader and to otherwise keep it "away from the common people." Offering his own vernacularizing hermeneutic, Ford offered an alternative: "After all, the Bible was written by men quite as human as you and I. Bible characters were plain people; we see them nowadays in colored windows, but they were just people after all." Criticizing reverent presumptions and ornamental understandings of Christian scripturalization and ecclesiastical history, Ford urged a more instrumentalist approach to biblical texts. "I look upon the Bible as a record of experience," he said. "No matter what knocks we receive in life, we find, reading the Bible, that others have received similar knocks. It is a true book of experience." While biblical scholars debated questions of textual interpretation and scientific authority in camps increasingly divided during this era along the lines of so-called higher critics and fundamentalists, Ford entered the fray with his own understanding—one grounded in a theory of progressive reincarnation as a process of experiential accumulation and proffered as part of his metaphysics of production that sought to privilege the masses. Approaching biblical characters as "plain people" and Christian scripture as "a record of experience" was not only a matter of right reading; it was also good science. To adopt a theory of reincarnation and the knowledge of "winning" power it affords people over the course of many lifetimes would, Ford agreed, help work toward "the real *scientific basis* . . . of what we term natural law and spiritual law." For Ford, reincarnation offered existential ease in contrast to the interminable ticking clock and sourced evolutionary change both in world-historic terms and in personified genius; it also afforded Christianity and its scriptures a scientific basis and a grounding in the common.[27]

Reincarnation further occasioned Ford's Christological account. "My belief is that Jesus was an old person, old in experience; and it was this that gave him his superior knowledge of life." Amid acknowledgments about the ineffable expression of that powerful force sometimes referred to as "God," Ford suggested that the Christ figure was a plain person, too—only different from other humans in the grand order of experience and knowledge. Affirming the high anthropology of both Social Darwinist discourse and New Thought, he suggestively theorized that divinity was a label for someone with superior knowledge and excess experience. Because "it may be that we all have our 'genius,'" he implied that divine surplus was a difference in degree more than kind. "God?" Ford responded to one reporter, "Why God is in everything, always working for perfection. . . . The whole process of reaching the ultimate perfection is naught but experience." In Ford's formulation, Jesus was an old person, perhaps the closest to "ultimate perfection," which was always, too, a work-in-process, a "reaching" in which any "ultimate" termination is endlessly deferred. "Life can not die," he reminded, "Longfellow was right—'There is no death.' It is not poetry, it is science. Life that can die would not be life." Ford's understanding of reincarnation was a progressive scientific process and a kind of perfectionist theology that accorded Christian divinity to experiential accumulation and lived assemblage. "Perhaps," the industrialist speculated during a conversation with Sufi mystic and Indian musician Inayat Khan, "that deeper wisdom is what Jesus referred to when He told us we must become as little children if we would enter the Kingdom." As we have come to understand through Ford's theory of reincarnation, the ongoing work of "becoming as little children" was a kind of literalism for Ford.[28]

Seeking Metaphysical Pasts

Like other progressive reincarnationists of the late nineteenth and early twentieth centuries, Ford sought proof of past lives, often finding it in the personal perceptions and experiences of what historians have detailed as a long-standing "science of the soul." Entangled histories of Baconian empiricism and post-Reformation theologies tell of the many ways European colonists and early American adherents— from Puritan divines and Shaking Quakers to evangelical converts and Spiritualist mediums—have sought to locate religious truth in practices of inductive and meditative reasoning, combining practices of empirical observation, data compilation, and assessment. Enduring links among Enlightenment thought, English natural philosophy, and Anglo-American religious practices situate Ford as far from idiosyncratic when he insisted on the porous boundaries between the religious and scientific, material and spiritual. "Science is not limitedly material. Religion is not limitedly spiritual," he asserted. "Matter and spirit are terms we use to make distinctions, which perhaps do not exist." As earlier Americans sought evidence in testimonies of faith, confessional witness, natural contemplation, bodily movements, reading and writing practices, emerging technologies like telegraphy and photography, and new therapeutic sources like hydro- and electrotherapy, Ford looked for corresponding evidence to substantiate the spiritual science he gleaned.

In contrast to those reincarnationists who asserted that the body contained no memory of prior existence, he contended that "the body, by its instincts, the soul by its intuitions, remember and utilize the experience of previous lives." Memories of past lives, however faintly retained, offered evidence of what came before and served as never-quite-raw material for a new combination in Ford's theory of progressive reincarnation. "What you call hunches I call the memories of things learned in past lives," Ford affirmed. Not just some kind of vaguely felt déjà vu, what was vital to understand about reincarnation as a verifiable truth of natural and spiritual law, Ford suggested, was to discover "the gist, the result of experiences that are valuable and remain with us." Though it may take some kind of catalyst to rouse the mind, bringing "scenes from the deep where they slumber on the surface of consciousness," they are not only there to be aroused within but "constitute an essential part of our being." In his view, past lives remain part of a human in memories not quite forgotten and in intuitions spurred from slumber. In these lingering lives, he identified immortal ontological presence, the very essence of a human's being. It is this that Ford also refers to as "native knowledge, knowledge born with us, which we inherit from a previous existence." The extended voyage of human living and dying and living again, was a continuous and perpetual journey, and Ford found in such inborn knowledge proof of lives past.[29]

As various media outlets began to report Ford's interest in reincarnation, a curious populous began writing to the industrialist about the matter. In the late 1930s and early 1940s, Ford—or in this case, at least, a Company secretary writing on his behalf—exchanged a series of letters with a correspondent named Edward G. Strobach. Early letters from Strobach, now held in Ford's corporate archives, primarily cast aspersions and make allusions to Jewish culpability for antisemitic persecution. Ernest Liebold, one of two personal secretaries in the Office of Henry Ford, apparently wrote a reply to this letter, though copies are suspiciously missing from the collection. Strobach's second letter asked about Ford's thinking on reincarnation. Having recently read about his professed belief in reincarnation in the pages of the *New York Times*, Strobach wondered if Ford had "ever given thought that there may be reincarnated in you, some previous person" and "who it could be." This time, a copy of Liebold's response on Ford's behalf remains in the industrialist's office papers. In it, Ford's secretary reiterated that his boss was "a believer in reincarnation." Noting that Ford had given several interviews on the matter, Liebold also offered his own recollection about how Ford had "given out some statement on the subject of having descended or have in his life the reincarnation of some other individual . . . back even to the date of the Egyptian Kings." Though Liebold hesitates to expound much further on the subject since, he wrote, it "opens up and becomes too broad for us to consider or even discuss," we glimpse how Ford seemed to have probed his own "hunches" and narrated the "gist" of his inherited knowledge, apparently stored in his very soul. Liebold's suggestion of a possible Pharaonic past for the industrialist is a telling one, particularly given the context of his correspondent's expressed antisemitism and the prominent role Ford's antisemitic publications have played in American fascism, something we will consider at greater length in later chapters. Never merely a philosophy that offered answers about life and death for Ford's otherwise unsettled mind, his ruminations on past lives "mapped layers of story and history" onto his present. What these brief moments of archival documentation offer the historian is not only evidence of his conception of reincarnation—however brief, indistinctly retained, or "hunch"-filled—such glimpses also bring forward questions about the ways that Ford, as businessman and corporate office, collected and archived the genealogical traces of his/its metempsychosis, thereby supplementing both his family and business histories.[30]

If Liebold hinted at the antisemitic orientalism of his boss's possible previous lives, Ford also looked toward the so-called mystic East to gain insight into the possibilities of reincarnated pasts. Like so many other orientalists of his era, the industrialist expressed a curiosity about what Catherine Albanese referred to as "metaphysical Asia," a reference meant to describe the ways that Americans sought Asian teachers and traditions through which to reinvent and invigorate their own metaphysical concerns. One notable example of this occurred in the 1930s when Ford initiated an inquiry into the story of a young Indian girl, identified in news reports as Shanti Devi from Delhi. Devi claimed to have been reincarnated, her account reportedly verified by "a committee of careful investigators" made up of local civic leaders. At Ford's direction, Frank Campsall, the industrialist's other personal secretary, prompted Ford Motor Company leadership in India to find out more about Devi's story, and to verify its authenticity. Seeking to confirm Devi's reincarnation story, Ford participated in a longer history of investigative rituals—rituals that, as many religious studies scholars have shown, perform religious work. As much as the investigation into Devi's claims was also part of the industrialist's efforts to verify Ford's understanding of a past ordered and reassembled incarnationally, the inquiry also showcases how the mechanics of Ford's metaphysics must be understood as inclusive of and inseparable from the corporate inquiries and global networks of his automotive empire.[31]

Not all of Ford's pursuits of past lives were cast so far afield. Others were much more intimately assigned. Historian David Nye reported that Ford was convinced that Dorothy Richardson Heber, the granddaughter of Henry Ford's cousin, was the reincarnation of Ford's mother, Mary Ford. The industrialist reportedly gave young Heber the Theosophical text, *Reincarnation, The Hope of the World* by Irving S. Cooper, a text that proposes that the "innate qualities of a child"—whether an inclination to handicrafts, untrained musical talent, the aggressive proclivities of a warrior, or the maternal instincts of a young mother who died too soon—"indicate quite clearly the general lines along which the soul of that child has been trained in previous incarnations." Later, Ford cast Heber as his mother in a short vignette that was included in an early Company film. Irving Bacon, an artist and advertising executive who was commissioned to paint many scenes from Ford's early life, was likewise directed by Ford to use Heber as his model when painting Mary Ford. Similarly, after the untimely death of his son, Edsel Ford, the auto-industrialist sought solace for his intense grief. According to Ford's close but not-entirely-trustworthy business associate, Harry Bennett, Ford "fell back on his theory of reincarnation" after Edsel's passing. In Bennett's telling, Ford affirmed to him: "[Y]ou know my belief—Edsel isn't dead." A close family friend, Mrs. Stanley Rudderman, also reported that Ford acknowledged that, while "he and Edsel had not always understood each other and at times could not see eye to eye," in the aftermath of Edsel's death, Ford felt that "before too long, he and Edsel would be together again" and thought that "there would be better understanding and they could continue working together" with such former experiences and the knowledge that accompanied them. Although these kinds of reported anecdotes resist additional corroboration in the archive, they point to ways that Ford's practices of past-making intersected with his metaphysical ideas of reincarnation. The identification and understanding of former lives seemed to promise Ford a way to more closely locate and more intimately render the stories and subjects of those who came before and of those he held dear.[32]

However much his theory of reincarnation helped Ford assemble, supplement, and systematize narratives of the past amid his prophetic charge of a coming Machine Age, for the industrialist both past and future were more fully understood as part of a protracted present, an extended now that simultaneously promised and postponed any "satisfactory fulfillment of one's own life" through infinite improvement and boundless accumulation. Ford's "gospel of reincarnation" offered the auto-industrialist a solution to the "mystery of life." It also lessened the pressure of the present. "We are pretty well shut up to this present phase of life so far as our conscious knowledge is concerned," Ford acknowledged, yet he was "never convinced that the present phase is all." Reincarnation offered a more encompassing conception of temporal existence, he explained, "and the fuller it is the more present the present is. . . . There is only this, going on, going on, and coming to itself more and more." Insisting that "there is nothing new but new combinations," Ford argued that "what is 'new' about each individual is merely a new combination." The industrialist's theorizing of reincarnation was itself a "new combination." He received it from Social Darwinist texts, and assembled it into an orientalist expression. He argued in vernacularized biblical hermeneutics and passed it on in Theosophical gifts. Finally, he located reincarnation amid longstanding practices of spiritual science, and connected it to other past-making practices by American reincarnationists. For Ford, life was a kind of assembly line of experience—always pushing out, going on, evolving, recombining, ceaselessly improving, accumulating, and coming to itself evermore through the use of available materials to increasingly efficient ends. Extending human temporality beyond any one human lifetime, Ford's theory of present-abundance can press us toward a new vantage on the auto-industrialist's modernity—one informed by the mechanics and metaphysics wrought through it and forms of experimental religion forded in the "cruel optimism" of its impasse.[33]

Mind Power and the Modern System

Ford insisted that the Company's new methods of mass production would address "the worst errors of competitive factory practice" and remake the world. Propagating a transition away from what both contemporary observers and later historians called the "American System" of manufacture, Ford insisted that its new method of mass production was a form of liberation for workers, a mechanically supported system that would free human thought from the drudgery of back-breaking labor. No longer preoccupied with mundane tasks nor having to race to and fro retrieving parts now brought mechanically to each workstation by moving conveyors, workers would be afforded time for "higher activities." Like the standardization of work processes and the sale of a single model of motorcar, the methods of mass production were, in Ford's design, intended to cultivate a deeper kind of thinking. "Everything you do, let it pertain to that one thing," Ford advised. "You have got to throw around it a great deal of mental power," he continued. This kind of concentration—of work and thought, of magical methods and mental power—would afford those "capable of and fit for freedom" a method through which to substitute "mind for muscle." Later chapters will consider in greater detail what Ford meant in his reference to the ability and fit-ness of workers. For now, the point I am homing in on is how he conceived the emancipation of workers from "physical thralldom," thereby releasing "man's energies from physical channels" into the hard work of thinking.[34]

Ford's industry was not simply about producing more and better cars (though, yes, that too). Mass production was, he urged, a way to improve human lives through abundant consumption and the energetic enterprise of right thought. It would offer opportunities for workers to recognize present problems and to identify solutions amid their ever-changing modernity. "The job of thinking is a real one," Ford argued, "probably the hardest work there is to do. Yet I believe that all the world's secrets are open to thinkers, and that whenever a problem comes to us, it can always be solved—otherwise it would not present itself." The carefully thinking worker—one freed from the tiresome toil of inefficient manufacture—would be more receptive to the "ocean of thought" that, according to Ford, "we shall always continue to live in . . . even though our form and the form of the universe and the things in it may change as we do." The metaphysics of mass production were wrought not only through the "long pilgrimage" of reincarnated living but also the right attunement of thought, and mass production offered the conditions for right reception. Ford's system of manufacture—centered on messianic machines cast to "liberate mind and body from the drudgery of existence"—would free up the "mental power" required for epochal advancement.[35]

Joining a long history of thought experiments in America, Ford insisted on the power of the human mind to think and experiment in active and lively ways. "I know a man's religion without asking," he declared, "just see how he acts, how he fronts life." As we have already seen, the ways that a person "fronted" life offered Ford a way to glimpse experiences acquired in past lives; he believed it also afforded a broader religious vantage. In the active confrontations of life, he identified the religious as a kind of experimental practice, one at least partly powered through the work of active thought. "Every man works out his own religion," he explained. "It comes partly through thought, partly through experiment." Imperially inclusive and commonly regarded, Ford fielded religion as both special and inseparable from the other domains of life: "I believe it is possible for us to experiment in the special field we call religion, and the points where most men are in fullest agreement may be regarded as the common ground of truth in that field. Not that I think religion is a field off by itself, separate. No, it includes everything, and everything includes it." As a thought experiment and agreement of the commons, Ford's approach to religion was influenced by and advanced in terms central to the New Thought movement, a religious formation that Kathryn Lofton identified as the "combinatory trope" of philosophical idealism and mind cure practices, often accented in the expressions of a protestant vernacular. Ford's intimacies with the New Thought movement and its emphasis on the power of the mind proved to be central to his experimental metaphysics.[36]

Ford once told Ralph Waldo Trine that the author's bestselling New Thought text, *In Tune With the Infinite*, had been a "great help" to him around 1914, when Ford and his associates "were working out some very difficult problems." Though there are many contenders, Ford did not elaborate upon just what those difficulties were. Ford's attention to Trine's work was no simple or passing interest. The industrialist engaged in a lengthy conversation with the author, later published under the title, *The Power That Wins: Henry Ford and Ralph Waldo Trine in an Intimate Talk on Life—the Inner Things—the Things of the Mind and Spirit—and the Inner Powers and Forces that Make for Achievement* (1928), and Ford kept stacks of Trine's other books in his office, reportedly to hand out to friends or associates whom the auto-industrialist thought would benefit from Trine's work. Ford was also "in tune" with several other expressions of New Thought. This included the work of writers James Allen and Emmet Fox, as well as related works from Theosophical and Spiritualist authors. So too did Ford send away for texts by William Walker Atkinson and Yogi Ramacharaka, which was Atkinson's ostensibly exoticized pen name, published by the Yogi Publication Society.[37]

Ford's connections extend well beyond reading practices and public conversations and place him firmly within a history of New Thought's inconstant institutionalization. While he maintained membership in the Episcopal Church throughout his life, archival materials also suggest substantial links between the industrialist and the Unity School of Christianity, an organization often identified by historians as one of the most significant and successful New Thought denominations in the United States. Founded by Charles and Myrtle Fillmore, Unity—as it came to be called—combined Hermetic philosophy, spiritualism, mesmerism, theosophy, homeopathy, Christian Science, and other forms of Christian liberalism. The founders embraced doctrines of reincarnation, and at least privately, Charles Fillmore reportedly thought himself the reincarnation of the Apostle Paul. As the Fillmores developed their ministry, though, they gradually sought to distance Unity from the "New Thought" label. One historian has described the language and practices of Unity as "earmarks of New Thought, even if clothed in slightly more orthodox terminology." Though they belonged to the International New Thought Alliance for several years and shared significant genealogical and intellectual ties to that movement, the Fillmores increasingly considered Unity to be more akin to what they called "Practical Christianity." Unity's "Christian" accent and its "more warmly evangelical emphasis than most other forms of New Thought" may have also helped Ford connect his thought experiments and mind cure commitments to the broadly Christian concerns he likewise purported. Indeed, Ford sought, and Unity gladly gave, official permission to Ford Motor Company to reprint an article on "God

Knowledge" in pamphlet form, likely as part of Ford Motor Company's non-serial imprints. Combined with the social gospel work of one-time Ford executive and Episcopal minister, Samuel Marquis, it is possible to begin gleaning how Ford helped reassemble from New Thought genealogies new forms of "Practical Christianity" in capitalized script and the mass production of machinery, men, and minds.[38]

One of Unity's central ministries, its affirmative prayer program, also proved to be crucial to Ford's thought experiments. The auto-industrialist sent prayer requests and at least one "very generous love offering" to Unity's program Silent Unity seeking aid in harnessing divine energy and to receive encouragement and support for the health and abundance of himself and several employees and friends, including Frank Campsall, P. E. Martin, Charles Boyer, and Frances Louise Jacobs, as well as Ford's physician, Roy D. McClure. In one such request, the industrialist asked Unity to help Ford Motor Company executive William Cameron in seeking "greater spiritual understanding and self-mastery." In response, Silent Unity sent prayer pamphlets for use by Ford and Cameron, assured Ford of "the great good he has done and is doing to increase the beauty and happiness in the lives of God's children," and affirmed that he "cannot fail to be richly blessed by this love in his heart." Additional correspondence between Ford's corporate office and Silent Unity includes prayers that, for example, affirmed that Ford and others in the organization "shall be renewed, revitalized, and filled with new life and energy, new strength and wholeness, new self-mastery and soul satisfaction." Ford likewise sought out Unity's prayer ministry around the time of his son Edsel's first surgery, which was undertaken to rid him of the cancer that was soon to take his life. In a letter sent just over a year before Edsel's untimely death, Silent Unity conveyed healing prayers and proclaimed, "a constructive, renewing, harmonizing power" was present and active "in each atom and cell of Edsel Ford's body." Reassuring the elder Ford that "your prayers and our prayers now unite in a mighty unison of faith," Unity claimed "perfect healing for Edsel Ford" and assured that God would free him "from every inharmonious condition." These documents from Ford's corporate archive demonstrate how the auto-industrialist found in affirmative prayer practices the kind of religious experimentalism and proper mental attunement that he lauded elsewhere as central to his metaphysics of mass production. In Unity's program of affirmative prayer, as in other New Thought idioms and ideas, the auto-motive was mechanized as a technology for health and renewal, self-mastery and the harmonizing power of faith.[39]

Through this series of practices, Ford said he found his faith. Collected experientially over many lives, stored in one's assembled soul, and fronted by the present-self, Ford explained that "faith is what we gather from experience." Theorizing "faith" in terms and techniques familiar to those in the New Thought movement while anchoring it in a materiality of his own corporate and corporeal assemblage, Ford contended that faith is a material substance, "solid and substantial," "the material out of which all the things that are yet to be are made," "an invisible and plastic substance capable of taking upon itself the reality of visible form." "Most people have yet to see how substantial faith is," Ford told Ralph Waldo Trine, "how material it is." "Forming and seeing an ideal—a mental pattern or print," he explained, "is faith." Yet, and here Ford is on solid New Thought ground, he went on to argue that faith was not only or even especially material; it was a force—a power of mind "to bring the invisible things into the visible plane where all men may use them." "I say 'material' where others say 'spiritual,'" Ford continued, "because I am thinking of the substance of life and the universe. Man is a universe of these little lives, and he himself is the Master Cell, if you like, the queen bee, that holds it all in order. Some call the man the Soul, but one name is as good as another." Through reincarnation, humans accumulated experience and gathered faith as a fundamental substance of life and a powerfully innovative force. Thus, Ford insisted, "natural law and spiritual law are one and the same—no difference." Unlike those who "may think we are thus emptying the heavens," he countered, "we are only clearing them for the greater things to appear." The point was not to populate the heavens, but to understand "what we are going to do with life after we learn how to live."[40]

"As to the religious aspects," Ford mused, "I don't know. I think it is all religious, for that matter. The whole system is what it is, and there can be nothing else." Promoting its industrial system as the broadest, most encompassing and inclusive solution to the difficult problems of the modern world, Ford proffered a new brand of prosperity—one mobilized in the mechanics and metaphysics of mass production. His auto-motive metaphysics was not crass consumerism, Ford assured, but a way of concentrating mindfully on "the welfare of the common man." Aspiring to a more expansive and experimental kind of materialism, he explained that this matter of thinking could not be understood as distinct from the religious, even as it—indeed *because* it—offered "the common man" a concrete way to secure his "bread and butter." Ford held that a "bread and butter" gospel of prosperity would help usher in the Machine Age. "The machine age is barely started now," he told a reporter from the *New York Times*. "In the real machine age which is to come the dirt and ugliness and confusion and noise and disregard of human rights which are all about us today will be done away with. This is only the ox cart stage of the machine age. I wish I might live to see the real thing when it comes." Ford prophesied that this new age would offer redemption from the insufficiencies and inefficiencies of an era on the verge of becoming past.[41]

Ford's advancement of mass production was no secularizing schema, if by that is meant merely some simplistic declension of "religion" in modernity. For Ford, the religious was to be worked out in the actions of life, through thought and experiment, across a continuously progressive assembly line of existence. He engineered a modernity that would come to be christened in its name, simultaneously congealing and culminating "now" and "then" in the perpetual motion of his relentlessly improved present-infinite. "Hidden in to-day is a root of distant to-morrows," Ford theorized, "and it is the man who knows the coming to-morrows who really sees most of life." Any system, and especially that which Ford called "the modern system," needed "able individuals to operate it." Amid the spiral of scientific management and (re)incarnational experience, the visionary mind of the engineer-prophet was necessary, he urged, to "do a kind of original work—read what few are reading, or read what isn't yet printed, reach original conclusions, deal with fundamental values which lie beneath and behind all other values." As industrial seer of that modern system, Ford worked to read "the signs of the time," and in so seeing, to cast them affirmatively into being.[42]

Not everyone was quite so convinced. Among the most famous criticisms was Charlie Chaplin's 1936 film, *Modern Times*, a moving picture featuring Chaplin's iconic character, the Little Tramp. It portrays the Tramp as a struggling factory worker tasked with screwing nuts at increasingly precarious speeds along an assembly line. Whether compelled by the necromancy of the enormous machine or the maddening rituals of constantly twisting and tightening bolts, Chaplin's character is quickly overcome by a kind of delirium. The Tramp runs through the plant erratically until, in one of the most famous scenes, the assembly line eats him alive, spitting him back out as an altogether different, perhaps crazed, person in need of institutionalization. In these scenes of industrial engineering, the temporal charge Ford heralded as the "modern system" came alive as an affective quality of mechanical quickening. Machines moving. Machines making. Powerful machines empowered, coming alive as something more than mere machinery, as the (not-quite or maybe-more-than) human. As monstrous.[43]

* * *

Ford's systemic assemblage incorporated products and processes into a new kind of movement and a new kind of time. His "religious" experimentation had many precursors, inspirations, and patterns upon which he drew to produce this assemblage. "Oh no," the industrialist once confirmed to a reporter in a flourish of understated assertion, "I am not orthodox in my religion." That unorthodox take included New Thought teachings and Theosophical gifts, orientalist examinations and Social Darwinist conceptions of reincarnation, vernacularizing hermeneutics and millennial mechanics, affirmative prayer practices and prosperity gospel promises. Disaggregating each conveyor of Ford's metaphysics would not show us the truth of his religious history. The force of Ford's mass production has always been in its assemblage.[44]

For Ford, experimentation in religion meant experimentation in "everything"—in it all, in the imperially inclusive and prophetically engineered All. In his undifferentiated approach to matter and spirit, Ford rejected any trump card kind of spirituality that suggested something above and beyond what really mattered. He advanced instead an understanding of material progress and spiritual engagement, of spiritual matters and progressive materialism, as one and the same. In Ford's brand of scientific management—written and promoted as "mass production"—he aimed to offer the public a need he comprehended, having read the signs of his times. Industrial engineering and religious experimentation meant greater efficiency and increased abundance, a way to spread the "bread and butter" of material plenty. Mass production was not to be just an engineering experiment. It was a populist-intoned prophecy of prosperity premised in and purchased from private enterprise. In Ford's endeavors to systematize life and engineer time—in assembly line conveyance and through reincarnated lives, in the magical and perhaps monstrously auto-motive, and in the machine age he heralded—we find material and metaphysical attempts to organize the world in correspondence with Ford's fashioning of modernity.

What is the relationship between Ford's metaphysical ideas and mass production mechanics? David Nye interprets Ford's adoption of the doctrine of reincarnation in 1901 as liberating the industrialist from the self-doubt that had theretofore plagued him, serving as a "catalyst" for his intense hubris and "unswerving purpose" by promoting intuitive impulses and "hunches" as reassuring evidence. I resist this causality, since it belies the messy interchange Ford argued repeatedly in his combinatory practices. More critically, drawing a causal link between idea's encounter and practical realization presumes a linear temporality in discursive construction. This is a linearity that my study of Ford seeks to interrogate rather than presume. That very appearance of linear relation—chronological or causal—is more often a product of careful assembly, an appearance that conjures clarity despite the non-clear fact of Ford's messy machinery, metaphysics, and myth-making. Rather than clean lines of causation that treat historical construction as an assembly line, I trace associations and draw interpretive energy to the spiraling dynamics of time—of Ford's and our own.[45]

Against those who asserted that history repeats itself and mankind "merely moves in a circle," Ford instead theorized: "Mankind progresses like a spiral. It goes upward and on. It only seems to move in a circle." This temporal swirl is what Ford's metaphysics engineered in and as a present-infinite, a modernity understood as an epochal moment and as characteristic of an ever-improving system of capital incorporation. Others have written about the temporalities of capitalism and of the spiral as a way to analyze notions of historical change that takes the form of something other than the timeline. In the next chapter, we will follow this fording of religion as an assemblage of the material and spiritual, physical and metaphysical, mechanical and messianic, into the ways that Ford also sought to incorporate the productive men around him. Ford explained to Trine that each person "is continually attracting *little entities*—invisible lives—that are building him up, and adding to and building up whatever he is doing." Human life, he believed, was built up in and over time through experience and accumulated knowledge, attraction and force. "There is nothing to me that is more thoroughly established than thought transference," the auto-industrialist argued:

> to my mind, thought is a force or thought has force—put it as you like. It is a stream of little organizations that go to and fro. . . . When thought goes out some of the energies of personality go out with it; these energies are around us all the time. . . . Yes, we attract them; each of us is an intelligence center. These living entities become a part of us; and then they work under our direction, and according to our character.

To accumulate lives and gather experience would bring into being increased depths of apprehension and more thorough organizational incorporation. Indeed, Ford proved to be a great organizer of the thousands of material entities, all those "invisible lives," he gathered, incorporated, and directed in streams moving to and fro. In the following chapter, we will pursue additional forms manufactured by and spiraling around Ford, as we home in on its wage and labor policies. Alongside mass-produced machines and minds, we find Ford "making men" into incorporated beings—"living entities" that become a part of Ford and then work under its direction, and according to his character.[46]

2

"Spiritual Hegemony" and Ford's Rite-to-Work Religion

The thermometer registered 9°F on January 12, 1914. Snow blew fiercely through the streets. Twelve thousand people gathered outside of Ford's glass and concrete factory in Highland Park, Michigan. Anxious job seekers had begun to line up the evening before, facing down weather reports that called for blizzard conditions through the late-night hours. To shield themselves from the forty-mile-per-hour winds, many in the crowd jostled for shelter near Ford's newly constructed plant, as they waited for the employment office to open. All in hopes of securing one of the thousands of new jobs recently announced as part of the Company's new wage and labor policy: the Ford Five Dollar Day.[1]

Though published details about the new policy and its requirements were initially few, Ford promoted the plan in headline-grabbing terms. It proclaimed that every worker—regardless of skill or experience—would be eligible to earn up to $5 per day, a sum far above the Company's previous rate of $2.34 per day. Ford suggested that this was only the beginning of its wage and labor reforms. "It is our hope to do still better by our employees in the future," Ford's second-in-command, James Couzens, said, "we want them to be in reality partners in our enterprise." Ford proffered the Five Dollar Day not only to employ more workers but also, it said, to transform industrial relations and advance social justice. "We believe that social justice begins at home," Couzens continued, in his announcement of the new plan. "We want those who have helped us to produce this great institution and are helping to maintain it, to share our prosperity." It was for this reason that Ford called the Five Dollar Day "a sort of prosperity-sharing plan."[2]

Newspapers around the country carried the Company's announcement for several days leading up to its commencement, and job applicants streamed into the area. Crowds gathered outside the factory every morning for nearly a week. Only a handful of people were ever actually hired those first few days of the new year, but need persisted. Squads of local police patrolled the scene, attempting to keep the crowd away from the factory gates. By the morning of January 12, the official day that the plan was to go into effect, more people had arrived outside Ford's gates than on any of the previous days. With the influx of so many people looking for work, so few getting it, and all of them bearing the frigid Michigan winter, the scene grew increasingly volatile. News reports say one police officer was attacked the evening prior, his uniform torn, and weapons confiscated, before reinforcements arrived.[3]

By 8 am, when Ford workers on the day shift were meant to clock in, the crowd had grown so large that roads around the plant were nearly unpassable. Employees and applicants mingled indiscernibly, shoving their way toward a single open door where Ford officials endeavored to admit only those with employment badges. When announcements were made that no new jobs would be handed out that morning, the unrest in the crowd surged. Police ultimately turned fire hoses on the masses, drenching some 3,000 of those pressed closest to the gates. For many in the crush of people there was simply no way to disperse. "We can't stand here and freeze to death," some of the men trapped near the front gates shouted, as the crowd pressed urgently toward the factory entrance. Some prospective workers' clothing froze stiff in the piercing temperatures, yet the police turned their water hoses on the crowd two more times. Some managed to scramble away, overturning vendor stands as they sought rapid escape. Others picked up bricks, stones, bottles, and other materials, throwing them in retaliation toward the officers who continued to weaponize the icy water. Some of the projectiles crashed through the factory's windows and doors. Five men were arrested as the crowd dispersed. The quieter tone was only temporary, though. Soon enough the crowd reconvened, this time seeking either revenge or basic sustenance or both. Ford's factory was bombarded a second time. Nearby eateries were taken over, and other buildings in the area were used for kindling. Police returned to discharge additional rounds of freezing water.[4]

News reports blamed the unrest on "the foreign element," apparently basing their claims on accounts of "much shouting and exhortation in foreign tongues." One account speculated that the following day would see further disorder by "the foreigners [who] mean to get inside the plant at any cost in the morning, believing that once there they will be put to work." There is no archival evidence supporting these descriptions, which mirror chauvinistic speech about immigrants. People did come to Ford from all over the world, anxious to be put to work. Hundreds of thousands of people were attracted to Ford's promises of industrial partnership and shared prosperity. Though only some would be elected to enter its gates and be put to work as "Ford men." Crowded and cold, most would be turned away. Some violently so. Above it all stood Henry Ford. "There is probably the chief reason we have made this plan," the auto-industrialist said during an interview held one of those same freezing, early January mornings. Gesturing toward the masses outside, Ford insisted that the Company's new wage and labor policies would uplift the anguished. Observing from on high those struggling for position outside his factory, Ford told reporters that the Company "wanted to give employment to more men."[5]

Ford's concern to give more to more was an organizing ambition in the Company's argument for mass production—of both automobiles and autoworkers. But its insistence that it was *giving* employment would also stand in perpetual tension with repeated assertions that the "Ford idea of welfare" was not the kind of charity offered by other forms of corporate philanthropy. "There will never be a system invented which will do away with the necessity of work," Ford proclaimed. "Idle hands and minds were never intended for any one of us. Work is our sanity, our self-respect, our salvation." Ford's brand of salvation was premised in and purchased through a focus on waged work as redemptive labor. And he blessed those rites of labor with salvific power. His was to be not only a method of converting the struggling machinist or shiftless laborer but also a system by which to set society aright. Heralding a new kind of industrial producerism, Ford reassembled an industry of and for the industrious, wagering that the value of labor is central to both industrial production and human salvation. Wages, Ford insisted, cut to the relational heart of what mattered in industry. The "fundamental truth of wages" is that "they are partnership distributions." What the Company wanted, the industrialist said, "is a better recognition of the human element in business," because "the secret of it all is in a recognition of human partnership."[6]

To study twentieth-century American industry is to find many stories similar to those that have opened this chapter—of desperate and dismissed workers and pompous businessmen eager to see themselves as figures of uplift. "That the American industrialists, starting with Ford, should have tried to argue that a new form of relations is involved, comes as no surprise," explained Antonio Gramsci, writing some fifteen years after Ford initiated the Five Dollar Day, "in addition to the economic effect of high wages, they also tried to obtain certain social effects of spiritual hegemony." Ford linked converted workers, a just society, and sacred authority in his corporation. "There is something sacred about a big business which provides a living for hundreds of thousands of families," Ford remarked in his first ghost-written autobiography. "The continuance of that business becomes a holy trust." The *Ford Sunday Evening Hour* radio show similarly heralded "the consecration of Business as a social ministry." Delving into the history of Ford's Five Dollar Day program and its related bureaucratic creations, this chapter details how, according to Ford, properly waged work and right industrial relations would redeem workers, consecrate capital, and ad/minister society. It contends that the study of religion offers important resources for understanding the Company's ritual endeavors to produce "a satisfactory human unit"—a laborer who would work harmoniously and productively for Ford, and would want to. Getting through the Company's gates was only the first step for workers at Ford. Writing about "what organization meant to Ford Motor Company," Charles Sorensen, an early Ford executive, explained that "the 'motive' came from a close-knit group of men who lived on the job" and for whom "work was play." "If it had not been play," Sorensen conceded, "it would have killed them. They were as men possessed." This chapter examines the relations of Ford Motor Company to its "human element"—both its human resources and its discursive recourse to the "human"—to better understand the "certain social effects of spiritual hegemony" obtained through Ford's possessive power. Ford's Five Dollar Day program offers a massive archive of institutionalized effort to regulate and capitalize human relations. The auto-industrialist advanced a ritual theory of labor, one that insisted upon work as an opportunity and an obligation to right one's self and one's relational world.[7]

* * *

"Ritual is, first and foremost, a mode of paying attention," Jonathan Z. Smith theorized, "a process for marking interest." As we trace the methods by which Ford began marking its interest in the "human element" of automotive production, we will draw together theories of ritual and histories of labor. Looking toward Ford's archive to understand the industrialist's systematizing significance in histories of capitalism and exploring ritual's "economy of signification"—which is to say "a means of performing the way things ought to be in conscious tension to the way things are"—we will follow Ford's metaphysics of mass production into the Company's policies and practices of labor relation and corporate affiliation. In the differential space between the "are" and the "ought," Ford focused productive planning and attentive scrutiny on its "human element," ritualizing labor in the mass production of its workingmen.[8]

At Ford, labor was ritualized. Exploring the connections between Ford's corporate projects and subjects that have been central to the study of American religion—from Puritan industry and Social Gospel reform to tropes of evangelical conversion, the making of family values, and twentieth-century civil religion—I describe the fording of what I call here a rite-to-work religion, a concern for work as the source of personal redemption and social justice. The process by which individual workers became effective corporate entities was a religious procedure, one in which the individuals in Ford's factory learned their essential value through the work they did and the relations they developed at the Company to serve Ford's process of industrial productivity.

My concept of a rite-to-work religion is an attempt to bring questions about religion and capitalism alongside studies of how "the human" has been conceived and adjudicated and how social relations have been regulated and commodified. Rite-to-work religion homonymically gestures toward ongoing debates about "rights" to work and workers' rights. Scholars have studied human rights discourse as it is entangled with genealogies of religion in the west, placing questions about changing conceptions of "the human" amid contemporary discourse on "human rights." Talal Asad traced the genealogy of the "right to work" clause of the Universal Declaration of Human Rights, locating its roots in sixteenth-century work requirements for vagabonds and vagrants, pursuing it into eighteenth-century debates about work as a civil right and national duty, and following it into twentieth-century Keynesian employment policies that emphasized work as an instrument for stimulating the modern economy. In Asad's genealogical trajectory, notions about a right to work were transformed from "a means of controlling the unruly" to "the means of managing a so-called national economy," and in each instance, work belonged to distinct and differently conceived notions of the human. The concept of a right to work is not a universal one. It has a politics that are far from neutral, impacting the ways we have historically conceived of the human and the humane.[9]

I pick up Asad's attention to the ways in which a right to work has been harnessed to conceptions of and—I want to press forward this language—the *ritual* work of conceiving, purifying, and incorporating "the human." It is for this reason that I turn toward "rites" rather than "rights" and ask how a study of Ford's concern for "the human element" might help us further grapple with that early twentieth-century moment in a larger genealogical and interpretive schema of the human. To name and describe the formation of a rite-to-work religion explains forms of sociality mass-produced at and by Ford Motor Company. Scholars have increasingly taken up the charge of redescribing "what is fundamentally social about Protestant reform," a kind of religiosity that has more often been described through a focus on the individualism of human salvation. Ford's experience with fraternal rites of affiliation as well as his relationship with and employment of social gospel minister, Samuel Marquis, yields further evidence of his social reform. Yet, I nominate Ford's rite-to-work religion as a product line distinct from Protestantism or New Thought; it was a religion assembled and mass-produced by and at Ford.[10]

Theorizing this religious formation is also an effort to describe what is "religious" at Ford and what ritual technologies the auto-industrialist employed to mass-produce "religion" in modern America. Rite-to-work religion explains Ford's form of organization and incorporation as a sectarian movement to automobilize individual human labor as corporate entity. A study of Ford's wage and labor policies and its approach to the "human element" offers a portrait of the longue durée of corporate relations. Rite-to-work religion is, then, an attempt to convey and critique the profoundly ambivalent effects and affects of Ford's labor policies and its mythic and material legacy, including what workers consent to and, perhaps, to begin to intimate why we tolerate corporate power.

Conceived with an eye to the broader product line of Ford's religious economy, the proposition of a rite-to-work religion serves as a kind of analytical ready-made of mass-produced religiosity. Ford obsessively argued that waged work was redemptive. Resisting that argument requires seeing how his efforts to salvage humans required their diminishment.[11]

Reassembling the Human Element

The Five Dollar Day program was an extension of ongoing wage reforms, shift changes, and job category reevaluations that the Company had begun in 1913. As Ford began mechanizing its production, armies of increasingly deskilled laborers came to work its quickening conveyors and soon confronted the monotony of the assembly line. This situation came to the notice of the Company through labor agitation and high rates of turnover. In reply, Ford began to raise wages and reduce shift times. Ford's Five Dollar Day plan was a continuation of those earlier changes meant to "keep the men in line and on the line."[12]

The main message conveyed publicly was Ford's promise that all workers, regardless of skill or experience, could earn up to $5 per day. In addition to a significantly higher compensation rate, the plan also garnered attention for reducing shift times, a change that labor organizers around the nation had been advocating for decades. The new shift-time policy also enabled the Company to accommodate a third full-time work period, thereby increasing Ford's total production time from eighteen to twenty-four hours a day. Initial reports estimated that hiring for the additional shift meant the Company would add somewhere between 4,000 and 5,000 new jobs at the Highland Park plant alone.[13]

Although pay rates, shift times, and job opportunities dominated early headlines, additional details about the new plan began to filter out as it took effect. What was novel about Ford's newest wage and labor reforms was the industrialist's commitment to a new, experimental "profit-sharing plan." A crucial detail was that the much promoted $5 per day total was to be divided into two different, itemized payments: hourly wages and "profits." Though every employee was guaranteed an hourly wage provided they were on the job, "profits" were contingent. Employees became eligible for profit-sharing only after the successful completion of a six-month probationary period and after they passed a series of rigorous examinations into their private behavior, health, home life, and finances. The elaborately surveilled process required a worker to "show himself sober, saving, steady, industrious, and must satisfy the superintendent and staff that his money will not be wasted in riotous living." Ultimately, the tests were based on and meant to maintain, Ford said, "certain standards of cleanliness and citizenship."[14]

Questions about Ford's plan arose soon after such details emerged. Yet, coverage in newspapers remained generally celebratory. One article in the *Detroit Free Press* heightened the Company's own promotional resplendence, calling Ford's profit-sharing plan a "munificent gift" of "bountiful beneficence," a deed of such corporate generosity that it would augur "the advent of the millennium" and "be as purely advantageous as the givers hope for it." Fawning local journalists were not the only celebrators of the Company's new program. Less obvious early supporters included the likes of Frank Martell of the Detroit Federation of Labor, who found Ford's new plan to be "a victory for the principles of union labor, and as satisfactory as if it had been brought about through union activity." The labor trustee asserted that, despite there being no formal labor organizing of Ford's plant, the workers there were "getting the prize for which labor organizing has been striving." "The profit-sharing scheme which Mr. Ford has announced," Martell continued, "is a great thing for his men and cannot but help advance the cause of labor generally." Likewise, *The Labor World*, a Minnesota newspaper published "for social justice, economic reform, and political progress," judged Ford's Five Dollar Day "a modern and just system of profit-sharing."[15]

Far less exuberant were Ford's fellow manufacturers. Many competitors speculated that the carmaker's announcement was an effort to insure itself "against possible labor troubles" and to head off possible state intervention or governmental regulation. The industrialist himself lent support to those who saw in the Company's profit-sharing plan a kind of prophylactic against further labor organizing in its plants. When a reporter from the *New York Times* came to Detroit to interview the industrialist about the Five Dollar Day, Ford disregarded the history of union activity around its plants, instead arguing that labor unions "have never succeeded in organizing our factory." The auto-industrialist insisted that this was because Ford paid better than anywhere else. But he conceded that its higher wages were not the only reason for the union's sparse success. "We keep close to our men," Ford explained. "I keep going through the shops all the time. We keep track of any talent that develops, and many of our men invent devices for assisting or simplifying our work. Such a man always gets advanced." In Ford's telling, its workers could advance their careers and their corporate interests through better work, and the Five Dollar Day was a way to help manage those efforts. If careful monitoring and tracking was needed, this surveillance was merely, in Ford's assessment, a requisite feature of a close working relationship.[16]

Workers bristled as the oversight in Ford's plant operated as a form of industrial espionage—one expressly designed to maintain an open shop. "We always had spies or agents to get information on the union," a Ford manager acknowledged. "It would just be a casual thing," a kind of rumor mill designed to convey information up its bureaucratic ranks. Ford's close working relations were governed carefully, if informally, through a network of both talent scouts and corporate spies. If the promise of successful advancement and career improvement didn't work, the threat of job loss might. Should Ford managers get wind of possible labor agitation, including walking off the job or soldiering (when "certain men who were working on certain operations . . . weren't going to do much work the next day"), the Company would recruit a ringer—a new worker or a subforeman from another department whom they could trust—to test the other workers, and subsequently fire those who tried to enlist the Company's loyalist to the union's cause. More organized efforts were dealt with even more decisively, often with the assistance of local police. Union organizers were regularly hauled away from the factory, including those who gathered considerably beyond Company property or outside of working hours. For instance, in 1913, as conveyors were first being motorized and Ford was beginning to implement its earliest labor reforms, five "socialists" were arrested for blocking traffic while speaking to "a number of the employes of the Ford plant." Less than a month later, two separate groups of organizers from the International Workers of the World were arrested. The second time, the Wobbly organizers reportedly drew a crowd of some 3,000 people, as "curious workers lined the factory windows and milled about in front of the lunch stands," but police moved quickly, arresting the speakers before they could address "a crowd of Ford employes . . . on a vacant lot behind the Highland Park

State bank." When the undaunted speakers returned the following day, far smaller crowds gathered because Ford "suspended outdoor lunch 'privileges'." The only kind of assembly allowed at or around Ford was that which the Company ordered and incorporated. In "keeping close" to its men, Ford endeavored to ensure the advancement of its assembly lines as well as the disassemblage of competing organizational power.[17]

It was these dynamics—worker organizing and union breaking—that brought Ida Tarbell, the so-called muckraking journalist, to Ford's factory not long after Ford's new plan was implemented. What she found there, she said, was something distinctly different from what she had initially expected. Having previously witnessed the not-so-benevolent corporate welfare practices of the Pullman Palace Car Company, Tarbell noted that she was instinctually skeptical of Ford's plan. However, upon spending ten days at Ford's Highland Park plant, observing and conducting interviews there, Tarbell concluded that the Company's brand of welfare "was not the paternalism that I dreaded," for unlike those "founded on a profound disbelief in the capacity of men to do for themselves," Ford's new plan "claimed that every man . . . could do for himself if you gave him chances in accord to his individual needs and handicaps." If Ford's practices to uplift the everyman were different from the prevailing paternalism of his day, Tarbell suggested it was because the auto-industrialist understood his workers differently than did other businessmen. Not only did Ford find workers capable of doing for themselves, the Company understood "that you literally could make men—make them out of the flotsam and jetsam of human life." At Ford, Tarbell explained, workers were a salvageable resource, able to be remade and mass-produced.[18]

Ford likely could not have agreed more with Tarbell's conclusions. "We want to make men in this factory as well as automobiles," Ford proclaimed. Even if men could not be manufactured precisely like cars, the analogy between automobile and autoworker was never far removed from the industrialist's investments and intonations. "It was only a short time ago that some one suggested that, since it paid to study the scientific management of steam and gas engines, it might pay to study the scientific management of men," Ford observed. The Company's metaphysics of mass production further insisted upon a rightly assembled and properly fit worker—a laborer who would work harmoniously and productively for the Company. This meant workers had to show up for work on the right days in accordance with the proper liturgical calendar. It also necessitated right care for the body—both individual and corporate.[19]

"Sickness, indebtedness, and fear and worry" could breed discord and result in lower production rates among Ford workers, one executive remarked. He went on to describe the plight of an anonymous drop-hammer operator whose production numbers suddenly plummeted after years of experience. The decrease was enough to draw the eyes and ire of Ford's increasingly meticulous production analysts, who quickly ascertained that the hammer itself was in good condition, as was the health of the worker himself. The drop-hammer operator proved to have no complaints about the Company, but upon probing further, interviewers came to understand that "things entirely outside of business . . . had crept in and had put a satisfactory human unit entirely out of harmony with the things that were necessary for production." The wife of the "human unit" had recently become seriously ill and could no longer care for the couple's children. The worker worried about what would become of his family and feared destitution from mounting debts. Once the Company made an effort to help the worker address the deteriorating conditions of his home life, his production rates returned to expected levels. The Ford executive offered no details about the specific steps the Company took to support the worker, but the incident and others like it apparently pressed Ford to "suddenly comprehend the intimate relations between an employee's efficiency and his home life, recreations, and sense of security or insecurity."[20]

Seeking to manufacture both a new kind of worker and a new kind of relationship with those workers, the Five Dollar Day endeavored to bring laborers into partnership with Ford by insisting that workers commit to the corporate relation and requiring that they enact those commitments. "The work and the work alone controls us," Ford asserted. Together, employer and employee would work for the interest of the Company. "We made the change not merely because we wanted to pay higher wages and thought we could pay them," he explained. That would be mere charity. Instead, the Five Dollar Day emphasized remuneration for both the value of work exchanged and of corporate profit produced. This form of payment would, Ford asserted, put the business "on a lasting foundation." No simple redistribution of wealth based on maudlin charity or philanthropic earnestness, Ford averred that his was the work of building a more stable, more durable, more secure future; for, he noted, "a low wage business is always insecure." Low pay precluded the commitment of real relationality because it pressed workers into precarious conditions and reduced their resultant productivity. The durable future, Ford forecasted, was to be built instead on the redeemed worker and the shared working relations of all those involved in the making of abundance through Ford's durable products.[21]

It would also mean the making of dependable workers who, according to Ford, should never be cast as dependent entities. While advocating and seeking to advance what he called the "arrival of the idea of humanity in industry," he warned that any humanistic approach to business "always had to reckon with the parasitic nature of men." As we will see in greater detail in the following chapter, the new working relation Ford sought to advance was regularly presented in contrast to the parasitical or non-working stockholder. But from the Company's initial announcement that it was investing some $10 million in the plan—an amount Ford claimed would have otherwise been allocated as dividends to the firm's eight shareholders—the plan was promoted as a way to enact a belief "in making 20,000 men prosperous and contented, rather than follow[ing] the plan of making a few slave-drivers in our establishment multi-millionaires." Amid the Company's promotional flourish, Ford placed its plan in an ambivalent relation to other paternalist economic systems, including human enslavement, a charge that would continue to haunt Ford. "By no means all employers or all employees will think straight. The habit of acting shortsightedly is a hard one to break," he observed, further stating that true social change could not be legislated or adjudicated by the state. Instead, the Company endeavored to initiate what it considered to be an age of enlightenment in industrial relations. "No rules or laws will effect the changes. But enlightened self-interest will. It takes a little while for enlightenment to spread. But spread it must."[22]

What was needed, the industrialist countered, was the guidance of private enterprise. "Business men do not think of themselves as leaders in social movements," Ford observed, "but they are." Because a businessman's "contact is constant and their influence unavoidable," the industrialist contended that corporate leadership was more influential than that exercised by politicians, teachers, or clergy. Ford said it was business that was responsible for guiding people into right habits and proper values. To bring about a better kind of corporate leadership, Ford set himself up as an enlightened exemplar, professing a pedagogical purpose in the social uplift of his workingmen.[23]

Though Ford is more accurately aligned with the rhetorical stylings of populist pundits, some of his competitors and critics began to label him a socialist, based in part on what they perceived as his efforts to redistribute wealth. In response to such charges, Ford pronounced that, as far as he understood socialism, "it is a doctrine which is popular among those who want to share other people's money without doing any work." Any such system, he insisted, was profoundly unappealing to him and certainly not part of his endeavors to uplift and reform. "We don't expect to pay anybody anything who does not work," he continued, "and we can tell here when a man shirks" or "is not doing his proper share." To Ford, socialism was a system inspired by shirkers wanting to share the spoils of others' labor. The Five Dollar Day was, according to James Couzens, a counter both to lazy forms of capital speculation and to the "socialist tendencies" of the era. Against what Couzens perceived to be the "asinine answer" of nationalized industry, the Ford executive insisted that the Company's new program would show that Ford could and would succeed on the corporate terms it supplied without the meddling of state regulators or capitulation to idle investors.[24]

Eschewing any label of socialism, Ford also rejected the idea of a solitary man "sufficient unto himself." Something more relational was required, and at Ford the relations that mattered were those that were rightly incorporated and properly waged. The manufactured relations at Ford offered a different kind of sociality, a less ecstatic one than many beatific visions of socialist solidarity promoted. "It is not necessary for the rich to love the poor or the poor to love the rich," Ford stated, "what is necessary is that employer and employee should try to do justice to each other." He offered a transactional but, he argued, no less fundamental relation—one that rewarded a more circumscribed corporate coupling between employer and employee. Industrial occupation, properly waged, could turn selfish elements into social justice. Work, the productive toil of labor, would deliver humanity from its idle greed. It would lead the way toward more abundant living and away from the perils of both moral and material poverty. "Poverty is not cured by charity," Ford argued, "it is only relieved." "To cure it the causes of the trouble must be located and then removed. Nothing does more to abolish poverty than work. Every man who works is helping to drive poverty away." According to the industrialist, work was not just a form of individual salvation and capital saving; it was the path to social redemption by offering purchase on what Brad Gregory has called "the Goods Life."[25]

Part of what made Ford's philosophy of industry unique was its simultaneous commitment to high wages and low prices. The worker on the line should, he thought, be able to purchase the durable good he was helping to produce. "What good is industry if it be so unskillfully managed as not to return a living to everyone concerned?," Ford provoked, insisting that a business was responsible for offering a return to those whose toil produced its profit. Even the Company's most unskilled worker was doing his part, Ford argued, and consequently has "the right to demand a wage that will enable him to maintain his family in moral and material environments that are healthful" and that, if used properly, "will give him shelter in his old age and spare him the disgrace of the almshouse and poor commissions." Unlike the "disgrace" of almshouses and other charities designed to placate the indolent poor, Ford argued that his plan put people to work, liberating them from a legacy of shiftlessness. In the process, he reproduced moralizing claims against those not otherwise graced with waged work.[26]

Work was, Ford urgently insisted, the only thing that offered real happiness, the only thing that could truly redeem one's venality. "So far from being a curse," he proclaimed, "work is the greatest blessing. Exact social justice flows only out of honest work." Sharing profits with those who really worked to be Ford's corporate partner—that is, among those whom Ford's processes of incorporation worked—would help bring about the justice Ford foresaw. "Human nature is essentially selfish," but never absolutely. "I have never met a man who was thoroughly bad," Ford explained; "there is always some good in him—if he gets a chance." If the opportunity was there, he thought, men could and would transform. "My idea is, aid men to help themselves. Nearly all are willing to work for adequate reward." In the rites of labor, Ford proposed redemption from the selfish self.[27]

Ministering and Administering the Ford Idea of Welfare

Ford regularly and publicly forswore any "belief in paternalism." For the auto-industrialist the disavowal of this much bandied-about term meant something particular: "[W]e are not in the habit of founding 'institutions' for [our workers] . . . we consider our employes as independent beings, and we do not believe they would relish paternalism any more than we." Ford claimed no interest in instituting anything like Carnegie's elaborate library system or Rockefeller's massive endowment to the entity that would become the University of Chicago. Instead of such philanthropic impulses, he appealed to what he called the "Ford idea of welfare" as the work of industrial occupation, a commitment to "provide a fair day's work, just pay, good working conditions, security of work, and a chance for every man to secure individual and personal consideration." Ford's idea, one executive explained, was to focus on corporate investment *through* its workers, not merely spending *on* them or *for* them. Spending *for* workers was what businesses did when they distrusted their workers. The executive described how some businesses worried that, if paid high wages, laborers would "buy diamonds, or drink, or do something else that might injure them." To avoid this, such companies put money "into gymnasiums, lunch rooms, swimming pools . . . spend[ing] this money for the employes in a way *they* feel would be beneficial to the men." In contrast, spending *on* workers was what companies did, the Ford executive continued, when they "give yearly bonuses to the men and then forget anything about the manner in which they might dispose of the same, thus relieving the mind of any further responsibility." Countering these approaches, Ford insisted that its way was different. Its interest was in "spending the money *through* the men." Unlike other employers, Ford claimed that his company trusted its workers as partners, "giv[ing] them money to do things for themselves in a way best suited to the needs of the individual."[28]

Ford also insisted that its thoroughgoing idea of corporate welfare would also help safeguard its own corporate investments because the Company was committed to encouraging and assisting workers to find practical ways for "investing this money for the benefit of both themselves and their families." The primary way that Ford protected its corporate investment *through* workers was by "making the getting of profits conditional and the continuance of profits conditional." In practice, this meant that the Company set rigid eligibility requirements for its profit-sharing plan. When describing those requirements, the Company claimed a kind of rhetorical simplicity: "[Y]ou have to live right to get [profit-sharing] and continue to live right to continue to get it." As we will see, at Ford to "live right" was anything but simple. It meant workers were required to understand and adhere to "certain standards of cleanliness and citizenship," as defined by the corporation. It was also far from simple for the Company to verify workers' uprightness or convert them to right living. To do so, Ford created an entirely new and increasingly sprawling bureaucratic entity, which it named, at least early on, the Sociological Department.[29]

Established as a centralized venue to assess and oversee employee eligibility for the Ford Five Dollar Day, the new department quickly became a kind of catchall, universalist entity for the Company's "human element." It was promoted as a place where a worker can go "if he does not know where to go, or if he fails to secure what he considers the proper hearing or remedy." In many ways, the department was the Company's early iteration of what would later come to be called a personnel office or human resources department. Endorsed as "the personal representative of Henry Ford and of the Company," it was likewise charged with being "a link between employer and employee where they may meet on a common ground and settle any real or fancied injustices." It was also the bureaucratic organ responsible for adjudicating the suitability of which workers were eligible to receive "profits." This meant employees in the Sociological Department were charged with ensuring that their colleagues were "living right" and in proper accordance with the standards set out by the Company. Among the conditions Ford outlined in its eligibility requirements for the new plan were traits that it understood to be central to establishing healthy and harmonious employee-employer relations. "Thrift, good service and sobriety will be encouraged and recognized," Couzens explained. If social justice was to begin in the home, Ford explained, "the man and his home had to come up to certain standards of cleanliness and citizenship . . . a man who is living aright will do his work aright."[30]

Once worker efficiency came to be understood as resolutely connected to environmental, familial, and social conditions, the home lives of Ford laborers were increasingly subjected to corporate oversight through the Sociological Department. In accord with Ford's professed concern for close-keeping, the Company promised the experience would be a personal one—not some abstracted experience through which workers were reckoned as an undifferentiated mass. To account for and rightly regard each worker as a unique individual, department investigators surveyed every worker one-on-one, both in the factory and at their home. They sought out conversations with workers' families and neighbors, and they maintained extensive personnel records for each person being examined for eligibility. Doing so, Ford reasoned, would help the Department "know the man as an individual, and to deal with him in relation to his home and environment." Through the creation and continual updating of these records, "a Ford man is no longer an unknown number" but instead "takes his place as an individual member of the organization, with a home and a family, with a position in the community and purposes and ambitions which the Company recognizes."[31]

The Department then used the personal information accumulated to determine workers' eligibility for the Company's profit-sharing plan. Despite Ford's regularly repeated insistence that it trusted its employees, the Company expressed concern that increased income among some employees would be a startling and confusing new circumstance, one that could lead to wasted time, money, and energy. And waste was something Ford could not abide. "It was clearly foreseen that $5 a day in the hands of some men would work a tremendous handicap along the paths of rectitude and right living and would make of them a menace to society in general," said John R. Lee, the Sociological Department's first head. Accordingly, investigators examined workers' living conditions, financial outlays, personal habits, and recreational activities, and they advised laborers on how to best utilize their new resources. Tasked with counseling and helping "the unsophisticated employee to obtain and maintain comfortable, congenial and sanitary living conditions" and to "exercise the necessary vigilance to prevent, as far as possible, human frailty from falling into habits or practices detrimental to substantial progress in life," department investigators ministered and administered Ford's idea of welfare and its related notions of social justice. To ensure that workers used their funds "advisedly and conservatively," department employees were also empowered to "take away [a worker's] share of the profits until such a time as he could rehabilitate himself."[32]

The Sociological Department conducted examinations using many of the primary tools of the early twentieth-century sociologist and social worker, including personal interviews and surveys, home visits, and statistical analysis; they also issued case study reports. Investigators mapped out and apportioned the city so that investigators could be clearly and efficiently assigned to the array of neighborhoods in which Ford workers lived. During meetings between investigators and workers, agents of the department would record answers on a prepared form with places to transcribe a host of information, including basic identifying information for the employee and all members of the workers' family along with much more detailed data—from years of residence, citizenship status, nationality, and religious affiliation to whether a worker drinks alcohol or smokes tobacco, the worker's doctor's name, any life insurance coverage and amounts purchased, debts and mortgages, any property owned or leased, the number of rooms occupied and the physical condition of a worker's home, the air quality and furnishings within, and the frequency and number of boarders taken, if any. In addition to this extensive reporting, Ford investigators noted whether they obtained the information with the help of an interpreter. They audited bank accounts and otherwise scrutinized "every available source . . . churches, fraternal organizations, the Government, family Bibles, passports—everything that would give the truth about these men." Documents from the Ford archive attest that police and prison officials worked closely with Ford investigators, too. In response to their findings, investigators advised workers on what the Company considered practices of "right living." The Department understood their responsibilities to include instructing workers on specific sanitation standards, familial order and obligation, property ownership and fiscal responsibility, and the successful use of Americanized cultural and linguistic expression. The Department checked whether Ford workers worked the way Ford wanted even when they were home.[33]

These elaborate inspections also brought investigators into traffic with established forms of religious reckoning. Accounting and surveying practices have long been part of the work of religion in America, whether by anxious Puritans intent on ascertaining signs of election or by promotional teams of social gospelers in advance of scheduled revivals. Conjoining evangelical conversion narratives with Social Gospel reckoning, Ford's Sociological Department was responsible for fulfilling Ford's missionary enterprise, in accord with the Company's designs of worker uplift and American assimilation. "I think that if we are persistent in following up what we have started to do, and are careful and diplomatic in bringing about a change of conditions in the living of our men," Lee explained, "and make them see what it is that Mr. Ford really wants them to do, that we will eke out the success for this scheme, even more than Mr. Ford has planned." The department therefore conducted repeated exams with workers, particularly early on in the program's history. It was crucial, Lee cautioned, to remain attentive to those who "have walked the straight and narrow path for fifteen or twenty minutes, and then dropped back to their old traits." As scholars of American evangelicalism have argued, conversion has rarely been understood to happen once and for all. If preaching to the choir was sometimes necessary to prevent backsliding, Ford investigators also found it necessary to examine and evangelize on a routine basis.[34]

By 1915, with the First World War under way, Lee was transferred to a different position with the Company, this time in Washington, DC, as government liaison, applying his sociological skill to diplomatic lobby. On his removal, leadership of the Sociological Department was turned over to Reverend Samuel Simpson Marquis, Dean of the Episcopal Cathedral in Detroit, and one-time personal friend and parish minister of Henry and Clara Ford. The liberal clergyman, known for his advocacy of improved relations between capital and labor and extensive ministry to the business community, had been advised by his physician to take time away from his parish for health reasons. Marquis had already been volunteering with the Ford Motor Company, advising Lee and his employees as they worked to institute some of the earlier, pre–Five Dollar Day labor reforms. Soon Marquis decided that what he really needed was a change of vocation. Rather than rest, what he needed was work. Where better for this minister to do so than at Ford? The minister quickly found there a new call and a new flock. When Ford asked him to take over the Sociological Department, the clergyman readily accepted. Using the nickname the auto-industrialist gave to his new employee, Ford reportedly urged: "I want you, Mark, to put Jesus Christ in my factory." In late

1915, the Episcopalian minister became the central administrator of Ford Motor Company's "human element" and the Christian executive overseeing and incorporating its social work. Ford's sociological project had for some time been engaged in the relational work of religious reckoning, with the Sociological Department intervening in individual work's moral lives. But Marquis's arrival amplified the most overt social gospel aspects of Ford's Five Dollar Day plan.[35]

Under the Episcopal Dean's leadership, the department was formally renamed. No longer the Sociological Department, by 1916, it was the Education Department. Its "investigators" were officially retitled "advisers." The Company continued to face questions about the paternalist properties of the Five Dollar Day, but during this time, Ford increasingly countered its critics by turning to its pedagogical role. While the educational aspect of Ford's plan had been suggested in its public pronouncements from the beginning, with Marquis's arrival, Ford's project was presented less often as employee investigation and inspection and more so as one of worker edification and examination. "Some people call the fifty-acre group of buildings out in Highland Park the Ford Factory. Well it is that," Marquis began, "but it is a great deal more—it is a school. Mr. Ford is more interested in men than in machines. He is, before everything else, interested in the education of his employees." If Ford was conducting a set of rigorous assessments among its employees, it was doing so pedagogically, the clergyman explained. Its point was not to police but to teach. Likewise, it was under Marquis's leadership that a new slogan gained steam. The former minister consistently asserted that Ford's sociological programs were fraternal rather than paternal, routinely repeating Ford's new motto: "Help the Other Fellow."[36]

Progressive Purification

The era of the Five Dollar Day was a time that many historians have since referred to as the Progressive Era, a period often perceived to be one of increasing speed—as expanding corporations raced for market dominance, muckrakers prompted sales alongside scandal, and labor hustled. Ford was resolutely a part of this moment, his machines quickening both production and consumption as workers pressed for labor reform. The auto-industrialist reportedly kept a signed photograph of his friend and engineering icon, Thomas Edison, in his office, and was known to reflect upon the image's inscription, which read: "To Henry Ford, one of a group of men who have helped to make the U.S.A. the most progressive nation in the world." The country abounded with reforming ardor. Fastidious hygiene campaigns among social reformers, settlement houses, philanthropic institutions, and missionary organizations sought to scrub dirt and depravity from modern city centers as much as in far-flung foreign locales. Photographers exposed the stain of poverty to cleansing light through works like Jacob Riis's *How the Other Half Lives*, meant to make more transparent the troubling realities of an increasingly industrialized nation. Diets and fasting fads developed. Temperance campaigns reinvigorated long-held concerns about alcohol consumption and self-restraint. Eugenics discourse sought to sterilize the unfit and control births. Curative practices reshaped medical programs, and hospitals became holy grounds as practitioners joined forces with reformers and corporate advertisers to disinfect domestic spaces and cleanse bodies as forms of spiritual progress and civilized living. Ford's particular brand of progressivism mirrored this assemblage of social reform, educational work, eliminative effort, and cleanliness campaign. Led by Ford's former parish minister, the Company's sociological investigations and managerial advice would become forms of both fraternal counsel and sermonic exchange.[37]

"Study the way you are doing things!" Ford exhorted. "See how many steps in any particular process you can eliminate. An inefficient process is almost invariably a 'dirty' one. All waste is a kind of dirt." Theorizing labor efficiency in direct opposition to dirt, Ford echoed the concerns of many of his contemporaries. Dirt, twentieth-century Americans seemed to instantiate at nearly every turn, simultaneously threatened to spread disease and dis-ease, jeopardizing healthy bodies, compromising productive practices, endangering moral rectitude, and risking social assurance. "Reflection on dirt involves reflection on the relation of order to disorder, being to non-being, form to formlessness, life to death," wrote Mary Douglas, an anthropologist best known for her structuralist theory of dirt as "matter out of place." "Whenever ideas of dirt are highly structured, their analysis discloses a play upon such profound themes," she argued. "This is why an understanding of rules of purity is a sound entry to comparative religion." At Ford, dirt polluted and endangered all that was presumed pure—from the spaces of its factories and the healthy bodies of its workers to the tidy homes and the American nation that the Company sought to inculcate.[38]

The sanitation of Ford's "human element" was central to the Company's techniques of scientific management and mechanized efficiency. Laborers and their homes, like the Company's machinery and factories, were to be kept "immaculately clean." The industrialist claimed that his mother's spotless kitchen established the cleanliness standards of his shops, but such pristine measures proved to be more than maternal model or domestic duty. They became rites of divine injunction and industrial prosperity. "There is a lot to that old Biblical statement that cleanliness is next to godliness," Ford told the Methodist minister and radio personality, William Stidger, repeating an aphorism commonly, if mistakenly, attributed to biblical texts. Although his citational practices were considerably less than immaculate, Ford's emphasis on ritual purification as central to right religion and industrial virtue does have a long and enduring history—one that scholars have increasingly recognized and chronicled. Plus, Ford added, cleanliness is not only proximate to the empyrean; "it is next to prosperity also." At Ford, practices of purification required scrupulous care and attention, and "besides that," the industrialist observed, "it pays."[39]

The human is "a three-cylinder engine in one piece" declared an early Ford imprint published by the Company and authored by Marquis prior to his arrival at Ford Motor Company. "Keep an engine clean and it's a better engine. Keep a life clean and it's a better life," Ford advised. "When you look under the hood of a human being and see slovenly disorder, watch for a smash!" Bringing its brand of scientific management to its "human engines," Ford urged workers to be properly fitted and carefully installed "with self-starting device and automatic control." Here we see the Company's managerial strategy as a discipline of the self as industrial technology. "Success in our case," Ford urged, depends upon "scientific self-management." The willingness and ability to reduce "possible waste in time and strength" would enable the worker to put themselves in proper working order—one that did not rely on either a benefactor or a boss to "tell us how to get the most out of ourselves."[40]

Antonio Gramsci theorized the concept of hegemony directly in relation to Ford's industrial system. If hegemony was "born in the factory," as the Italian revolutionary described, it was also a project that he said extended well beyond the plant floor. Ford prescribed both greater productivity and increased prosperity, and it both invited and insisted that workers get on board with its corporate mission by demonstrating their commitment to Ford's notion of right living and laboring. This was the opportunity and the obligation of all its industrial partners. Ford's Sociological Department administered the Company's millennial mission and pedagogical program, ushering workers into what Ford prophesied as a new age of advanced industrial relations. To be successful Ford workers needed to demonstrate their own clean living while affirming Ford's corporate fellowship and industrial fitness.[41]

Home Visits and Right Consumption

In 1915, Ford published *Helpful Hints and Advice to Employes* as a supplement to its Sociological Department employees' domestic inspections and advisory duties. It instructed workers to "live in clean, well conducted homes, in rooms that are well lighted and ventilated . . . [and to] avoid the congested and slum parts of the city." Profit-sharing, Ford explained, would be granted only to those with clean and wholesome surroundings. The homes of recent immigrants drew special attention from the investigator-advisers. "In visiting the homes of foreigners," another Company imprint that was published the same year detailed, "the Advisors explain to the people, through an interpreter if necessary, the joy and healthful advantage of cleanliness and order, and . . . try to impress this fact especially upon the housewife." Employees were advised not to sleep in rooms occupied by more than one other person. Foul smelling locales were to be avoided, and toilet accommodations were of particular olfactory focus. "Employees should use plenty of soap and water in the home, and upon their children, bathing frequently," Ford's *Helpful Hints* pamphlet advised. Interior and exterior spaces were to be kept tidy. Vegetable gardens and flower beds were lauded, as were covered garbage cans. To accompany their supplementary prose, the pamphlet also offered pictures for its employees' edification. "Study the pictures," the Company publication instructed, "with the aim in view of drawing as much comfort and satisfaction out of life as possible, by leading clean, moral, and self-respecting lives, and to provide for the future and old age. . . . Each employe[e] should feel that he is one of a big organization, and take a personal interest in its welfare." If the investigations were a way to personalize workers in Ford's growing organizational structure, they also expressly directed employees to incorporate the organization's welfare as their own.[42]

The department's records of investigation served as a repository for the newly made man, manufactured with pen and paper if not fully fleshed out. A few of these were published as examples of the work undertaken by the department. For instance, the "record of investigation" for Stanislaw Danzch, a forty-two-year-old worker who was initially denied profit-sharing, was published in the November issue of *Ford Times* in 1914. A recent immigrant from Lithuania, Danzch and his family inhabited two rooms in a large home, the rest of which they let out to boarders. Mary Danzch, Stanislaw's wife, operated the boarding house and made a fairly sizeable income doing so, though Ford emphasized instead how the work ran her ragged. The Danzch's bank account had a healthy sum in it. But neighbors complained about the Danzch children, and the department's investigator-adviser, R. Roe, took issue with both the tough working conditions of Mary Danzch and the meager comforts of the family's rooms. At Ford, thrift was not a synonym for living as cheaply as possible; it was a form of "intelligent saving"—a smart kind of keeping that did not compromise domestic comforts oriented on right purchase. Through the work of the Sociological Department, "the foreigner" was urged to understand that the national bargain was not relentless economizing. Instead, Roe and his fellow investigators required workers to ever-more-fully realize "the meaning of the phrase, 'American standard of living'." To scrimp and save endlessly was devalued in the mass-production of Ford's economies of scale. Such behaviors were not "really living" but instead "merely existing." Investing in and properly valuing oneself and one's family was Ford's formula for success. "It is possible even to overemphasize the saving habit. . . . You are not 'saving' when you prevent yourself from becoming more productive," Ford advised. "You are really taking away from your ultimate capital." Workers should not squirrel away their lives or their family's livelihood. They too needed proper investment. "It is not the possession of money, but the right use of it," Ford asserted, "that goes to make a man's future." Roe initially withheld profit-sharing from Danzch because "he had denied himself and his family every pleasure and comfort that were rightfully theirs and which men, who were earning much less, as a rule, were willing to accord their families." Money, like workers, needed to be put to work.[43]

For Ford, a properly principled worker was also expected to be the primary breadwinner. Ford required men to "live with and take proper care of their families," and to do so, Ford "had to break up the evil custom among many of the foreign workers of taking in boarders." Homes were not for money-making. Earnings were to come from outside the home. Ford advised workers against "regarding their homes as something to make money out of rather than as a place to live in." As factory labor methods changed alongside increased mechanization and standardization of both the job and the product, Ford's profit-sharing plan and the sociological education it meted out contributed to Ford's reconception of acceptable forms of masculinity and right family-making. The responsible head of household became a defining characteristic of what it meant to be a man at Ford. That is, to be a Ford man, to be forded as *man*, was to be the provider, an American family man.[44]

At Ford, the workingman was never only an individual. He was also a citizen and householder, responsible for contributing to both domestic and national welfare. Ford understood that this meant the corporation had to pay them accordingly—on "conditions." Those conditions necessitated that the worker demonstrate his commitment to the same principles of upright living and corporate welfare. A clean home and living conditions improved a worker's production, and the Sociological Department would administer the Five Dollar Day profit-sharing plan to incentivize those standards. Importantly, too, from Ford's perspective, increased production from the "householder" enabled his dependents to consume rather than to take on some other "hideous prospect," like "being forced out to work." For Ford's men, industrial work offered redemption. For "mothers and children," heralded labor was that which happened in the home and with the family. Home labor economies, though, like manufacturing, would be increasingly mechanized, according to Ford. So, if the automated factory offered the opportunity for higher thinking, as the automaker insisted, the industrialized home would advance right purchase. Through the leadership of American industry, Ford explained, "wives are released from work, little children are no longer exploited; and, given more time, they both become free to go out and find new products, new merchants, and manufacturers who are supplying them." It is for this reason, he argued, that there is an intimate relation between domestic life and industrial production, "the prosperity of one is the prosperity of the other . . . the solution of one helps in the solution of another."[45]

In the salvation schema of Ford's rite-to-work religion, wages revealed not only right corporate relations between employer and employee; they also exposed the ways in which consumers were to appropriately orient to products. Wages marked productive partnership as well as the value of acquisition. In his third autobiographical account, Ford explained this consumptive wager: "An unemployed man is an out-of-work customer. He cannot buy. An underpaid man is a customer reduced in purchasing power. He cannot buy." A rightly remunerated worker has proper purchasing power, he suggested, and part of that power is best exercised by the worker's family. Ford insisted that the country "is maintained by work" and that "the evidence of work is wages," but it was the employer who "has to create customers." Part of what made Ford such a success, at least in the industrialist's successfully self-managed telling, was the "first-class customers in [his] own company." Productive, salvific work that would remake workingmen and reform social relations was not only to be found in the factory. It was also located in the consumptive practices among workers and their families. "There can be no true prosperity until the worker upon an ordinary commodity can buy what he makes. Your own employees are part of your public," Ford advised, "if you cut wages, you just cut the number of your own customers." His mission of industrial conversion was an errand extending to the bodies and homes of workers and their "dependent" families. The fording of "family values" happened in industrial experiment and domestic economy.[46]

With the help of an interpreter, Investigator Roe advised Stanislaw Danzch "as forcibly and comprehensively" as possible about Ford's standards of cleanliness, citizenship, and consumption. He sent Danzch to learn English in the Ford English School, which was operated by the Sociological Department, and Roe took the worker to witness first-hand "what other men, employees in the Ford factory and born under similar circumstances, had done for themselves and families." Soon after his field trip with Roe, Danzch moved his family to "a comfortable cottage with six rooms, large back yard upon which much labor had been expended, as was evidenced by the grass, flowers, and vegetables," in a new neighborhood in Highland Park's suburban environs. The *Ford Times* article did not detail how the family financed such a move, but it did assert that "clean living and healthy quarters had taken the place of the dark, crowded, dismal and neglected two-room arrangement." According to the Company, the profit-sharing plan, with its social and educational disciplines, had rendered Danzch's home and family life anew. Harkening tropes about the optimistic affects and youthful futurism of conversion, Ford emphasized the "contentment [that] was written upon the face of the wife, and the children in school promised a bright future." Ford publications held up cases like Danzch's and his ethnic brethren as proof "that if a man is treated in man fashion, given the practical recognition in human equality; given equal opportunity and all around freedom in initiative and living—the 'square deal'—he will respond like a man."[47]

Work was, consequently, not the only ingredient in Ford's prescription to right its human element. Production was always harnessed to consumption. This included not only domestic products and familial purchase but also the goods ingested into workers' bodies. To combat pollutants of both human and social bodies, Ford became an outspoken supporter of Prohibition. "Liquor never did anybody any good," Ford said, "I'm against it in every form. I wouldn't have a laborer who drinks. He can drink neither on nor off duty. . . . Business and booze are enemies." The Company later teamed up with federal and local Prohibition agents to enforce the Eighteenth Amendment in Detroit's neighborhoods. Even more vociferously, Ford was a fierce critic of smoking, publishing an extensive booklet on the evils of the cigarette or what he termed "the little white slaver." Drawing on statements by scientists, inventors, military officers, journalists, teachers, YMCA officials, boxing champions, the Women's Christian Temperance Union, juvenile court judges, and an array of corporate and industrial leaders, Ford compiled an advice manual meant to appeal to young men who might be tempted to take up the "dirty" habit. "The world of today needs men," he wrote, "not those whose minds and will power have been weakened or destroyed by the desire and craving for alcohol and tobacco but instead men with initiative and vigor, whose mentality is untainted by ruinous habits."[48]

Ford was also a vocal advocate for and investor in the industrialization of food, insisting that good food would yield more goods through the labor of rightly productive people. "I believe that most human ills are directly traceable to food," he told a reporter from *Popular Science*. As part of Ford's larger factory hygiene campaigns and sanitation squads, including the formation of an official Safety and Factory Hygiene department, the Company established "a little bacteriological lab" and conducted regular analyses of the food served in their corporate lunchrooms and concessionaries in order to monitor appropriate "food values" and ensure "that they had sufficient food qualities." "In manufacture you cannot make your product better than the materials you put into it, and food supplies the materials from which the body is built up. From proper food a strong body comes, from improper food a weak body." Like the machinery and industrial processes in his plant, productive workers needed to be rightly examined and carefully maintained to avoid excess and eliminate waste. "It isn't work that kills men," Ford told Bruce Barton, "work lengthens their lives. It's eating—just the way you can ruin a boiler if you let it choke up with too much coal and cinders and dirt."[49]

Such consumptive accounting and bodily maintenance was, for Ford, a matter of expressly religious work, a rite of responsible well-being that evinced and affected righteous living. Eating, Ford said, was "part of religion." In an interview with a reporter from *Redbook Magazine*, Ford explained: "[Y]ou cannot have a thorough-going complete religion without it." Clergy should "teach people how to eat," he advised, "instead of cluttering up religion with a lot of things that do not belong to it." Ford set out to do just that. Aligning himself with the Christian physical culture movement, he reprinted and distributed to its workers a sermon by Reverend Ralph Welles Keeler of Crawford Memorial Methodist Episcopal Church, who preached about the close relation between right religion and healthy living—"not in the magic sense" of religionists like Mary Baker Eddy, "but in a more normal way, as evidenced by our physical and cultural make-up." Greater recognition of that relationship would, Keeler said, "hasten the day of the Kingdom of God on Earth" and ensure "we would have a race more fit physically." Dissociating itself from Eddy's Christian Science, Ford's imprint urged instead a Christian millennialism in healthy consumption, orderly physique, and mental upkeep. "A disordered, run down, or worn-out body affects both mind and soul," the pamphlet explained. Consciousness of this "would drive us to the best possible physical condition, in order to not cloud our thinking, or mar the vision of our soul." Drawing on a passage from Romans, Keeler's sermon continued to herald bodily sacrifice as religious practice, describing the "perfect body . . . as a fitting demonstration of one's spirituality." "Religion makes insistent demands that we keep ourselves physically fit," the homily explained: "It asks that we consider our bodies living sacrifices for the service and use of God among our fellows. The man who is religious accepts this challenge and finds the body remarkably free from many of his former ailments. For he treats his body as a gift from God. . . . [A] body that is as it should be, bids the soul take the throne and rule." In Ford's prosperity gospel of health and wealth, workers were urged toward a new form of muscular Christianity through the laborious upkeep of robust bodies, abundant living, refined consumption, and physical fitness.[50]

In studying "food values" and instructing people about the soul-affirming value of imbibing rightly, Ford furthered its administration of proper religious incorporation. Ford's rite-to-work religion yoked production to consumption through the embodied regime of waged work, domestic hygiene, and healthy eating. To reform his human engines, Ford sought to root out ruinous habits, expanding his rites of purification and incorporation into the bodies of his workers. To cultivate and manage health and wellness as necessary industrial resources, masculine habits of householding and perfect fitness became a larger project for Ford—a task that prompted the Company's errand to extend out from the machinery on its factory floor and into Ford's workers' bodies and homes. "While the Company has specialized in methods, materials, and machinery, and a single model of car," a Ford promotional pamphlet explained, "it is also . . . specializing in MEN." Like its "Universal Car," Ford sought to mass-produce a new kind of "universal" manhood. Whitewashed like the walls of Ford's factories by its roving sanitation squads, these newly standardized, industrially civilized, racially reformed workingmen were to be part of the larger material product line emerging out of Ford's *man*ufactories.[51]

Sacred Waste and Human Fitness

"One of the principal requirements Mr. Ford makes of his associates is—Health!" emphasized one Ford employee. The Medical Department was one of the first things a new worker encountered, through the employment physical. If these tests helped avoid future claims for preexisting conditions, Ford insisted that they were also intended to align workers with the right job. The Company claimed worker dissatisfaction and lower rates of production correlated with worker fitness. If a worker could be fit carefully to an appropriate job, his production rates and his own individual level of contentment would be higher. "A man with weak lungs is not put at dusty or confining work," Ford explained, "a man with a weak heart is not placed on a heavy lifting job." To fit workers to appropriate jobs, the Medical Department was tasked with conducting strict physical exams of all new hires. It helped that the medical exam room was located right next to the Employment Department at the Highland Park plant. Medical staff, Ford contended, were in excellent positions to "exercise a sort of watchfulness over men." "Besides their medical and surgical work," he explained, "the doctors have to do a sort of sociological work in looking after the employes." The Ford method, the auto-industrialist said, was to "straighten up men who show evidences of not keeping to their standard" by putting them into the right job and keeping them busy. Marquis affirmed this approach, urging a group of industrial physicians and surgeons to appreciate "the social value" of their work as "a great and sacred responsibility."[52]

According to one Sociological Department executive, Ford was concerned for worker health and fitness "because he regarded the body as a machine; how to improve it and make it last longer; how to keep it from growing old—the old problem of cleaning the rust off and shining the brass." The Company's concern for worker health and medical care was promoted as part of Ford's broader efforts in material salvage. "There are literally thousands of other economies religiously practiced in the Ford organization," proclaimed one Company publication. Historians of religion have noted the ritual work of caring for and disposing of "sacred waste." At Ford sacred waste was carefully contained, rigorously reinvested, and ritually incorporated. Ford exercised multiple economies of religion in its plants and, as we will see, his concern for re-collecting sacred waste helped guide historic preservation projects in his creation of a sprawling Americana reliquary. Machines and industrial materials weren't the only elements the industrialist claimed to salvage religiously at Ford. Humans were too.[53]

"One of the features of the General Salvage Department is its salvage of men," the Company attested. Work would reform all for social salvation, Ford insisted. But it also sought to reinvest in its human units, especially in those it said were otherwise too often wasted, devalued, or needlessly cast out. Trading in the moralizing tones and racial science projects of his day, Ford heralded employment practices that directly sought to incorporate—that is, to simultaneously produce and dissolve difference—a range of applicants typically marginalized from industrial labor. "There are many here who have lost an arm or a leg, are deaf or blind—yet each is happy and self-respecting, holds down a good job and does his work well." Producing and designating human difference in dis/able-bodied terms, the Company celebrated in condensed and condescending terms its employment of thousands of men across a range of physical abilities. The "maimed and the halt" or "the blind man or cripple," found work "among the great number of different tasks" in Ford's growing industrial empire. Those workers would, Ford promised, "receive exactly the same pay as a wholly able-bodied man." By the close of the second decade of the twentieth century, the disabled population of Ford's workforce constituted not quite a third of the total number of men employed at Highland Park. If carefully fitted to the task at hand, Ford contended, disabled workers could and would perform their work with equal, if not greater, productivity. One contemporaneous critic of Ford attested to the role of disabled workers in Ford's plants, grimly confirming the Company's detailed and precisely reckoned reinvestment in the productivity of all its human engines:

> When a worker hurts himself, he receives medical attention and must return to work. If he has broken his right arm they give him a job for which only the left arm is necessary: he becomes one of the many "substandard men." Thirty-five hundred ninety-five types of activities (in total there are 7,882 in the Ford factories) must be completed by the crippled, of these 670 by those missing both legs, 2,637 by those missing one leg, 2 by those without arms, 715 by the one-armed, and 10 ten [sic] by the blind.

Welders work even in the hospital. Black oilcloth outstretched on the bed serves as a work area on which the patients screw nuts into bolts. . . . Whoever is not able to continue working not only receives no paycheck but also receives no medical support.

Handicapped and disabled workers had considerable value at and for Ford—value forged through their efficient and rightly fitted labor.[54]

Yet, Ford claimed, if all labor had the power to re-form men, it was also the case that humans were distinctly unequal—not just differently distinct but also hierarchically ordered. "Men are not equal in mentality or in physique," he asserted; "any plan which starts with the assumption that men are or ought to be equal is unnatural and therefore unworkable." As we have seen, those human inequities were not to be excused or avoided. For Ford they were evidence of divergent experiences and progressive promise. What was needed was the saving power of work—ritual toil understood as a way to get ready, to prepare, to acquire, and to accumulate the experience needed to advance in the long pilgrimage of human reincarnation. Ford insisted that his corporation did not condescend to crippling charity; instead, it offered work. It offered a new life, in and through labor, the right to and rites of work.[55]

"Thinking men know that work is the salvation of the race, morally, physically, socially," Ford wrote. "Work does more than get us our living: it gets us our life." At Ford, all lives and livelihoods were valuable and valued through mass production. Drawing on eugenic idioms of human "fitness," the industrialist's incorporation of labor value also machined difference onto workers' bodies through the historical discourses of racial and ethnic distinction. During the time of the Sociological Department's administration of the Five Dollar Day, around 70 percent of Ford's workforce was foreign born. In the years following the plan's introduction and in the wake of the First World War, immigration from abroad fell significantly, abetted by restrictive federal legislation. However, increasing numbers of Black workers migrating from the American South to northern cities like Detroit meant increased numbers of African Americans in Ford's factories. The Company garnered a (sometimes celebrated, sometimes lamented) reputation for employing a great many immigrant and black workers. In Ford's plants it was understood that otherwise ethnically and racially marginalized men were paid rates equal to their white and American-born counterparts. Importantly, though, once hired, these workers were much more often assigned to particularly difficult jobs, ostensibly based on their examined "fitness," diagnosed in part during the employment exam. This was especially true for Black workers, who were much more frequently placed in or transferred to foundry jobs.[56]

Between 1918 and 1947, Black workers were disproportionately placed in jobs around the blast furnace, coke oven, iron melting, and other hot and hazardous areas of the factory. Lloyd H. Bailer, an early analyst, writing in 1940 after performing independent statistical analysis and conducting interviews with officials in the automotive industry as well as with both Black and white auto workers, described foundry occupations as "the most undesirable in the industry." They are, Bailer continued, "extremely hot, dirty, and demand exceptional strength. The accident rate is higher in the foundry than any other department in automobile plants. Workers are subject to hazards such as burns from molten metal, flying sparks, and touching heated machinery and metal parts." Labor economists have since shown that in Ford's Rouge plant nearly half (46 percent) of Black workers were assigned to foundry jobs, whereas only 5 percent of whites were. In fact, by the 1930s, nearly all workers in foundry jobs were categorized as Black, and by the end of the decade, "Ford essentially stopped hiring whites for foundry jobs." Although the implementation of the Five Dollar Day prompted a turn to wage equity in Ford's plants, such that Black and immigrant workers were all eligible to earn—conditionally—an income equivalent to every other worker in the plant, and at a wage that was, at least for a time, considerably higher than other industrial manufactories, they also were subject to much more difficult working conditions. "Ford captured the negative wage differential that the outside market attached to black labor by masking it with a positive differential for difficult work," one group of labor economists concluded. "In this way, Ford could profit from discrimination elsewhere without generating major differences in the observed wages of its own black and white workers." Exploiting racialized differences in outside alternatives available to Black workers, Ford was able to exercise an arbitrage strategy that proved exceptionally profitable to the firm.[57]

All workers could be redeemed, all could be forded, through Ford's rites of labor. "The Negro needs a job, he needs a sense of industrial 'belonging,' and this ought to be the desire of our industrial engineers to supply," Ford editorialized. The industrialist insisted that the chance to work—the opportunity to labor in return for wages—was the most liberating of all initiatives, enabling the formation and reformation of working men. "Freedom is the right to work a decent length of time and to get a decent living for doing so," he reasserted. Through the Five Dollar Day, Ford claimed to be transvaluing the worth of deskilled work through the thing Ford understood as most central to labor valuation and corporate relations: wages. "There is no reason why a man should be penalized because his job is menial," Ford explained. Such jobs were paid at the same rates as any other because "they are useful and they are respectable and they are honest." Ford thought it "absurd" to insist on equality across all humanity, but, he said, "I am for the kind of democracy that gives to each an equal chance according to his ability." As we have seen, equality was an absurdity in Ford's understanding, not least because of the way that different experiences ordered human lives. To earn the experience required to move up in Ford's spiraling pilgrimage of life, one had to work at it.[58]

Ford's rite-to-work formation not only offered up labor as the prescription for proper advancement, it also reproduced and worked to naturalize racialized notions of "fitness." If, in the longue durée of one's career—a notion Ford understood to last over many lifetimes—work would enable advancement through acquisition of experience, it also meant you had to start somewhere. Proper placement meant examining closely where a worker rightly fit. The placement of most Black and some immigrant workers in the most challenging working conditions reveals how the Company forded racist assumptions about the supposedly innate capabilities of African Americans in industrial occupation, while also embedding Southern and Eastern European immigrants as "problematic" ethnicities in need of civilizing correction.

Scholars have frequently turned to Ford to discover the creation and reformation of racial and ethnic categories. George Paris Loizides has shown the ways that "race" and "ethnicity" came to be understood as related but distinct categories at Ford. Southern and Eastern immigrants were "ethnics," whereas Black and Jewish workers were "races." Beth Tompkins Bates has described the ways that Ford's views about racial difference aligned with his support for residential segregation and antisemitic sentiments. Most recently, Elizabeth Esch has shown how Ford constructed and surveilled a variety of racial regimes across the globe as crucial elements in its capital accumulation, with the color line cutting through Ford's still uneven and still unequal methods.[59]

In Ford's telling, unlike the ethnic civilization and proper Americanization of immigrants, racialized human difference made "the assimilation involved in social 'equality' as impossible for the African as for the Asiatic element of the population." Even as he claimed that African American workers were "entitled to opportunities to develop . . . and enjoy [their] natural human rights," the racial "fitness" of some workers—notably Black and Jewish laborers—placed them, according to Ford, at a naturalized disadvantage. Among biographers of Ford, historiographical focus has often fallen upon William Perry. Perry cut trees on the Ford family farmstead in Dearborn during the 1880s and is said to have been Ford's first Black employee. In renderings of Henry Ford, the twenty-something young man is said to have come out to join Perry in his labor, taking hold of one end of a two-man crosscut saw and working with Perry to cut the wood. Nevins and Hill, Ford's authorized historians, point to this story as early evidence of the industrialist's philosophy of race: "the colored man at one end of the log and the white man at the other." In hagiographical accounts of the industrialist, Perry is thereby cast as Ford's first labor "partner," but the story is more suggestive of a particular kind of separate-but-equal form of racism. Ford's conception of race was also put to work in fording notions of an American nation in nativist terms. If Ford's America could not assimilate his conception of racial difference, Ford's industrial assemblage nevertheless promised corporate belonging to all.[60]

Investigator Testimonials and Ritual Conversions

In January 1915, to celebrate the one-year anniversary of the Five Dollar Day, Ford had its investigator-advisers reflect upon their various experiences and turn their documentary records into published testimonials. The result was a large book of case studies, or "human interest stories," as the department called them. The testimonies by Sociological Department employees about Ford's "human interests" manufactured patterns of change and reform that would be generally unsurprising to those familiar with histories of missionary discourse. Though historians of missionary projects have long noted the varied results and often inconclusive projects of reform and conversion, missionary journals and other promotional materials often reproduced romanticized and sanitized stories of such efforts both at home and abroad. A quick review of Ford's Sociological Department testimonials reveals a familiar set of themes and tropes: workers transformed, families rehabilitated, homes improved, drunks cured, immigrants assimilated, bank accounts and cottages built up, furniture and clothing purchased, gratitude and new-found faith in Ford Motor Company earnestly expressed. Yet, closer readings show considerable angst on the part of Ford investigator-advisers. In his advice to his employees early on, John Lee recognized that "we are afraid they are shamming this improved manner of living." One regular concern among investigators pertained to the marital status of workers and their own in/ability to verify it. Testimonials from investigators describe workers lying about being married, forging documents, or even hiring neighbors to pose as wives or family members. Some accounts mention assumptions by their fellow workers about their investigations, noting that they were often avoided by other workers "as they would a plague." Even those that recounted successful relations with their colleagues who had finally come to "fully realize that the investigator is the personal representative of the Company, and consequently their best friend," nonetheless maintained that it was "a sure thing" that any workers who continued to object to an investigator's questions had "something to hide and has been doing something underhanded which he is afraid will be found out." The point is that amid celebratory tropes of corporate success, it is possible to read the testimonials from Ford's Sociological Department as also hinting at the furtive ways that workers negotiated, resisted, or even conspired against the missionary impulses of Company programs.[61]

The auto-industrialist's producerist idea of capital investment was not only a kind of industrialized economic logic. It was also a crucial component of the religio-racial identity and white nationalism manufactured and administered through the fording of right domesticity and properly propertied consumptive values. We can see this in two testimonials included in the Sociological Department's anniversary book. Together they showcase what historian Stephen Meyer referred to as "assembly-

line Americanization," which I take to be a political economy and technological regime oriented on racial capitalism and national assimilation.
The first "human interest story" is of a recently immigrated, Russian
peasant named Joe Kostruba, who lived with his wife and six children in
what the Ford investigator described as "a filthy, foul-smelling hole"—
until, that is, the fraternal commitment of the Company stepped in to
help Kostruba "make a start toward right living." The second account is
of a young Turkish Muslim worker named Mustafa Kectcheli who lived
"with his countrymen in the downtown slums in a squalid house" until
a Ford investigator "advised [him] to move to a better locality." Written
by Sociological Department employees, each case concludes with the
worker reformed and, ultimately, deemed eligible for Ford's Five Dollar
Day profit-sharing plan. The workings and wages of whiteness among
immigrants like these has been described and analyzed by many historians, most prominently by David R. Roediger and most recently by
Elizabeth D. Esch. What I want to emphasize here is how Ford's project
was affected ritually, including through the testimonial rites of Company
investigator-advisers. If Ford's reforms were always more ambivalent
than its investigators wanted to admit, the testimonies they compiled
showcase the ways that the Company narratively shaped the lives of
workers into neat and tidy stories of corporate conversion.[62]

After the freshly clothed Kostruba family moved into their newly furnished five-room cottage with instructions from the Ford investigator
to use "a liberal amount of soap," the family gathered in the backyard
of their former residence. "Their dirty, old, junk furniture" was heaped
into a pile and set aflame. "There, upon the ashes of what had been their
earthly possessions, this Russian peasant and his wife, with tears stream-
ing down their faces, expressed their gratitude and thanks to Henry
Ford, the *Ford Motor Company*, and all those who had been instrumen-
tal in bringing about this marvelous change in their lives," wrote the
investigator charged with administering the profit-sharing plan for Joe
Kostruba, refusing to recognize that there may have been many reasons
besides simple gratitude that the Kostruba family may have shed tears
that night. While the Kostrubas were reassembled in right relation to
Ford and its American standard of living through this "ritual of fire," the
story told of Mustafa Kectcheli is one that features a new ritual relation
both to the worker's employer and to Islam. Although Kectcheli had pre-

viously washed his hands and feet between three and five times a day as part of his religious practice, his conversion to a Ford Five Dollar Man found him clothing himself in new ritual garb. He "put aside his national red fez" and no longer wore "baggy trousers," but dressed instead "like an American gentleman." After his domestic relocation and upon having begun to learn the English language, Kectcheli also "voluntarily took out his first naturalization papers." When M. G. Torossian, the investigator assigned to the case, interviewed Kectcheli, the worker was no longer performing daily ablutions or offering regular prayers. Instead, according to Torossian's testimony, the Muslim worker petitioned: "Let my only son be sacrificed for my boss (Mr. Ford) as a sign of my appreciation of what he has done for me. May Allah send my boss 'Kismet.'"[63]

Although Ford's sociological associates sometimes assisted workers with naturalization papers, it was in the English School where an "American standard of living" was most directly taught as practical idea, national ideal, and disciplined virtue. Origin stories about the Ford English School often recourse to the challenges of bureaucratic communication and workshop safety. According to one early study of Ford methods, the Company originally printed notices and forms for employees in English, Italian, German, Polish, Greek, Turkish, Russian, and Romanian. However, at the bottom of every one, it also demanded in large print: "LEARN TO READ AND WRITE ENGLISH." Like other efficiency techniques being developed in the factory, Ford increasingly sought to standardize the language of his workforce. He set aside special classrooms for the instruction of all workers who did not know the language. Initially staffed by one man with twenty students, the school increasingly took on both new instructors and new pupils. Eventually operated by English-speaking employee-volunteers across job categories, the lessons were designed to provide a working knowledge of English in less than one year, with an average time-to-completion of approximately six months. All non-English-speaking workers were expected to attend, and it was an eligibility requirement for all immigrant workers seeking "profits." "They had to go to school," one Ford employee remembered. "There were many, many men who never would have thought of learning English if it hadn't been for that." In the first three years of the school, there were reportedly between 1,600 and 2,700 students enrolled at the Highland Park plant at any given time, and lessons that included issues of practical living in America were central to the school's curriculum.[64]

In addition to English sentence structure and vocabulary, Ford workers were also taught a cultural grammar for American citizenry. One account describes lessons in "such matters as the proper care of the body, bathing, clean teeth, etc.; daily helps in and about the factory, including safety first and first aid; matters of civil government of the state and the nation; how to obtain citizenship papers, etc. In a word, the lessons are based on environmental conditions and their improvement." Civics and etiquette were regular and important aspects of the Ford program. "In addition to the basic principles of civil government, the simple fundamentals of table manners are taught, such as how to sit down at the table, how to place the napkin, how to put sugar and cream into coffee and how to drink from a cup and not from a saucer," the Company detailed. "The men are taught how to use a knife and a fork; that a knife is made to cut with and a fork to convey food to the mouth." As Ford sought to fit employees with productive forms of bodily wellness, instill proper consumptive habits, and advise on how to keep a healthy home, in the English school, the Company was also fording a new manner of American citizen.[65]

By the time of the Class of 1915's graduation, Ford Motor Company was apparently teaching English to men who spoke more than fifty different languages, establishing itself as a kind of "cosmopolitan university containing all the human elements of sturdy American citizenship." Ford's graduates were issued diplomas upon completion of the entire course, and the school required that all students not only be able to pass language examinations but also understand "the basic principles of civil government." Indeed, Ford's English School extended significantly beyond the teaching of the English language; it was an Americanization program institutionalized for industry. A diploma from the Ford English School was even accepted by the US government as an acceptable form of documentation for the first stage of the naturalization process, exempting its holder from initial examination.[66]

The Company's graduates and graduation ceremonies attested publicly to Ford's nationalist endeavor. Ford debuted its infamous "melting pot" as part of the school's annual graduation. The stage featured "the towering side of an ocean steamship," as if docked at Ellis Island. Graduates processed down its gangway into a huge, papier-mâché cauldron, which the Company understood to be "symbolic of the fusing process which makes raw immigrants into loyal Americans." Ford publications rightly observed how "the 'Melting Pot' exercises were dramatic in the extreme," detailing its ceremony at length:

> from the ship came a line of immigrants in the poor garments of their native lands. Into the gaping pot they went. Then six instructors of the Ford school, with long ladles started stirring. "Stir! Stir!" urged the superintendent of the school. The six bent to greater efforts. From the pot fluttered a flag, held high, then the first of the finished product appeared waving his hat. . . . Many others followed him, gathering in two groups on each side of the cauldron. In contrast to the shabby rags they wore when they were unloaded from the ship, all wore neat suits. They were American in looks. And ask anyone of them what nationality he is, and the brief reply will come quickly, "American!'" "Polish-American?" you might ask. "No, American," would be the answer. For they are taught in the Ford school that the hyphen is a minus sign.

In this elaborate ritual, Ford remade its working men not only into a new kind of efficient, productive manhood but also into an American porridge, amalgamating human materials in national fusion and nativist calculation. With fluttering flags and hats held high, Ford's American reduction offered a stirring tableau. Its human element forded into productive citizens, "eager with stimulus of the new opportunities and responsibilities opening out before them."[67]

Fraternal Rites

At Ford, fellowship was component to monetary policy and managerial strategy. Waged work was designed to make laborers into partners. Ford shortened shift times and raised pay to increase labor efficiency but, equally as important, it claimed, was the Five Dollar Day's contribution to winning a worker's good will, "gain[ing] his cooperation and fill[ing] him with enthusiasm for his Company." Ford executives reckoned their success in the Company's significantly reduced turnover rate. In Ford's telling, the Five Dollar Day not only raised overall employment numbers; it demonstrated that more workers were also sticking around. Marquis attributed the Company's new staying power to the Five Dollar Day's expression of fraternal spirit: "The attitude of the Ford Motor Company toward its employees is not paternal, but fraternal. The 'Help the Other Fellow' spirit runs through all we do. The men catch this spirit and are practicing it in their relation toward one another." Appeals to Ford's fraternal spirit were undoubtedly part of a larger response to ongoing charges of paternalism. They also echoed practices of fellowship and camaraderie elsewhere attested to in Ford's archive.[68]

One central area of fraternal membership that proved crucial to Ford's understanding of corporate fellowship and ritual society was the industrialist's participation in American Freemasonry. Ford was familiar with Masonic imagery from his father's membership and engagement with it. His father, William Ford, proudly displayed the characteristic all-seeing eye from the Masonic plaque in the family's parlor, and Henry Ford took his own pledge as a young man. Advancing through successive Masonic degrees, Ford was raised to the Sublime Degree of Master Mason in 1894. Later in life, he was conferred the title Sovereign Grand Inspector General and named an honorary member of the Northern Masonic Jurisdiction's Supreme Council upon initiation into the highest and last degree of the expanded rite.[69]

It might be easy to file away the industrialist's Masonic participation as part of the expected, though never innocuous, practices of American businessmen and boosters. In some ways, it was. Like church membership, fraternal clubs and civic associations were part of the standard practices of twentieth-century public life for entrepreneurs like Ford. Though he remained a member of the Masonic brotherhood throughout his life, he was never a very active participant in lodge activities. Those close to Ford have suggested that if Masonic dues hadn't been paid out of the Ford Motor Company coffers, his official membership probably would have lapsed at various times throughout his life. Yet, Freemasonry does play a valuable role in understanding how Ford understood the social rites and disciplinary virtues of fraternal relation, which became central to the practices of corporate assemblage and socialization that Ford manufactured and mass-produced. Scholars of American religious history have described Freemasonry as a combination of enlightened, scientific artistry and republican gentility with the esoteric symbolism of

Hermetic secrecy, mystical initiation rites, ever-expanding degrees, and colorful public ceremonies. Histories of Freemasonry have also shown how advancement in the brotherhood was a way for elite, white men like Ford to establish respectable relations to a pan-protestant political economy—one where politicians and businessmen ritualized their relations, ascended hierarchy by degrees, and played out right headship of the American social body.[70]

Dana Logan has shown how Masonic initiation invested in subjects like Ford a form of ritually controlled and hierarchically arranged sovereign power, even as they repeatedly invoked ideas and ideals about inclusive democracy. Celebrating the promise of republican civic association alongside overt marginalization of non-elite, non-white people from the social body, Masonic initiation rites enacted the "royal remains" of monarchal sovereignty—a quality present in all corporate bodies but which Logan shows took a more literal form in Freemasonry's elite fraternity. Freemasonry's rites of initiation featured highly choreographed and artfully staged violence—often through plots of men being "hunted, punished, and raised from the dead." Participation in these rites offered powerful men like Ford a way to attest (to themselves as much as to others) that they "had earned their position through a meritocratic process, even if that process took place behind closed doors." Ford and his Masonic brothers used initiation rites to demonstrate to themselves that their social status was not simply a by-product of privilege but was proper and deserved. While Freemasonry's elaborate ceremonies were public affairs, the audience for initiation was the Masons themselves—an awkward training, Logan argues, that instructed the brotherhood in practices of "virtuous discipline that could be put on and taken off," teaching them to inhabit multiple, flexible, impermanent, and even dichotomous roles, "both subject and sovereign, active and restrained, individual and corporate." For Ford—human founder and corporate brand—that kind of supple duality was a necessary and profoundly valuable enactment. Logan's insight provides a way to better glean the rituals that authorized whiteness and popularized a pan-protestant metaphysics of sovereign violence and democratic appeal. Ford drew upon and reproduced these rituals and metaphysics in his own manufacture of fraternal spirit as corporate wager and industrial duty. In Ford's Masonic initiation and advancement, we glimpse the disciplining of self that the industrialist sought to administer and, eventually, automobilize through the work of the Company's Sociological Department and its related programs.[71]

The fraternal appeal and elite camaraderie Ford found in the formalized fellowship of Freemasonry echo, too, in the industrialist's more informal but no less influential relationships. Among the most prominent was his friendship with a group of men—Thomas Edison, Harvey Firestone, and John Burroughs—who coined themselves "The Vagabonds" in honor of the annual car and camping trips they took together. The inaugural event was in February 1914, just one month after Ford's Five Dollar Day surge in job applicants, as the industrialist ventured into the wilds of the Florida Everglades with Burroughs and Edison. The men reunited for what would become a roughly annual road trip a year later when, after gathering at the World's Fair in San Francisco, the group ventured by car down the California coast with Firestone to pay a visit to the celebrated agricultural scientist and eugenicist, Luther Burbank. Over the next decade, the men took nine more expeditions together in various configurations, with one or another of the group sometimes having to lay off for a year. Communing with nature and showing off their strenuous character, Ford reminisced about how the Vagabonds "gypsied" through forests in automotive caravans and "slept under canvas." He was always game for competitive sports and outdoor recreation, and the men often arranged physical contests for entertainment. On one journey, Burroughs and Firestone competed to see who could sheave the most oats, and Ford organized a rifle-shooting tournament and a high-kicking match. On another trip, Ford lost to Burroughs in a tree-chopping contest. "The trips were good fun," Ford recalled, "except that they began to attract too much attention." The outings did indeed become popular news events and served as important publicity generators, as a cadre of journalists began to accompany the men on their meandering excursions through the Adirondacks, Alleghenies, Appalachians, and across the upper Midwest. The trips boosted Ford's and his friends' statuses as folk heroes and nurtured the role of automobiles as aids to those who adventured into the recreational wilderness to escape the stress of modern living. "We grow weary of our luxuries and conveniences," Burroughs recounted. Reflecting on his reaction "against our complex civilization," the naturalist explained that the Vagabonds "cheerfully endure[d] wet, cold, smoke, mosquitoes, black flies, and sleepness nights just to touch naked reality once more." Their rustic rituals also helped promote a brand of rugged capitalism that resonated with contemporaneous campaigns for a more muscular Christianity.[72]

If the fraternal rites of the Vagabonds tended to affirm and help popularize Ford's concerns about right physical culture and strenuous masculine conversion, they also renewed his connections to a longer history of American Transcendentalism, to which Burroughs first introduced him. Given that Burroughs had previously referred to the motor car as a "demon on wheels," the men's friendship seems rather unlikely. Ford, upon hearing of Burroughs's distaste for the automobile, sent the naturalist a car meant to convince him that "machines would not kill the appreciation of nature." Ford's gift worked a conversion. As others before him, Burroughs soon found that the machine in the garden "greatly enhanced" his enjoyment of the natural world and contributed to a new, if often nostalgic, gratitude for his place in it. "Out of that automobile grew a friendship," Ford wrote, "and it was a fine one." The two men quickly found that they shared a fondness for birds and for the great Seer of Concord, Ralph Waldo Emerson.[73]

Ford was considerably younger that Burroughs and never met Emerson personally, but Burroughs did. The naturalist greatly admired Emerson, especially in his younger years, and was eager to share his understanding with the industrialist. "He taught me to know Emerson," Ford wrote, reflecting on his relationship with Burroughs, for "not only did he know Emerson by heart as an author, but he knew him by heart as a spirit." In 1913, before their excursions with The Vagabonds, Ford traveled with Burroughs to Walden Pond and Concord, Massachusetts, on a pilgrimage to some of the most popular shrines of American Transcendentalism. As workers in his Highland Park plant were beginning to experiment with the moving assembly line, Ford and Burroughs visited Emerson's home and his grave at nearby Sleepy Hollow cemetery, where Henry David Thoreau is also buried, and they were guided around the area by Emerson's friend and biographer, Frank Sanborn.[74]

As harbinger of the auto-industrialist's white nationalism and broadly Christian nativism, Ford would have found in Emerson's *English Traits* (1856) a kind of orthodoxy of Anglo-Saxon whiteness in and for America. Nell Irvin Painter convincingly referred to Emerson as "the philosopher king of American white race theory," based on his success synthesizing and popularizing ideas and ideals of whiteness, particularly around traits of virility, beauty, and national productivity. For Emerson, the Saxons or "Norsemen" were the most important historical arbiters of Englishness. As Painter explains, "alongside the Saxons, all others are lesser." Indeed, Emerson essayed, "race works immortally to keep its own," but alongside race's defining contribution to "national life" was also the work of "civilization" and the physiognomic countenance of the "religious sect." In Emerson's telling, the "traits" of a nation were "an anthology of temperaments"—a conjunction of racial, cultural, and religious factors. Through the "breeding" of the Saxons, England managed to maintain its "power of blood or race." In Emerson's telling, the Anglo-Saxon inheritors of England demonstrated "vigorous health" and "good feeding." "They have more constitutional energy than any other people," he wrote, and engaged in regular "manly exercises" as "the foundation of that elevation of mind which gives one nature ascendant over another." Such bold and brawny men, Emerson said, "box, run, shoot, ride, row, and sale from pole to pole" and "live jolly in the open air." Ford and his Vagabond friends would have heartily assented. Elsewhere Emerson heralded qualities of vivacity, precision, and efficiency as characteristics that the "Saxon founders" came by honestly. Likewise, in a gesture that Ford would later echo, for Emerson it seems "race" only had as bold a power—either as a "controlling influence" or as being of "appalling importance"—for Jewish and Black people, respectively. Though Emerson did not elaborate, Ford did. As we will see in the following chapter, he described the hearty and wholesome frontiersmen of "pioneer blood" and compared them to the dark specter of "international Jews," which would soon occupy so much of Ford's imagination. Indeed, as much as Ford's English school was a crucial component to the Company's larger Americanization efforts, Emerson's Anglo-Saxon ideals of a strong and lively nation added historical and poetic ballast to the industrialist's corporate commitments and institutional programs. Ford's rhetoric and rituals of fraternity and fellowship were never disengaged from long-standing American appeals to a healthy nation and fit human, notions the industrialist approached in antisemitic and white supremacist terms.[75]

Although Ford eschewed the category of socialist and insisted his industrious economy could not be properly characterized in relation to it, the term took hold as a powerful descriptor of his efforts among many influential figures in Germany throughout the early twentieth century. Stefan Link has detailed the way that "not a few German readers" perceived in Ford's industrial philosophy "a kind of socialism." This included Friedrich von Gottl-Ottlilienfeld, a leading voice in the German historical school of economics (alongside more well-known figures like Max Weber and Werner Sombart). Gottl found in Ford "the contours of a distinctive political-economic ideology"—a system Gottl referred to as "Fordism," one of the earliest uses of the term—and insisted that this new form of political economy conveyed modernity past the "dense web of capitalist obligations" and toward a "white socialism of pure, active conviction." Notably, the "socialism of leadership" that the German economist located in Ford's example was closely connected to a notion of "service" (*Dienst*) that was also "meant to invoke an ethos by which individuals cheerfully submitted to a larger purpose or directed their energies to the presumed benefit of the *Volk*." In Gottl's rendering of Ford and Fordism, any industrially spurred crisis of meaning—what Gottl called the "'spiritual emergency' of modern factory work"—was understood to have been alleviated. In Ford's industrial system, workers began to understand themselves as "part of an enterprise of larger meaning and purpose." At Ford, that enterprise was organized corporately and built upon structures of whiteness through rituals of American assimilation and the enduring missionary work of proper socialization. For many observers, including Gottl and his ilk, Ford remedied the "antagonisms of industry" between employer and employee, capital and labor, and served as a "bold ethical example" of right production and racial leadership. The boys club that Ford incorporated as a fraternal entity of rightly converted, carefully purified, and highly waged workers offered not only new kinds of ritual inclusion in a larger project of Anglo-American reform. It also served as a model for many crusaders across the globe endeavoring to remake modern society in accordance with an increasingly powerful set of fascist ideals, including economic self-sufficiency, protectionist politics, racial purity, charismatic masculine authority, and other virtues that Gottl's "white socialism" heralded—concepts and values that would surround much of Ford's subsequent history throughout the mid-twentieth century and beyond.[76]

* * *

The violent scenes that opened this chapter—with mobs of job-seeking men icily turned away at the gates of Ford's factory—along with the intimate and often contested details of the Company's investigations into its workers' lives to satisfactorily guard against "riotous" practices, reveal that Ford's reform of industrial relations was never without the exertion of coercive force. Yet we also know that Ford's promises of prosperity and its promotion of industrial partnership proved alluring to many workers seeking to improve their varied circumstances. Ford's institutional programs and labor policies always exercised both: improvement and oversight, regulation and advancement, betterment and obligation, surveillance and progress, domination and persuasion, social uplift and social control. Hegemony, Gramsci reminds us in his early twentieth-century analysis of Fordism and Americanism, must be understood as a system of strategic power exercised through both force and consent. But we cannot and should not leave off at the "both/and" address. Such a recognition must be the beginning of an analysis of how this is—how Ford became—our standardized conception of capital power in modern America. What becomes crucial is to understand *how* such authority comes to cohere, if only for a time and if always incompletely. In Ford's Five Dollar Day, its bureaucratic organs, human organization, and social reforms, we can begin to see both the force of Ford's remaking of relations and workers' "ambiguities of consent" and attachment to Ford's engineering.[77]

In Ford's efforts to focus Company attention on its human element, we see a set of practices that other historians and sociologists have variously referred to as Americanization, socialization, masculinization, sanitation, and education. Ford's endeavors are all of these things. That is the presumptive power of Ford's manufacture. Rather than parse them, Ford demands that we understand them corporately. He saw a diffuse power in the masses of individuals laboring in his factory and living in his community, and he put them to work. In examining the wage and labor policies, socio-educational disciplines, and religio-racial regimes at Ford, it is possible to see how corporal and corporate relations connect. Humans manufacture and orient themselves to ordinary and extraordinary forces of power through ritual action. Powerful entities, like Ford Motor Company, authorize and are implicated in processes of human corporality and conception—and never innocently so.[78]

In the iconic branding of capital and the lived negotiations of labor, "the social effects of spiritual hegemony" can be located. Ford helped normalize these effects in twentieth-century America, and perhaps considerably beyond. He advanced and institutionalized a ritual theory of labor through which religion was redefined in the making and conversion of humans, proclaiming redemption for workers through the improvement of all that was inefficient, impure, effeminate, and immigrant. At Ford, *through* Ford, the prosperity of workingmen and their families was proffered through an industrial partnership of salvific power. Ford mass-produced religion in and through these corporate relations. In so doing, the industrialist forded a new religious form—a rite-to-work religion.[79]

Of course, not everyone agreed with Ford. Randolph S. Bourne issued his critique of "melting pot" Americanism the same year that Ford debuted his papier-mâché version. Calling instead for a "trans-national" America, one of the first utterances of the term, Bourne urged acceptance of "a dual spiritual citizenship," one that would better serve as "an enterprise of integration." In Bourne's transnational "spiritual welding," a "cosmopolitan spirit" would form, which would not only make the country "infinitely strong" but would, he said, also continue to serve as a kind of missionary enterprise for other, inferior civilizations. If Bourne was promoting a different kind of "trans-national" Americanization, he nevertheless found its possibility in another kind of American exceptionalism. He said that the hybridized, hyphenated subjects of his day, mobilized in migratory economic exchange, would serve as civilized missionaries with "a sense of the superiority of American organization to the primitive living around them." It was with "the pioneer spirit" of America that Bourne's cosmopolitan intelligentsia would traverse the globe, "educating these laggard peoples from the very bottom of society up, awakening vast masses to a new-born hope for the future." Despite their very real differences, Ford and Bourne also shared very real commitments to the forms and promises of American exceptionalism. These wages of history and framings of freedom do not offer us innocent exemplars. As we will see in the following chapter, Ford also insisted upon a pioneer spirit intent to convert the masses. Yet, in contrast to Bourne's vision of the "international mind," Ford asserted antisemitic portraits of the "international Jew"—a figure he understood as parasitic and against which he positioned the productive American that he continued to work hard to manufacture and properly incorporate.[80]

3

Capital Service and Ford's Supersessionary Secularism

The year 1915 was a busy one at Ford. The assembly line made its public debut at the Panama-Pacific Exposition in San Francisco, and the one-millionth Ford car officially rolled off the line in Highland Park. Horace Lucien Arnold and Fay Leone Faurote wrote and published a detailed analysis of work processes in the Ford shops. The industrialist testified about the Ford profit-sharing plan before the US Commission on Industrial Relations, and Ida Tarbell publicly eschewed assertions of paternalism at Ford Motor Company's plants. The Ford English School graduated its first class of students. Lee's general labor reforms had been in effect for about two years, and Samuel Marquis was brought in to replace him as the new head of Ford's Sociological Department, renamed that year to the Educational Department. Amid these assorted happenings, 1915 was also the year when Marquis and his new boss, Henry Ford, joined a group of anti-war crusaders on a dramatic international voyage to negotiate peace in war-torn Europe.

In the years leading up to 1915, the automaker had commented regularly about his pacifist position. With much of the same brazenness but also in decided contrast to those arguing for US "preparedness," Ford had begun to insist that diplomatic efforts in Europe were moving too slowly. In 1915, Ford entered the political fray of international diplomacy with the bravado of a man now very much used to getting his way. As the year was coming to a close, the automaker insisted that more could be done and could be done more quickly. "We're going to get the boys out of the trenches by Christmas," Ford proudly declared on November 24, 1915, publicly announcing his plan to commission an ocean liner, the SS *Oscar II*. In less than two weeks' time, Ford explained, he and a group of delegates would travel to a still-to-be-determined slate of neutral nations in Europe to negotiate world peace. The man who had recently claimed to have harmonized industrial relations in his much promoted Five Dollar Day was now asserting the power of his purportedly pacific hand, inserting it into the politics of international relations. Like Ford's profit-sharing plan, this new endeavor proved to be a headline-grabbing one. Unlike that earlier initiative heralded by so many at the outset, this one almost immediately provoked more widespread ridicule than cautious commendation. World peace proved elusive, as did Ford's tacit declarations for neutral mediation.[1]

Historians have understood this moment of failed political partiality as at odds with Ford's otherwise steady industrial hand. A broader view of Ford's enterprises shows that they were anything but neutral. The Company's concerns for progress and efficiency, productivity and prosperity, were always also campaigns for a particular standard of human comportment and national countenance. Studying Ford's media empire reveals how these campaigns contributed to Ford's religion-making practices and its secular manufacture. This chapter examines that twinned production (of religion and the secular), extending the study of the Company's assertions about the rightly incorporated worker to better understand how Ford conceived, condensed, and plotted human difference in racial and religious terms. It reveals how the auto-industrialist mass-produced these dynamic classifications—of race and religion—not only in its making of an Americanized workforce but also through specific modes of technological mediation. Drawing on a designation of the modern as a "doubly asymmetrical" process of mediation and purification, I observe Ford's mass production of ostensibly purified categories of human differentiation—what the industrialist referred to as the pioneer, the parasite, and the primitive—and consider them as workings of Ford's modern-making. Ford's print publication and film creations operated as technologies of religion, race, and nation in the early twentieth century. These classifications were mediated in and dissociated from one another in Fordist image and idiom, and they were manufactured as nationalist projects for civic reform. In its never-innocent, always-complicated social makings and systems of valuation, Ford advanced a particular notion of "service," one sacralized through a critique of investor capitalism. That theory of service was grounded in and suffused with the supersessionary logics of what he described as the broadly Christian. What I find in Ford's advocacy of this broadly Christian form of capital service is a driving form of industrial producerism, one he conveyed in forms of media and in demanding regimes of factory discipline.[2]

Before we examine Ford's media materials and disciplinary methods, let us first pause to review two moments that have routinely operated as signal events in this history. First, we return to the scene of Ford's shipping for a new peace accord, which he claimed was meant to bring an end to the emerging world war. It is a moment in Ford's history that the automaker narrated as a kind of revelatory occasion. It is also revealing in how the gleam of Ford's enlightened industry seemed to ghost a tragic farce only the world's most popular manufacturer could supply. As Ford ventured into international waters, he returned to nativist concerns. After an evaluation of this conjunction between peace-mongering and anti-immigrant sentiment, we turn to one of Ford's many courtroom dramas in which the figure of the "parasitic" stockholder emerged in opposition to Ford's purported approach to business as a sacred service, an institution to be managed and directed for public benefit and productive capital. Together, these two mythic moments in Ford's modern-making offer particularly potent views into the dynamics of the industrialist's mediations. They reveal his power to mobilize media events, and they display the supersessionary logics and entangled motivation of Ford's producerist ideals, racialized differentiations, capital economies, and international interventions.

Ship of Fools

Ford did not conceive of the Peace Ship. He was the person who transformed an initial idea of creating a commission of interested nations and independent American pacifists for peace mediations into a much more elaborate affair. Touring the United States as a lecturer for the American Peace Society, Rosika Schwimmer, a Hungarian peace activist and longtime advocate for equal rights with the International Congress of Women, introduced Ford to the idea. Ford's public professions of pacifism had enticed Schwimmer, along with her new colleague and collaborator, Louis P. Lochner, formerly of the International Federation of Students, and the two sought out the automaker for help. Once Ford became convinced of the value of the activists' aims, he significantly took over the project, funding and publicizing the trip in a way only he could. He also sped up the timeline of departure in a predictably Fordist manner. He arranged for himself and a group of some eighty-plus unofficial delegates, along with an army of newsmen, photographers, and support staff, to make the trans-Atlantic voyage. He invited a slew of famous figures to accompany him and sought the blessings of President Woodrow Wilson. But, in a move that surprised the self-assured industrialist, Wilson refused to give it. Many of the most well-known names on Ford's list of anti-war allies also declined his invitations (among them Thomas Edison, Jane Addams, William Jennings Bryan, Washington Gladden, John Wanamaker, Luther Burbank, and Cardinal Gibbons), though nearly all expressed general support for his equally general ideals. Nevertheless, the industrialist remained resolute, and over protests from even those in the American Peace Society who worried it was all moving too quickly, Ford reportedly retorted, "If you don't act, I will." And he did.[3]

The turmoil never managed to remain behind closed doors. The reservations and declined invitations from Ford's friends and apparent allies cast significant doubt on the venture, and the voyage's hurried planning lent an air (and an actuality) of disorganization to the activists' efforts. Pacifists in much of the country supported Ford's ideals and basic intentions, but in the press, most commentators were gently bemused by the affair. Satire was the primary mood for reporting on Ford's plan, though some articles alluded to more polemic interpretations. In time, news accounts grew sharper in their ridicule of the venture, suggesting it was a naïve effort at political intervention by an overconfident businessman vastly out of his depth. Cartoons were published widely, playing up an image of Ford's so-called ship of fools or showing a puttering Ford in or as his Model T automobile, guilelessly approaching a looming front of icy war. Another cartoon lamented Ford's "quick peace" promise, picturing the automaker in a strained battle with William Jennings Bryan, who was Secretary of State at the time. The two men pulled in opposing directions at the Dove of Peace, as a diminished Jane Addams stood nearby insisting that, at this rate, even within the pacifist community "there will be bloodshed."[4]

Despite the negative press coverage and the wary response of his contemporaries, Ford remained stubbornly resolute. He was determined, after all, to get as much publicity for his cause as possible. In a kind of "no press is bad press" approach, he doubled down on his peace plan, organizing an elaborate launch party for the ship. An enormous gathering—perhaps as many as 15,000 people—showed up at the Hoboken, New Jersey, pier for the group's departure on December 4. The affair grew into a kind of carnival scene, instigated, some said, by the best showman on Earth since P. T. Barnum. The crowd burst into song at least once, and two Peace Ship participants used the inauguration of the voyage as a time to get married. Mixing, and sometimes shouting at one another, were groups of pacifists, pro-German, and pro-Ally attendees. Amid the hubbub, someone sent a messenger boy with a cage that was thought to carry a live dove for release as the ship pulled away from the docks. Instead, when the cage opened, two squirrels ran out and a sign was revealed reading, "To the Good Ship Nutty." The slogan and its mascot caught on and commentators repeatedly insisted that the animal's affinity for nuts was a better symbol than the dove of peace when considering those aboard the vessel. Later, reporters named the two squirrels "Henry Ford" and "William Jennings Bryan," the most prominent pair of political animals who were "nuts" for peace. Charles Sorensen, the now-former Ford executive, reportedly remarked that not since Noah's ark had such an odd assembly of passengers been seen.[5]

As the vessel traveled across the waters, much was made in the press about Ford's earnest, even admirable, but altogether too inexperienced diplomatic efforts. The extravagance of the trip's cost and the lack of a known itinerary became regular news copy. Many onboard grew extremely seasick, and later the flu spread to several of the delegates and crew. Ford had secured a wireless transmitter aboard the ship, and both his emissaries and the journalists aboard used it daily. The resultant broadcasts swung widely between optimistic assertion, generic boredom, and utter chaos. As the days passed, the passengers were reported to be fighting amongst themselves in a kind of satirical story of mutiny among peacekeepers. Reactions of those aboard came into sharp conflict as they endeavored to determine how to respond to the ongoing news from Europe and, especially, to President Wilson's newest policies. The President had, while the ship traversed the seas, publicly announced the nation's neutrality while also proposing increased military preparedness by building up the number of soldiers in America's standing army. Debates escalated about whether the group aboard should oppose the presidential position and advocate international disarmament instead. Not everyone would agree to a public resolution countering the nation's highest executive, and the group had to wrestle with ongoing questions about their role as unofficial diplomats amid such tense political developments.

Accompanying reporters jumped upon these newsworthy controversies as a kind of journalistic gift. Likewise, there was a latent but rumbling distrust about Schwimmer's connections to and agreements with actual European heads of state as well as the broader peace talks that she was organizing upon the group's arrival on the continent. Amid the rousing fanfare of their departure, these misgivings seemed especially prescient when the ship finally ported two weeks after its departure but failed to draw any celebratory crowds at its Norwegian destination, where the temperature that early, cold December morning was close to −12°F. For his part, Ford grew increasingly distant and disillusioned over the course of the trip, as the group argued amongst themselves. Like others onboard, the industrialist's health was reportedly faltering, causing him to retreat to his own quarters both on the ship and once they made land in Norway.

The expedition continued on to later stops in Sweden, Denmark, and Holland, and some in the party helped form the Neutral Conference for Continuous Mediation, which met for almost a year in The Hague. But Ford was not to be among them. Instead, he unceremoniously exited the ship upon their arrival at the first stop in Norway. He spent several days there convalescing, before returning to the United States accompanied by his friend, Episcopalian minister, and now Ford Education Department head, Samuel Marquis, on the first ship sailing back across the Atlantic. Ford was, as one historian pithily observed, "the only one who would make it home from the war by Christmas."[6]

Ford continued to fund the Peace Ship's subsequent stops and donated money to the American Peace Society's ongoing projects. While blustering in positive terms about the value of the voyage publicly, many noted that he was privately chastened by the trip. Ford said as much later, too, especially once he began to attribute the Peace Ship's failure to end the war as part of a larger set of nefarious forces he understood to be at play in global politics. He had to admit the Peace Ship didn't work, but he didn't have to admit it failed because it was a bad idea. Instead, he increasingly cited populist and antisemitic tropes about a cabal of "international bankers" who were seeking to profit from the war. Profit-seeking people kept his proclamation of peace from happening, he said. "It was the Jews themselves that convinced me of the direct relation between the international Jew and war," Ford asserted in the pages of the *New York Times*. "They talked so long and so well that they convinced me. . . . We were in mid-ocean and I was so disgusted that I would have liked to have turned the ship back." Ford's account of his botched peace talks became the context for his public pronouncements against Jewish people. It was after this encounter, Ford claimed, that he became "determined that the situation should be made clear to the people of the United States." He needed to let everyone know what he understood.[7]

Disseminating this information would be a problem, however, because Ford was increasingly distrustful of the press. They had, in his telling, ridiculed and sabotaged his peace plan and none could be found "that dared print the truth." "Then a funny thing happened," Ford recounted, "an old chap in Dearborn came to my office and wanted to sell the local paper, *The Dearborn Independent*, a weekly newspaper." Ford narrated this moment as if it were an awakening: "The thought came to me like a flash. Surely some place in the United States there should be a publisher strong and courageous enough to tell the people the truth about war. If no one else will, I'll turn publisher myself. And I did." Ford—tinkerer, engineer, industrialist, educator, diplomat—turned publisher, too. Motivated to spread the word about what he decided was the Jewish role in warmongering, Ford became a newspaperman.[8]

The *Dearborn Independent* was soon one among many of Ford's burgeoning media productions. Through articles in the *Dearborn Independent* and subsequent publications in the *International Jew*, Ford lamented, in familiar antisemitic tropes, "the lines of business controlled by the Jews of the United States . . . those which are really vital, and those which cultivated habit." Among a long list—sugar and tobacco production, jewelry stores, grain and cotton industries, liquor and loan businesses— Ford included newspaper and magazine publishing along with the theater and motion picture industry as being controlled by Jewish interests. The industrialist entered media in order to combat what he saw as Jewish dominance of it. He used media to argue against certain forms of "racial" identity and in favor of particular tropes of American triumph.[9]

Alongside the assembly line, universal car, sociological survey, sanitation and salvage projects, and educational curriculum, these new media operated as technologies for Ford's corporate programs and nativist projects. They headlined the bitter allegations Ford most wanted to distribute, and they sold copy. His media empire was an information industry built on a craving for the ostensibly neglected. Curiosity and an appetite for the unfiltered were offered in simplified terms, and these print media products enabled Ford to make bold what the industrialist took to be so common. His surplus could spill onto the page, objectified in paper and ink, as the neglected made true. The worst that he wanted to think could be impressed and purchased as tangible information distributed widely but engaged in intimate ways—held between one's fingers, tucked neatly beneath one's arm, or used as background lining in daily life, wrapping sandwiches or helping secure cherished pieces of domestic decor. We could call this production of social life "reification" if, as Angela Zito has already noted, it would not imply that "someday de-reification would come and we could live in an im-mediate reality." But we know that any such sense of that immediacy "is itself a mediated effect." Like our own knowingness about the mediated reality of our affected immediacy and promotional publics, Ford's newsreaders knew this, too, to varying degrees. Ford's "Chronicle of the Neglected Truth" disclosed his exclusive ownership and published his ideals on his own page. Ford's objectified truth—expounded in linguistic singularity, commodified for consumption, and circulated en masse—accumulated its own excess and helped incorporate his spiraling surplus.[10]

Dodgy Shareholders

The blatant antisemitism of Ford's origin story of the *Dearborn Independent* notwithstanding, the automaker had, indeed, faced an increasingly critical press in the years after the Peace Ship shenanigans. During this period, Ford was embroiled in one of several legal cases that helped secure his general suspicion of governmental regulation and adjudication and aided his self-aggrandizing assertions of persecution by state regulators, jealous and greedy competitors, and sensationalizing journalists. In a three-year-long lawsuit against the *Chicago Tribune*, Ford insisted that the paper had committed libel when it referred to him as an anarchistic enemy of the nation and an ignorant idealist who profited ungratefully from a military that protected his interests. Although the event eventually ended up furthering Ford's self-cultivated status as a folk hero vying against urbane newsmen, it also fed his enduring contempt for the press and served as yet more fodder for his invectives against a warmongering media.

The *Tribune* trial was not the only court case Ford was fighting in this post–Peace Ship period. In 1916, John and Horace Dodge sued Ford Motor Company, charging it with purposefully withholding dividends that had accrued to minority stockholders, among whom the Dodges were included. The largest and most profitable automobile company of the time, Ford Motor Company was raking in the returns. But Ford was also plowing huge amounts of the Company's earnings into further capital investment—expanding plants, building new ones, growing into international markets, and buying up suppliers. As minority shareholders, the Dodge brothers balked at the effect of these practices on their own dividends and called Ford's business decisions "reckless and unwise." Ford had, indeed, recently begun to enter the mining industry by purchasing vast ore deposits, and had plans to construct giant blast furnaces to smelt the material in the Company's new plant in Dearborn. This new plant was to become the massive, vertically integrated, River Rouge factory. Earlier the same year, Ford had further reduced the sales cost of the Model T, and the Company extended the Five Dollar Day policy to women working in its plant.[11]

The Dodges argued, in an enduringly controversial case, that the primary purpose of a business was to earn profits for shareholders. They demanded that Ford distribute as dividends up to 75 percent of the Company's surplus, and they obtained an injunction to prevent any further plant expansion until he did. The brothers further accused the Company and its founder and president, Henry Ford, of "reckless expenditures of the company's assets." What is more, Ford's elaborate expansion plans were, they said, an endeavor to make the Company into an automotive monopoly at the expense of minority stockholders. As majority shareholder, Henry Ford exercised dictatorial control of the Board of Directors, they argued, and his refusal to issue special dividends was an arbitrary decision meant to deprive them, as minority shareholders, of fair and reasonable returns upon their investment. The Dodges suggested that Ford was trying to avoid healthy competition, withholding dividends because he knew they would use their share as capital for their own car company. Accrual of excessive amounts of cash reserves was, they further insisted, outside legal capitalization limits and, therefore, not in the best interests of the Company.[12]

In Ford's moralizing counterargument, the practice of issuing dividends went against everything he thought "business" was ultimately for. Ford used the Dodges' legal dispute to make his case both in court and to the public. "I do not believe we should make an awful profit on our cars," Ford told the *Detroit News*, "a reasonable profit is right, but not too much." Similarly, in his widely cited court testimony, Ford insisted that the vast majority of profits earned by a business should either be redistributed to workers and/as customers (through higher wages and lower prices) or reinvested in capital equipment (like the blast furnaces Ford had planned). Company profit was expressly *not* for the benefit of stockholders, he said, or at least not in large part. Instead, he contended that his Company's ambition was "to spread the benefits of industrial system to the greatest number, to help [employees] build up their lives and their homes." To do this, Ford testified, "we are putting the greatest share of our profits back into the business."[13]

Ford's arguments can and should be read as savvy marketing talk. They were also more than that. More accurately, they *did* more than that. Ford's was a sales pitch for a booming automotive company. But, for him, the stakes were much higher. Like many corporate institutions throughout US history, Ford Motor Company repeatedly insisted that its purpose went beyond money-making. It was not (only) about profit but prophecy. Ford understood it was remaking the world, ushering in a new industrial system, a "consecration of Business" to be held in "holy trust." This approach to business, Ford observed, results in "surprisingly enormous benefits to ourselves," too. When the case came to trial, he insisted on the witness stand that the purpose of the Ford Motor Company was not really to make profits but instead "to do as much good as we can, everywhere, for everybody concerned . . . to make money and use it, give employment, and send out the car where the people can use it." For Ford, the purpose of the Company was only to "incidentally make money." "Business," he proclaimed, "is a service not a bonanza." In his heightened rhetoric, both in legal testimony and business slogan, profit was gleaned as mere by-product of the rightly serving corporation. Business, Ford insisted, was an amenity employed for service, not a speculator's jackpot.[14]

Despite Ford's ability to impress his devoted public with his populist appeal even amid his great wealth, the Michigan Supreme Court issued a complex, split ruling on the subject. It dismissed the Dodges' concerns about capitalization limits and ultimately refused their charge of monopoly. Citing the Company's articles of association, it held that Ford's proposed expansion was not *ultra vires* the corporation, nor was the Company in violation of anti-trust laws. Ford's plans to expand the business vertically did not fall outside the Company's legal powers as authorized by its corporate charter, and the Court judged that Ford's endeavors to integrate its supply were not incidental or arbitrary to the corporation's primary purpose. Affirming part of an earlier circuit court's decision and declining to interfere with Ford's expansion plans, the Michigan Supreme Court commented that "judges are not business experts," in an early expression of what has since come to be known as the business judgment rule. Yet, if the Court remarked favorably upon the judgment of Ford's business leaders, it considered his philosophy of business less legally compelling. The rest of the decision went largely against Ford, with the court ultimately ordering Ford Motor Company to issue some $19 million in special dividends.[15]

"Inasmuch as business corporations are constructed for profit," the circuit court ruling stated, "they must not bend their energies in any other direction." The Michigan Supreme Court affirmed and elaborated upon this judicial direction about corporate construction in commentary that many scholars and legal experts have since interpreted as judicial dicta (an observation or suggestion not otherwise legally binding). After acknowledging the "certain sentiments, philanthropic and altruistic, creditable to Mr. Ford," the Michigan Supreme Court remarked:

> A business corporation is organized and carried on primarily for the profit of stockholders. The powers of the directors are to be employed for that end. The discretion of directors is to be exercised in the choice of means to attain that end, and does not extend to a change in the end itself, to the reduction of profits, or to the nondistribution of profits among stockholders in order to devote them to other purposes.

The purpose of profit, questions of its constituency, the function of a business, and the role of a corporation, particularly relative to philanthropic work, emerged as central to this case—one that has since been deemed "corporate law's most controversial." As legal experts have frequently noted, the full holding of the *Dodge v. Ford* case is narrower than popularly presumed. Yet, the case's ruling (in)distinctions—between arbitrary acts and reasonable decisions, what is said in passing and what is binding precedent, *obiter dictum* and *ratio decidendi*—has remained central to the case's enduring popularization and critique. Legal experts have importantly recognized the way *Dodge v. Ford* gets cast as "the basis of the so-called shareholder primacy doctrine"—"Exhibit A for commentators seeking to argue that American law imposes on corporate directors the legal obligation to maximize profits for shareholders." As such, it operates as a kind of origin story for enduring debates about the shareholder primacy model in contrast to a stakeholder theory of the corporation. Indeed, commentary on the case, historical and contemporary, seems to quickly and forcefully shuttle participants into urgent deliberation about corporate purpose and social responsibilities, majority-minority control rights and litigation as a promotional tactic, business judgment and designations of public good. These were questions for which Ford insisted he had the right answer. The court said he did not. When the $19 million in dividends had to be distributed, majority shareholder, Henry Ford, received the largest percentage. As one Ford executive later wrote, for Henry Ford, "it could have been worse."[16]

Despite the fortune Ford was just court-ordered to distribute to himself, the founder resented the decision—a lot. His profit policy, he later insisted, "does not agree with the general opinion that business is to be managed to the end that the stockholders can take out the largest possible amount of cash. Therefore, I do not want stockholders in the ordinary sense of the term." In 1919, Ford executed a complex series of events that culminated in a complete stock buyout of all minority shareholders. Ford's reason for the corporate takeover was that, in his estimation, stockholders "do not help forward the ability to serve." While many titans of industry had dominated their corporations through majority interests, as Ford's corporate historians Allan Nevins and Frank Hill rightly noted, never before "had one man controlled completely an organization the size of Ford Motor Company." Even the likes of John

D. Rockefeller and J. P. Morgan held only relatively small shares. "Ford wielded industrial power as no man had ever possessed before," Nevins and Hill exclaimed, "and what a consummation it represented!" By 1920, all of Ford's enterprises—including the newly formed Dearborn Publishing Company—were consolidated into Ford Motor Company stock. Henry Ford subsequently transferred some shares to his wife and son. After that, Ford was an entirely family-owned corporation.[17]

Effectively the sole owner of Ford Motor Company, the fifty-six-year-old founder now had no shareholders to appease. The trials and tribulations Ford understood himself to have endured effected his liberation from dividend payments and divided purposes. With the eviction of all those who might challenge his control, Ford's industrial ambitions could finally be fully integrated and rightly incorporated. Company policy closely held in his masterful hands, this insular new empire seemed to promise the automaker the undivided ability to focus all his capabilities and capital on the productive capacities he alone selected and sought to serve. Always and at once a talking point for Company press releases and a prophetic claim of public purpose, a fuller understanding of Ford's concept of service will reveal the implications and effects of his theory of consecrated business more broadly. Rejecting "awful profit," Ford insisted the corporate service he supplied would not only spread his automotive goods to more buyers but also do good.

Serving Capital

Some readers are now perhaps wondering: do I not realize the material violence of Ford? The Mussolini of Highland Park! The Flivver King! Ford was decidedly not some benevolent humanitarian. "His fordship" was the named inspiration of dystopic divinity in Aldous Huxley's *Brave New World*. "Do as much good everywhere, for everybody"?! We need only reflect on accounts of worker intimidation, surveillance, union busting, and the nervous condition laborers called "Forditis" to recognize that not "everybody" was being well-served by or at Ford. This is a fact importantly recognized not only in the cautious footnotes of Ford's biographical hagiographies but also in the lengthy annals of labor history. Although harsh and erratic treatment, harassment of union organizers, and a persistent speedup culture were long part of Ford's

labor policy, this reputation grew in the 1920s under the driving figure of production manager, Charles "Cast-Iron Charlie" Sorensen. His
was the era when Ford's previous social and education programs were
increasingly defunded. In the 1930s, as the nation was plunged into economic depression and greater employment insecurity, the Company
found itself even more significantly and publicly at odds with labor leaders. During this time, Ford began to battle unionization in its factories
increasingly vehemently—so much so that the intimidation and strikebreaking practices at Ford's plants during this time became infamous,
particularly as they were carried out through tactics of physical threat,
personal violence, and industrial espionage by men employed in Ford's
Service Department.[18]

Headed up by Harry Bennett, a former boxer and navy sailor, the
Service Department was formed as a corporate police force at Ford, and
in the wake of Samuel Marquis's exit from the firm, the department also
took over all personnel responsibilities at the Company. Throughout the
1930s, Bennet and his Servicemen—a group that one historian referred
to as "Ford's Brass Knuckles"—patrolled factory floors, pushed for efficiency standards by further speeding up line production, spied on workers and licensed auto dealers in the community, and disrupted union
campaigns throughout the Company, all while building the world's
largest private army to do this work. Ford's Service Department and its
violent opposition to unionism in the auto industry during the 1930s—
supported by Ford's antisemitic statements—earned it the label of
"Ford's Gestapo." Physical assault and personal intimidation of workers
were regular practices by Ford Servicemen, and violence erupted repeatedly in response to what one labor activist called the "terror regime of
the Service Department." The Ford Hunger March in 1932 and the Battle
of the Overpass in 1937 at Ford's River Rouge industrial complex were
only the most public of confrontations between Ford and labor. In both
of these encounters, Ford's private army joined with local police to violently put down union organizers and former Ford workers, including
firing directly on the crowd, and killing and wounding many of those
gathered. In the days after the Battle of the Overpass, as Ford continued
to openly spurn the Wagner Act, legislation passed in 1935 to guard the
right of private sector employees to bargain collectively, the United Auto
Workers pronounced: "Fordism is really gangsterism, fascism, and feu-

dalism." For racially marginalized workers, like many of the Black laborers who were hired in greater numbers at the Rouge plant, the realities
of work at Ford, in the sharp words of one historian, could be "better
described as man-killing than man-making." It all seemed a far cry from
the notion of service that Ford so brazenly testified was the orienting
force and corporate concern of his industrial enterprise.[19]

What needs to be clear is that Ford's concern for what he deemed a
"serving" industry need not presume some innocent version of Ford's
consecrated business. This is a crucial point and one that joins those of
other scholars who have similarly argued that "incorporating debates on
the purpose of corporations and who is to benefit into analyses of religion is particularly fruitful because religions tend to be idealized, both
legally and discursively, as selfless communities that enjoy tax benefits
as contributors to the public good." Recognizing that Ford's theory of
right business as "service" was also a particular religious formation, it
is also possible to recognize the never-neutral realities of religion as an
historically wrought analytic and categorical assertion fraught with all
the ambivalences of its making and reformation.[20]

There has been significant work to uncover how frequently and how
vigorously Christian-affiliated businessmen (and some women) have
espoused principles of service. But it is not always entirely clear exactly
what this principle of service has meant. It is most often connected implicitly, and occasionally explicitly, to notions of Christian stewardship.
"Service" is also commonly heralded by sets of conservative businessmen who tend to claim a dual role for themselves as entrepreneurs and
evangelicals. Yet, for his part, Ford would likely never be cast as an evangelical, and he certainly never claimed to be one. Rather, his marked
Christian commitments would instead connect him—at least in church
historical terms—to forms of Christian liberalism. The industrialist himself also directly eschewed the language of orthodoxy when describing
his own religiosity. Ford was, though, formative in presenting a particular understanding of service—and its sacralization in big business—as
a kind of corporate orthodoxy. Part of what Ford offers historians and
scholars of religion is a way to explore an earlier era of service work in
corporate enterprise than it has commonly been conceived. The notion
of service he offered was one that connected masculinized, producerist critiques of finance capital to driving regimes of industrial labor.

Drawing on tropes of muscular Christianity and purifying industry and incorporating his rite-to-work religion, Ford helped to advance the systems and semantics of what would become a global service economy. His vision of service promised a new kind of conscientious capitalism and promoted the benevolent presence of a corporate soul. Those promises echoed many of Ford's earlier assertions. In metaphysical strains of New Thought and in antisemitic tropes of finance capitalism, he demonstrated that the religious economies of service were never only the work of evangelical Christians. The widespread appeal of service as an unmarked but productive idiom of the broadly Christian allowed it to move equally broadly throughout American business enterprise.[21]

Ford not only issued his talking points about service as a script for his show trial. If the language emerged there most publicly, it was also a slogan he maintained and reproduced regularly. "I regard business profits above a small percentage as belonging more to the business than to the stockholders," Ford argued forcefully in his autobiography. The Dodge Brothers' suit might have brought to the fore Ford's assertion of business principles based upon an ethos of service through the work of industrial producerism. But it also helped Ford to demonstrate how that very business philosophy was routinely posited against a particular understanding of finance capitalism. In his telling, stockholders "ought to be only those who are active in the business and who will regard the company as an instrument of service." As "an instrument of service," Ford implored that right business was not "a machine for making money." If his Company made large amounts of profit—and he said it would because "working to serve forces them to be large"—those profits should also in similarly large measure be "turned back into the business," not distributed to its stockholders. The stockholder who was truly active in the business would appreciate such a business strategy, Ford suggested, because "the working stockholder is more anxious to increase his opportunity to serve than to bank dividends." Ford personified those who would not appreciate this approach as the broker, the banker, and the minority shareholder. Together, these figures signified what the industrialist sometimes called "absentee owners" or the "non-working stockholder." And, he noted, "we have no place for the non-working stockholder."[22]

Reflecting later upon his "serving" approach to business, Ford explicitly connected his ideas about wages with those of capital, and he asserted their sacred status through proper use. Philosophizing in homespun terms, the industrialist asserted, "there is something sacred about wages." Too often, business leaders considered wages merely as calculations on financial reports or numbers to be figured. But "out in the world," Ford remarked, wages "represent homes and families and domestic destinies . . . bread boxes and coal bins, babies' cradles and children's education—family comforts and contentment." What was decidedly not sacred, according to Ford, were profits used to merely "swell a personal fortune." Nevertheless, he countered, capital could be "just as sacred" if it "is used to provide the means by which work can be made productive," if it was reinvested "to provide a sounder basis for business, better working conditions, better wages, more extended employment." In that instance, Ford contended, "it is for the service of all, though it may be under the direction of one," and "capital thus employed should not be carelessly tampered with." Confronted with a challenge from Ford's minority shareholders, the industrialist insisted and continued insisting that his business was a sacred one. Unlike those who profanely demanded dividends, Ford posited himself and his company as the corporate interest rightly committed to accruing surplus as a service and holding capital in trust.[23]

Under the direction of one, Ford said he alone could be trusted to employ capital with productive care. "Capital that a business makes for itself, that is employed to expand the workman's opportunity and increase his comfort and prosperity, and that is used to give more and more men work, at the same time reducing the cost of service to the public," he restated, "that sort of capital, even though it be under single control, is not a menace to humanity. It is a working surplus held in trust and daily use for the benefit of all." Ford explained that as "holder of such capital," he "scarcely regard[ed] it as a personal reward . . . for he did not create it alone." Ever the advocate for a more corporate interest, Ford insisted that even under his sole direction, Company profit was "the joint product of his whole organization." The one was the All in such trusted surplus holdings. "A surplus has to be held somewhere," he shrugged, "the truly honest manufacturer holds his surplus profits in that trust." The alternative, he averred, was mere profiteering. That unsound, useless method of profit-making, he insisted, was the preferred practice of "the speculators, the exploiters, the no-good element that is always injuring legitimate business," the very people Ford defined himself and his business philosophy against. Around the same time he was buying out his "non-working stockholders," he put this differential distinction in starker terms. One was, he said, either "producer or parasite—take your choice." Ford knew what he claimed.[24]

Ford contended that shareholders were too often merely akin to stockbrokers and bankers, whom he described as "parasites thriving on the present system." Unlike them, Ford recurrently sloganized, "the only stock I take any stock in is the stock in the stock room." The automotive business that he was industrializing was to be a massively productive one, and not just figuratively. Harkening an almost mercantilist perspective, Ford posited his producerist industry against brokers and shareholders, those he understood to be mere gamblers playing games in corporate boardrooms and Wall Street offices. "The gears of a slot machine are figured out so that in the long run the machine wins. The stock market is like that," Ford asserted. Unfortunately, "the brokers of the country" couldn't see the version of casino capitalism he did. "They will continue it as long as they can," he lamented. "You can't argue with a parasite."[25]

* * *

Ford extended and expanded his classificatory language—of business or bonanza, producer or parasite, speculation or service—beyond the conflict he had with his Dodgy minority shareholders. Ford's capital classifications became a way for him to understand and organize justice in and for the world. Like the rest of Ford's resources, both human and machine, capital too had to be put to work. "The highest use of capital," he explained, "is not to make more money, but to make money do more service for the betterment of life. Unless we in our industries are helping to solve the social problem, we are not doing our principal work. We are not fully serving." Principled industry was a social service and a curative provision in Ford's accounting. "The principles of service cannot fail to cure bad business. Which leads us into the practical application of the principles of service and finance." Capital was not just for accruing; it also needed to be put into "practical application" for the world.[26]

Good, principled business was, in Ford's view, the primary force for progressive change in the world. Industry was the newest and best leader for his spiraling, progressive modernity. "The world has always needed leadership," Ford noted. "Yesterday that leadership was military and political. . . . But times have improved and today political and military leadership cannot serve the people as well as industrial leadership." As a leading force in the world, Ford asserted that his good business was not only serving people with better principles for social reform; it was also the best hope for civility on a global scale. In the wake of the first world war, he agitated: "though we won the military contest, the world has not yet quite succeeded in winning a complete victory over the promoters of war." Good business, Ford's "serving" industry, was the best hope, he said, in defeating those shadowy forces. He did not leave his own understanding of this power unsaid. He needed to make known those he said preferred to otherwise remain obscured. The hidden warmongers he imagined were "men with vast powers of control" even as they "belong to no nation whatever." They were an international power, with a clever and unconscionable war cry that ultimately benefited from the resultant confusion of national interests. As countries across the globe panicked, Ford said these profiteers "run off with the spoils." "War is an orgy of money," he explained, "just as it is an orgy of blood." In his telling, good business—not just "profitable business"—aligned with a trusted press he controlled, would counter the debauchery of those vague powers who got rich from the blood money of war. Against the "techniques" of such "manufactured evil," Ford positioned the service of his expanding manufacturing industry. "We should not so easily be led into war," he insisted, "if we considered what it is that makes a nation really great." "Take the industrial idea; what is it?" Ford prompted: "The true industrial idea is not to make money. The industrial idea is to express a serviceable idea, to duplicate a useful idea, by as many thousands as there are people who need it." Ford insisted his ideas were what people needed and he was ready to distribute them. One of those ideas was that when capital held in trust is responsible for distributing the good(s), a nation could "become great." The alternative to such an approach was, he reasoned, mere opportunistic assumption: "The negation of the industrial idea is the effort to make a profit out of speculation instead of out of work." As he consolidated his corporate holdings and capital enterprise, Ford found language to characterize that which he supposed himself to be organizing for, and against.[27]

The brazen antisemitism of Ford's utterances must be acknowledged directly. His antisemitism is notorious and well-documented. Yet, while Ford's antisemitism has been much described over the years, the connections between it and corporate theories of "service" and "work" have been considerably less so. These idioms and intonations were further iterated in the automaker's media productions. In them, Ford mass-produced an economic logic for industrial capital, fabricating his as a business of conquering growth premised in material production and serviceable ideals. That economic logic also forded a corporate personage. In news copy and filmstrip, Ford became the trusted director of industrial expansion and national advancement. Not interested in remaining unknown, he wanted all to understand what he alone knew of the "definite techniques" of manufacturing. In his media empire, Ford proffered his own techniques and applied technologies through a press designed to chronicle a truth that he insisted had been neglected and in motion pictures designed to move the nation forward into greatness.[28]

A Nation of Pioneer Blood

Ford's foray into newspaper publishing came in late 1918, when he purchased the small local weekly, the *Dearborn Independent*. He set out, he maintained, to tell the people the truth that others in the press dared not reveal. The publication would also be a way to get around the partialities and prejudices that he contended the American media too often advanced. "I am very much interested in the future, not only of my own country, but of the whole world," Ford explained; "and I have definite ideas and ideals that I believe are practical for the good of all, and intend giving them to the public without having them garbled, distorted, or misrepresented." After purchasing the *Dearborn Independent*, the industrialist decided to replace the paper's old press with a new and special one. Ford acquired the machine from Sprague Publications, a company known for its "wholesome" reputation based on its publication of the *American Boy* periodical. Just a few months later, in January 1919, this new press issued its first newspaper under the auspices of Ford's recently formed subsidiary, the Dearborn Publishing Company. The title of the news organ was to remain unchanged, but he added two new subtitles to the *Dearborn Independent*'s masthead, "The Ford International Weekly" and "Chronicler of the Neglected Truth."[29]

Ford's newspaper appeared without commercial advertising. Other than its name on the masthead, initially at least, not even Ford enterprises were promoted. The *Dearborn Independent* included an array of articles, including a special section called "Mr. Ford's Own Page." But it gained national and international attention when it began to publish the antisemitic materials that made it infamous. The first article decrying the "international Jew" appeared in May 1920, and many of the articles that followed in its wake were drawn directly from the notorious forgery, *The Protocols of the Learned Elders of Zion*. By the beginning of 1921, Ford supposedly had so many requests for reprints of its articles that he began to compile previously published pieces into a separate text issued under the title, *The International Jew*. Over the next several years, Ford continued to publish articles and books on the same general subject, and *The International Jew* was translated into several languages. It gained attention among antisemitic supporters of Ford. It also provoked considerable ire. The articles and derivative texts were controversial in their own time, but public controversy was something Ford was long used to by then, perhaps even something he courted.[30]

It was during this same period when Ford published yet another text based upon content from his newspaper. Made up of nearly one hundred different issues of "Mr. Ford's Own Page," Ford Motor Company released its newest print publication, *Ford Ideals*, in 1922. This publication has received considerably less attention than the automaker's other texts, but it offers a useful lens to study the ongoing mediation of race and religion in Ford's efforts to forge an American nation. While William Cameron, the editor of the *Dearborn Independent*, later testified that the articles printed in *Ford Ideals* were ghostwritten, the preface also confirmed that Henry Ford was personally engaged in "every essential part" of the preparation of the selected articles:

> He supplies the ideas. Very often he supplies the words in which his ideas are set forth. He does not manipulate the typewriter nor does he occupy himself with the detail of seeing the copy through the press, but the entire inspiration, the point of view, the resistless analysis, the ripeness of judgment are his. Without him there would be no "Mr. Ford's Page."

It was to be an account of Henry Ford's ideals and his ideas. The book, it said, was meant to celebrate Mr. Ford's "independence of thought" and "common sense," and the selections included were determined based upon "the principle of popularity as expressed by our readers."[31]

The "Mr. Ford" gathered in this text was, consequently, some mix of Henry Ford's independent ideas, ghostwritten maxim, and the popular principles of the paper's reading public. The book's ninety-eight chapters covered everything from utilitarian economic theories, statements on inflation, and managerial philosophies to Ford's position on charity and welfare work, his love of the farmer as "nature's partner," his concerns regarding party politics, and his preference for the small town over city living. The book also introduced a specific American ideal: "the pioneer." The pioneer was a mass media production, shaped in the pages of Ford's publication and mobilized in later film productions. Idealized in "Mr. Ford's Own Page," the pioneer conveyed a racial imagination and depicted the industrialist's fighting pacifism in nativist terms. A direct cipher for the Americans Ford most wanted to celebrate, the pioneer was not to be defined through his—decidedly masculine—position on the frontier but rather for his characteristic spirit of adventure and innovation. "Where we lack lands and seas to explore," Ford stated, "we are making up by conquering new continents of life." The American "of pioneer blood" was originally an immigrant with roots "overseas," but he also "visioned cities on the prairies and came half way round the world in search, not of a new country, but a new life." No dusty remnant of the past, remembered in nostalgic affection, Ford emphasized that the pioneer was "bred in the very fibers of our bodies." Drawing on eugenic discourses of innate biological human difference rendered in Social Darwinist terms, he linked his concern for a productive American to an ideal of freedom understood to be waged in the labor of productive, unencumbered movement. Automobilized by his ideals and inventions and coursing with the "blood" of conquest, Ford proclaimed a daring exceptionalism and "prophetic vision" in this pioneering figure of the United States. He celebrated the pioneer as "a superior sort of man" who scorned the idea of war waged for material profit. In him, Ford placed "the spirit of initiative, the very bloodstream of high daring, the vital urge to rest nowhere until Opportunity is attained." Superior and unencumbered, the pioneer was made in *Ford Ideals* to be the productive obverse of the "parasite" in Ford's schema of the First World War. Through this prophetic and conquering character, "the vanguards of Humanity," Ford posited his vision of "a nation of pioneer blood" in contrast to the international forces of unscrupulous speculators he summoned. Inscribed and idealized in Ford's print media, the pioneer figured Ford's modern position in proper form—rightly American, rightly productive, rightly mobilized. A modern invention mediated in purified terms, Ford manufactured the pioneer as his preferred form of the American primitive.[32]

Americanizing the Primitive

What I want to make clear is that Ford became a media mogul in part to propagate a specific idea of primitive modernity. This is to say that the primitive Ford pioneered was as much a modern invention as the automobiles in his factory. Notably, both of these products (the pioneer, the automobile) were quickened through other creations from within his media empire. Around the same time that the Company began its first large-scale experiments with assembly line production, Ford also entered the filmmaking business. By 1914, he officially opened a department for the express purpose of making both still and moving pictures. In April of that year, Ambrose Jewett, then a staff member in the Company's advertising department, was recruited to head up the new division, and he moved quickly in this new position to amass staff and supplies. Jewett oversaw implementation of an assembly line approach to photographic and film equipment in the fourth-floor laboratory of Ford's Highland Park plant, and by mid-summer of 1914, now with a staff of twenty-four in addition to six cameramen, the department produced its first of many films, *How Henry Ford Makes One Thousand Cars a Day*.[33]

From 1914 to 1916, Ford's standard film production was a ten-to fifteen-minute newsreel under the title, "Ford Animated Weekly." Cameramen traveled around the United States and Europe to take footage of whatever was deemed "news" at the time—bottle feeding a calf, a competitive swimming race, tractors plowing a field, panoramas from scenic locales, the crowning of one Jeff Davis as the "King of Hobos," the loading of a freighter ship with coal, a "War Dance" from Buffalo Bill's Circus, and several different winter sport recreations. Similar to Ford's policy for the *Dearborn Independent*, no official advertising was included in the weekly newsreels, except for an occasional shot of a Model T and the title card, which featured the grill of that now-famous automotive vehicle. Ford distributed his "Animated Weekly" to theaters and movie houses around the country for free, and more than three million people in more than two thousand venues viewed them.[34]

By 1916, the cost of gathering such ephemeral news footage led Ford to turn toward a title production with more staying power. The "Ford Educational Weekly" became the new central vehicle for the department's footage, and it likely also helped fulfill an early interest Ford had in the medium's didactic power. The Ford Educational Department and the English School were in full swing, and Ford's new educational movies became a central medium for the industrialist's larger civic and pedagogical pursuits. The Ford Photography and Film Department produced these new movies on a wide range of themes, often reusing footage as interchangeable parts in a typically Fordist way—from pictures about the industrial development of rug making, soap production, and the meatpacking industry to a description of "Frontier Days" in Prescott Arizona, a "pilgrimage" through early colonial sites in Massachusetts and Rhode Island, and an introduction to the benefits of occupational therapy for injured veterans. These films were similarly distributed to theaters and offered at no cost, though in late 1918, Ford switched from doing its own motion picture distribution to licensing this out to Goldwyn Distribution Company. "Ford Educational Weekly" films were soon showing at more than four thousand different venues—by some counts perhaps as many as seven thousand—and were seen by around five million Americans every week. Ford features were also produced with subtitles in eleven different foreign languages to be shown in theaters across the globe. By 1918, Ford Motor Company was not only the first business in America to create an in-house film department; it was also the single largest motion picture producer in the world.[35]

If the moving picture machines' efficiency and educational opportunities attracted Ford to the medium of film, by the late 1910s and early 1920s, this technology also promised to help him combat the cultural conditions he understood to be increasingly deteriorating. He worried about the loosening morals of the emerging "Jazz Age" and set about trying to correct them. Ford's new filmmaking enterprise was of a part with his other media productions, an effort to cultivate and educate his public about the corrupt forces treading upon his, and his America's, ideals. The in-house newsletter, *Ford News*, noted in 1922 that "the Ford film department believes that the long-neglected and dormant educational value of the motion pictures sacrificed in the desire for money grabbing, will be taken advantage of to carry out its fundamental purpose of true usefulness." In Ford's films the auto-industrialist mediated his primitive modernity, particularly through the Company's newest series, the "Ford Educational Library."[36]

The "Ford Educational Library" films built upon Ford's weekly productions, often reusing footage and narratives from those earlier films, but interspersing them with new inter-titles or cutting older footage with new film. However, the "Ford Educational Library" series also expanded its topical coverage, moving into an array of concerns, including agriculture, transportation, geography, physics, medicine, zoology, history, and civics. During this same period, Ford began to experiment with films designed to help sell its product and promote its brand more directly, and in many ways, these films returned to themes the Company began with in the early years, showcasing new production methods and industrial facilities. In the 1920s, many of these films included material about newly integrated operations that Ford was initiating as part of its expanding Rouge complex, including coal mining, railroading, and lumber production. These movies were shown in a variety of venues—dealer showrooms, parks, churches, fraternal lodges, schools, clubs, country fairs, YMCAs, chambers of commerce, prisons, agricultural colleges, and sometimes even outside on billboards or on the side of a building. Throughout the 1920s, Company sales and promotional caravans took Ford films with them into rural venues and international markets. These caravans often helped initiate events in small towns, using Ford's motion pictures as a particularly popular draw. The audience for these films was, therefore, quite diverse, extending far beyond the workers in Ford's factories or those who could afford time off and a theater ticket.[37]

Pueblo Indians (1921) was among the films Ford produced and distributed as part of this latest series of educational films. The motion picture promised a lesson in US history, beginning with the "discovery" of Pueblo Indians by Spanish explorers in 1540. The film describes and depicts "the arid Southwest," its dry and rocky terrain, desert vegetation, and the ways in which "Indian" homes "remain today as then," not quite four hundred years earlier. Footage cuts between shots of rugged plateaus and gorges, homes of "the ancient Cliff Dwellers . . . ancestors of the Pueblos," and adobes in a nearby valley. Its people are portrayed as "sturdy and happy," clad in moccasins and large-patterned blankets, and engaged in age-old labors. "Separating chaff from wheat in a primitive way," women are shown shaking the grains from a basket onto a large blanket beneath, "grinding corn into flour on the stone or metate," baking bread, weaving baskets and blankets, and making pottery "as in primitive days," while the men, it is explained, are the hunters and metal workers, fashioning silver jewelry with simple tools. Amid its portrait of purportedly ancient practices, the film rarely catches worker's faces, obscured in shadow despite the glare of the sunny scenes. The working life of the Indians is also positioned between settings of religious life: "a Spanish Mission Church in a village" where "for three centuries the bells have pealed their message," and "a sacred dance of the Indians." The film concludes with images of the pueblos at some distance with a title slide that reads: "The Pueblo Indians have changed little since America was discovered." Situated as historical subjects for the study of US history, these native peoples are presented as if preserved in time, serving as a window into a past little changed. Ford's primitivist vision in *Pueblo Indians* is one of an ancient chamber of unchanged order, a racial and religious assembly of static living and laboring.[38]

Produced one year later, *Democracy in Education* portrays a distinctly different view of a primitive America. Issued as part of the Company's civics and citizenship series within the Ford Educational Library, this motion picture begins by offering a less geographically particular vision than that of *Pueblo Indians*. *Democracy in Education* reveals an image of America's "pioneer" past. It casts "the early days of our country" as being peopled with "a sturdy race of resourceful, independent, clear-thinking men." These men endured the "hardships of pioneer life in the open" and "rebelled at tyranny," signing the *Declaration of Independence* to "establish a democracy in which life, liberty, and the pursuit of happiness are guaranteed to all." This pioneer life of democracy is shown in footage of log cabins, fife playing, and the stylish signature of John Hancock. Like the natives in *Pueblo Indians*, the pioneer is portrayed as sturdy and resourceful. Unlike the indigenous group, this pioneer past is a specifically Americanized primitive—one characterized as revolutionary, liberal, and democratic. Never stagnant, the film conveys this pioneer past being made into a "new republic," a new state that "grew, prospered, and became a rich, mighty nation." Indeed, the film suggests it might have grown too much and too fast. "In 1916, there were many who thought that the crowded conditions and manifold temptations of city life . . . had completely destroyed those ideals so firmly established by our forefathers," the film cautioned, amid scenes of street life and skyscrapers and city apartments strung with drying laundry. But the tides were turned, so the film narrates, as the country pulled together to fight against those who would challenge its people's pioneer ideals of liberty and democracy. The mighty and prosperous mobilized against "the challenge of autocracy," the motion picture proclaimed, with footage of soldiers marching in formation and taking up arms. "Wars and rumors of wars may continue for a time," the film continued, but eventually it suggests the formation of a "parliament of man, the federation of the world," in which "a new struggle will arise, a battle of wits and diplomacy." To "make the world safe for Democracy," the Ford film explained, a new kind of preparedness must come about—one performed in the schools, training students in "those qualities which are essential to the happiness of the individual and to the strength and vitality of the nation." Those qualities included "self-direction," "self-appraisal," "self-control," and "co-operation." Together these characteristics were said to make up "the fundamental spokes in the wheel of education." Amid panoramic footage of a city skyline and the US Capitol building alongside intimate portraits of students reading literature and practicing the violin, Ford's educational film promised that such qualities, established in school and practiced in life, would "develop this country into the greatest nation of all time . . . spurred to surpass any previous efforts." Cast in Hellenic terms, it affirmed "the United States will stand as a modern Greece, giving unselfishly a full share of its attainments to the world." In *Democracy in Education*, America's pioneer past is rendered as dynamic change and panoramic virtue. Ford's film showed the Americanized primitive as simultaneously classic and contemporary—a modern nation with origins in ancient democracy but shorn of any indigenous static or tribal nation.[39]

If Ford's *Pueblo Indians* film insisted on the antiquated primitive as part of a stable American history, its subjects are only remainders to a modern nation on the move. *Democracy in Education* conveys an alternative primitive as pioneering movement. Indeed, the subjects of *Pueblo Indians* cannot be a nation in Ford's framing. Rather, the Americanized nation of that primitive past is pioneered through the democracy of the United States. Unlike those in the southwestern pueblos, Ford's American pioneers discovered and moved and developed and surpassed. They prospered. In the Company's *Pueblo Indians* film, Ford produces a vacated landscape with few lingering ruins, in hearty human and natural form, exhibited in "little changed" terms. In *Democracy in Education*, Ford shows streets full of jostling children and erect skyscrapers. The past and the future are portrayed in both of Ford's film presentations, but only in *Democracy in Education* is the Americanized primitive (the pioneer) rendered as party to revolutionary industry. Ford's pioneer portrait in *Democracy in Education* reveals a rendering of industrial revolution that is also a restoration of prior rebellion, a resourceful race that moved modernity and advanced democracy. Unlike the "cliff dwellers" in *Pueblo Indians*, the American settlers used advanced tools to construct first its log cabins and constitutional government, and then later its crowded skylines, capital buildings, and world parliaments. If both films convey a past primitivism, in Ford's logic only the settler subject of the Americanized pioneer could conquer the future in its pedagogical preparedness and cultured prosperity.

Ford and the "Jewish Question"

Significant evidence has already revealed Ford's well-known antisemitism. This feature of his modern-making was something advanced by him and identified and debated among his contemporaries. Ford issued vicious statements in the popular press, through his own newspaper and print publications, and in his autobiography, *My Life and Work*, which was published in multiple editions in the United States and England, distributed serially in France, and translated into German, Finnish, Danish, Norwegian, and Swedish, as well as in Braille. Ford was a favored author of the twentieth century's most notorious genocidal leader, Adolf Hitler, and the industrialist publicly accepted (and directly refused to return) the Grand Cross of the German Eagle, which was awarded to Ford by the Third Reich in 1938 on the occasion of the automaker's seventy-fifth birthday.[40]

The prevailing account of these and many other details about Ford's antisemitism is Neil Baldwin's *Henry Ford and the Jews: The Mass Production of Hate*, in which Baldwin traces a long and enduring history of Ford's antisemitic activities and attitudes. Baldwin describes how this abhorrent aspect of Ford's industry was cultivated in Christian reading practices, nurtured by many of Ford's closest company executives, namely Ernest Liebold and William Cameron, and encouraged by a casual brand of Midwestern populism, which Ford adopted and helped advance through slippery epithets of Jews as both warmongers and moneylenders, Wall Street bankers and parasites of a military industrial complex. Baldwin, like other Ford biographers, has also carefully considered the weight of culpability surrounding Henry Ford's antisemitic statements, which were published under his name though ghostwritten by others, as were so many of Ford's reported assertions. Despite what Ford's underlings claimed amid public scandals and historical inquiry, most scholars have argued that the Company's eponymous founder was decidedly and directly involved in the mass production of these assertions, if not always or exactly responsible for their precise written formulation.[41]

I am persuaded by these conclusions, though my own approach to Ford's antisemitic productions has attempted to turn toward a slightly different set of concerns. Rather than ask about the biographical particularities and psychological dynamics of Henry Ford's anti-Jewish pronouncements, I have sought to focus critical interpretations on the ways in which Ford's myth-making institutionalized a particular assemblage of racial and religious classification through the media of his automotive empire. That the industrialist contributed to some of the most brutal atrocities wrought in modern history should never be overlooked. Accordingly, I have endeavored to follow his language—written and visual—across his media to better understand how his concern with the so-called Jewish Question can offer insight into his modern, and the notions of race, nation, and religion forged and reformed in its making.

State-building has historically gone hand-in-hand with racial and religious identification and differentiation. As European powers set themselves up as the metropole endeavoring to colonize the peripheries of the globe, these Christian imperialists increasingly found themselves encountering newly proximate others. The comparative race and religion projects that were entangled in these colonial relations were also political programs through which religious and racial differences were named, constructed, and classified, and by which "questions" about right rule were forged. These same productions and deliberations of difference were fashioned closer to home, too, and over the course of the late eighteenth and early nineteenth centuries, as colonial governments extended and were occasionally successfully resisted, questions about how the emerging, "secular" nation-state would govern and administer the religious life of its variously racialized citizen-subjects gained increased attention. It was in this context that writers like Bruno Bauer and Karl Marx began to refer to "the Jewish Question." What was at issue was whether emancipation for Jews predicated on the privatization of religion and on racial assimilation could be achieved in a secularized Christian state in Europe. The Jewish Question was, thus, tied inextricably to questions of the nation-state and its ability to both ensure and adjudicate religious freedom among racialized "others." It was also profoundly implicated in the historical expansion of capitalism as a system of economic exchange.[42]

In the late nineteenth and early twentieth centuries, Jews in Eastern Europe and elsewhere, including in the United States, began facing increased persecution. The language of religious freedom seemed to offer little protection for these groups in this period, and by World War I, some Jews in America began to draw less often upon the language of religion than they did on either "national" or "minority group rights." This was particularly true among Zionists in the period, though this movement for the formation of a Jewish nation in Palestine was a controversial one, both within and outside Jewish communities. As Tisa Wenger has described in her study of the Jewish Question, when language about Jewish nationalism or group rights was used, it was most often deployed in order to advocate for Jewish people abroad, though that changed in the years after the First World War. By 1918, the Zionist movement was increasingly recognized as among the most representative voices of American Jews, both within and outside Jewish communities. This new voice on the international scene, though, also had intense critics—again, both among Jews and not. Some of those critical opponents outside the Jewish community brought with them a renewed form of antisemitism, while some supporters of minority rights in America, like President

Wilson, returned to language of religious liberty rather than nation in defending international rights for Jews. Likewise, American law did not have in place many structures for the advocacy of minority rights in terms of nationalism within the United States. For instance, libel statutes were written for the protection of individuals, not groups, and as yet no laws against hate speech were on the books. Consequently, while the logic of religious freedom was limiting in its ability to address the complex identifications of Jews (and often indigenous groups in the Americas, too) as simultaneously religious, racial, and national, it was still the prevailing way in which freedom for minoritized populations in the United States was adjudicated, if not imagined. Much of this is familiar terrain in the study of religion, and the so-called Jewish Question's legacy lingers in ongoing debates about the secular. If Ford's antisemitism has been much described and analyzed over the years, his participation in the tangled categorical terrain of religion, race, and nation has been much less so. Yet, Ford left little ambivalence about his commitment to an American nationalist and nativist campaign against "international Jews" wrought on decidedly racial and religious terms, terms he thought he resolved in recourse with the "Jewish Question."[43]

Sometime in 1926–1927, Samuel Crowther completed a typescript for syndicated publication in magazines and newspapers around the United States under the title, "Henry Ford and the Jews." The 2,500-word article was to be the first of three texts later written by as many authors with this name. While the subsequent texts were later critiques and exposés of Ford's antisemitism, Crowther's was an apologia, and an updated one at that. It was based on a previous text, ghostwritten by Crowther and published under Henry Ford's byline as part of the industrialist's 1922 autobiography. In fact, some parts of Crowther's later typescript are drawn directly from that earlier text, published some five years prior. Amid all this reinscription and replication, Crowther's article is presented as an attempt to set the record straight, to tell the real story, and to describe earlier events with an insider's apparent clarity as well as seemingly benefiting from the disinterestedness of hindsight. Crowther begins simply: "Henry Ford, it is generally believed, is not only anti-Semitic but violently so. This is not true." The rest of the article is structured as a series of questions and answers, posed as if it were a thorough interrogation of the industrialist's reasons for publishing articles about Jews in the *Dearborn Independent*, lawsuits related to the published articles, and Ford's "personal feelings," general relations, and financial dealings with Jewish people over the years. The answers, Crowther noted, "are not in Mr. Ford's words, but they accurately represent his sentiments and have been approved." Setting himself up as the authorized but neutral arbiter of the evidence at hand, Crowther sought to counter popular assumptions about Ford's antisemitic reputation, insisting that "Every fact in the whole matter has been exaggerated either by the proponents or the opponents of Mr. Ford."[44]

Among the facts Crowther aimed to explicate was the "impersonal" nature of Ford's dealings. He advanced an industrialists' version of the "I have Jewish friends" defense—noting that Ford had "availed himself of the business and artistic ability of Jews whenever possible." Crowther also worked hard to dissociate the industrialist's articles from any "racial feeling whatsoever," even as he went on to describe how Ford "considered the Jews as a race and not as a religion." Ford seems to have been suggesting that he considered Jews to be a race but also wanted to claim that was not why he had written against them. Drawing on a confluence of national and religious definition, Crowther further asserts that Ford was "not and never has been anti-Semitic, just as he has never been anti-German, anti-French, or anti-British. . . . He has and always has had the greatest respect and admiration for the Jewish religion." Ford maintained he was not, even perhaps could not be, antisemitic because he held no animosity for Jewishness as a religion. Jews, again, according to Ford, were a race, but for this, Crowther claimed, Ford had no hostility. Rather, Ford's critical focus was on those Jews "who are said to have forsworn the faith of their fathers . . . the international Jew." In Ford's telling, these Jews were something beyond or between or somehow otherwise not quite national; they were inter-. "Mr. Ford believed that the international Jewish financiers were men without countries," Crowther wrote, trading in familiar antisemitic tropes, "and, as the inventors and manipulators of the money system of the world, used their power to promote war—because, no matter who lost, they stood to win."[45]

Here, Ford's vaguer gestures to parasitic brokers and warmongers took on the more direct moniker of the Jew. "That was and always has been the main point in his mind," Crowther emphasized. He eschewed "any kind of prejudice, except," he wavered, "it may be a prejudice in favor of the principles which have made our civilization." His prejudice was a civic principle. In Ford's assertion, "our civilization" was being damaged, not only by war but also by "a marked deterioration in our literature, amusements, and social conduct; business was departing from its old-time substantial soundness; a general letting down of standards was felt everywhere." Ford's declension narrative was placed at the responsibility "not of the robust coarseness of the white man" nor the "rude indelicacy . . . of Shakespeare's characters." At fault for civilizational decline, Ford said, was "a nasty Orientalism." Against this "Orientalizing" of Ford's civilization, he urged protection of "Christian society." What that meant, in Crowther's reporting, was that Ford's pioneering civilization needed to resist the "nasty Orientalism" that characterized Jewish practices "to make America Jewish," working instead and explicitly to "make Jews American." How or even whether this could happen seemed something like a converting impossibility since Ford also suggested in his sociological efforts that Jews could not be fully Americanized. This may have been the point. "The genius of the United States of America is Christian in the broadest sense," Crowther wrote and Ford approved, "and its destiny is to remain Christian." Ford's autobiography, *My Life and Work*, includes the same statement, followed up with additional explanation. For Ford, to speak of an America as "Christian in the broadest sense" was to advance "no sectarian meaning." Instead, his broadly Christian ideal was "a basic principle . . . in that it provides for liberty, morality, and pledges society to a code of relations based on the fundamental Christian conception of human rights and duties."[46]

Ford reminds here that the social good he purportedly sought to serve was also, in his "broad" understanding, a distinctly Christian one. For Ford, Jewishness was a designation of difference never to be fully incorporated into or by his purifying mediations. He claimed that his "Studies in the Jewish Question" were merely the latest in a longer history. Yet, his "studies" were exceptional in their media reach and in their impact on those who purported to be proffering the "final solution" to this "question." Baldur von Schirach, leader of the Nazi Students' Federation and the Hitler youth movement, testified during the Nuremberg war crimes trials that Ford's writings convinced him of Jewish culpability for world affairs when he was seventeen, and Hitler himself drew on material from Ford's newspaper in public speeches, cited Ford admiringly in *Mein*

Kampf, and kept a picture of Ford on display. Ford may not have originated the hate, but he certainly raised the stakes of its mass production.[47]

The scholar of Ford's material is, then, left with a conundrum—a question. Not of the Jewish type, but of Ford's. Of its systematizing power and corporate form. Of Fordism. To describe Ford's assemblage and mass production of religion, race, and nation, one must guard against reinscribing his terms and techniques. To merely retype his words, often so vile, is to hold uncomfortably close the real dangers of reinscription and reproduction, a theme and a question to be confronted anew in the following chapter. Amid Ford's many tangled and abhorrent assertions—as he disclaimed and enacted his racism, denied and affirmed his antisemitism—this material returns us to the Ford Question, to the problem of Ford and his corporation. To understand the modern he endeavored so urgently to make, scholars must contend anew with the religio-racial nationalism and broadly Christian, nativist Americanism Ford promoted.

Stefan Link, in his transnational study of Ford's "Nazi connection," has proposed the language of "illiberal" or "postliberal" modernism to describe Ford's producerist promotion as the most influential global strategy in the 1920s and 1930s attempting to "transcend" liberal capitalism from the Right. Aligned with much of the language we have traced above in Ford's distinction between his pioneering producer and the speculative parasite he imagined, Link locates in Ford a "producerist *critique* of liberal American capitalism." Link likewise describes how Ford's form of illiberal modernism was compatible not only with Nazi Germany's antisemitism but with many critics of capitalism, from National Socialists to Soviet planners. Link's assertion is that, while post-1945 liberalism became the "unchallenged *telos* of modernizing projects," in the 1920s and 1930s, "illiberal productivist alternatives" like Ford's still seemed to be a viable option. Ford's form of modernism, Link proposes, "still struck a note worldwide among radicals who thought that the time was ripe for an economic system that would supersede liberal capitalism." I find in Ford's form of illiberal modernism, or what Link later refers to as a modernism that "spoke with equal force to the insurgent left and the postliberal right," a pioneering religio-racial claim for a supersessionary secularism, a religious formation and a political project of broadly Christian nativism that proffers progress in pioneering pursuits.[48]

The Ford Question, then, urges us to interrogate the industrialist's supersessionary logic and its "broadly" Christian implications, its relation to an ethos of service, and the forms of nationalism wrought through the assemblage of it all. Ford did not deploy the language of the secular or pronounce his system of political economy as a kind of secularism. Despite the fact that most readers likely think of him as a largely secular subject, Ford was much more comfortable asserting religious vocation and vocabulary. Yet, in gesturing toward the category of the secular and secularism, I build upon the vast and ever-growing field of secular studies that approaches the concept of secularism as a managerial project of articulating, regulating, and assessing the religious from the not-religious, and seeks to govern right from wrong religion. In Ford's brand of supersessionary secularism, the industrialist inscribes a pioneering form of power and advances material progress in producerist critiques of finance capitalism. As scholars confront the Ford Question—the problem of Ford's corporation—it is worth considering how and why his antisemitic dreams and conspiratorial promises might yet remain appealing to some observers today. The Ford Question submerges us into messy histories, dangerous racism, supersessionary logics, and broadly Christian cadences of a "service" economy forded in the "neglected truths" of Ford. The Ford Question may likewise prompt us to return to producerist critiques of capitalism. As we do so, we would do well to ask anew whether a critique of Ford's producerist critique of liberal capitalism can only ever lead us back to liberalism. Or, might such a critique lead us elsewhere? And can that elsewhere be rendered in terms other than the rite-to-work religion and supersessionary secularism Ford strove to supply and service? My suspicion is that it might. By interrogating and critiquing the corporate relations, producerist populism, articulations of the primitive and the modern, and the supersessionary frames of capital service Ford mass-produced as a form of secular governance in and for the twentieth century, perhaps we can at least open a space of critical concern and alternative workings.

* * *

Antisemitic representations of Jews in Ford's print media became a way to connote non-productive, parasitic, international capital against which Ford rendered his pioneering, American production. The pioneer was not just a nostalgia. It was a proposition for a certain vehement idea about the nature of industry and the necessity of growth through nature's conquering. Nor was the pioneer a sidebar trope for Ford. The pioneer was the star ascription and eclipsing contrast, the direct opposite in his framing of Jewish people, indigenous groups, and speculative shareholders. The pioneer figured right subjectivity—a character of broadly Christian, "pioneer blood"—for Ford's supersessionary secularism, a political-economic structure that reassembled and governed a set of conditions, sensibilities, and logics through which that pioneering subjectivity was disciplined, ordered, and reproduced as a broadly Christian advancement over and against the "international Jews" and "non-working shareholders" that Ford conjured in antisemitic plots of threatening and expired subjects. These antisemitic tropes and supersessionary logics, advanced by and through his empire of industrial producerism and American primitivism—in print media, in rhetoric against minority shareholders, in early industrial photography and film, among others—became a way for Ford to connote non-productive, parasitic, international capital against which to render his rightly pioneering, American producers and his productive industry.

As we will see in the following chapter, Ford's commitment to a "pioneer" Americana extended well into the 1930s and 1940s through the museum and historical village he established late in the 1920s. This historical project became a way for him to continue to teach truths he considered otherwise neglected and to order right industry. Prescribing the pioneer through transmedia enterprises, Ford thought he debunked media representations outside his corporate command. He thought, too, that he "enlightened" the world's industrial production, as he worked tirelessly to show what was right and what needed to be stamped out by the right kind of pioneer.

4

Harrowing History and Ford's Run-of-the-Mill Relics

In late 1929, Wall Street investors panicked over plummeting prices, dumping millions of shares of stocks. The ensuing "crash" ushered in years of unemployment and economic struggle. Historians have since marked the darkest of these dim days "Black Tuesday," designating it the inaugural event of the greatest economic depression ever seen before, or since. Only a week before this historic rending, Ford commemorated a world blessed with electric light. "Light's Golden Jubilee" celebrated Ford's close friend and industrial mentor, Thomas Edison, on the fiftieth anniversary of his invention of the incandescent lamp. Named by General Electric and organized by Edward L. Bernays, the so-called father of modern public relations, the Light's Golden Jubilee was an elaborately coordinated national affair. Joining Edison's invention to the language of "jubilee," the anniversary linked religious and economic projects. For Ford the occasion was also timed to celebrate Edison as namesake of the auto-industrialist's newest venture, the Edison Institute of Technology. Situated on over 200 acres of land near the Company's experimental laboratories in Dearborn, Michigan, the Edison Institute was comprised of two parts: an industrial museum and an adjacent village of living history. "The history of our people," Ford explained, was "written into the things their hands made and used." He would collect those things and put them on display. The Edison Institute was to be "a living epitome of American history," a place where history was "not only to be seen but to be heard and felt."[1]

Edison's was an innovation that, according to Ford, not only helped initiate a "whole new system of electrical power" but also inaugurated modern industry. "It is the fashion," Ford acknowledged, "to call this the age of industry. Rather, we should call it the age of Edison. For he is the founder of modern industry in this country." In one densely illustrated guidebook for the new Edison Institute, Ford described how "our ancestors groped their way from the primitive to the enlightenment" and pondered "the effect on human progress" if Americans "could turn back the leaves of time and stand successively where stood the great men of our pioneer—and of our recent—past." The lessons Ford taught celebrated a "pioneer past" as American pedigree and positioned Edison's inventive mind and experimental conduct as its origin. The auto-industrialist especially admired his friend's ability "to organize himself into a research and inventing institution and make his brains more effective by having conducted under his direction many more experiments than he could possibly conduct himself." Not only a model of engineering ingenuity, Edison was to Ford an exemplar of mass organization and effective institutionalization. "Edison is in himself a great research institution— probably the greatest in the world," Ford admired. "He stands alone among inventors in having organizing as well as creative ability."[2]

Observers of the Jubilee quickly understood Ford's ambition. Perceiving the shadowy forms of Ford's hulking River Rouge plant located just beyond the gates of his newest venture, commentators said the factory's "mass production of 8,000 cars a day, seemed to symbolize the industrial advances made since Mr. Edison's lamp began to challenge the night."[3]

Ford was interested in the past even as he advanced a dramatic futurism. The quickening conveyors in his factories and the automobiles manufactured there increasingly hurried workers and consumers into a Machine Age that Ford helped propagate. More than a decade before the Jubilee celebration, Ford boldly proclaimed: "History is more or less bunk. It's tradition. We don't want tradition." The establishment of his museum and village of living history suggests that Ford's historical occupations were less antagonistic to history than they were an eager argument for a particular kind of it. "We want to live in the present," he continued, "and the only history that is worth a tinker's dam is the history we make today."[4]

Ford's newly dedicated museum and village housed his growing collection of historical artifacts and served as a venue for his newest foray into industrial education and Americanization. Museum spaces and buildings in Greenfield Village were used as classrooms. But more important to Ford was the Institute's ability to provide hands-on learning and vocational training in its machine shop, blacksmith, pottery, glass plant, gardens, sawmill, and array of domestic living spaces. Pedagogically reproducing a gendered division of labor and an ideology of separate spheres that organized the industrialist's own nineteenth-century education, girls were taught home economics and practiced hostess duties in buildings like the Daniel Webster House. Their male counterparts practiced traditional arts and learned skilled trades in the "village industries" portion of the Institute. Pupils were both educated on "old-fashioned equipment" and taught "how to do things the modern way." By "trying the jobs which their forefathers carried on," while also learning the skills Ford said were most valued by twentieth-century industry, the Edison Institute's curriculum was designed to give students the chance not only to witness but to reenact a "continuity of progress" that the auto-industrialist insisted was "too often lost sight of" in other schools. Ford wanted everyone to understand the industrial practices of yesteryear so that they could better appreciate the "magic methods" of mass production he propounded. Whatever economic downfalls occurred, Ford was certain human beings would celebrate always the modern industry he and Edison innovated.[5]

Crucial to Ford's pedagogical principles and methods of historical production were the "many precious relics" he assembled. The term "relic" was Ford's. I draw upon it first as a term indigenous to the auto-industrialist's archive, but it is also an important second-order category in the study of religion. It is a term that scholars have approached etymologically through the Latin verb meaning "to leave behind" and have typically used in relation to practices of collecting the bodily remains of venerated persons or sacralized objects. Gregory Schopen has described the way that the relic brings with it an "unflattering anthropology" wrought through the heavy polemics of Protestant reformers and colonial missionaries in their encounters with others—Catholics first and then those they reckoned less proximate, including South Asians, indigenous Africans, and Native Americans. Linked to "savage magic," the language of "relic" brings with it claims about those who Protestants deemed wrongly religious, impossibly exuberant, or absurdly superstitious. A clutter of abuse and stupidity, reverence and virtue, the relic's colonial history complicates any engagement with it. Some historians have suggested that the category has been effectively desacralized over time, coming to mean something more commonplace and simplified into a mere synonym for "old things." Yet, Ford was ever disobedient to secularizing schema rendered in religious declension. The relic is not so easily cast out, as so many Protestant reformers wanted. It "confounds our categories," Schopen rightly asserts. Situated at the boundaries of living and dead, animate and inanimate, immaterial and what matters, Ford's practices of material religion can be glimpsed in his careful collecting of and scrupulous concern for the relic, and it reveals his enchanted approach to relics and reliquaries in twentieth-century America more than any quick gesture to "old things" would otherwise suggest. In this interpretive move, I draw upon the language of magic and enchantment from the study of religion to bring Ford's specific historical summon of relics into sharper relief.[6]

According to Ford, textbooks too often forgot the work-a-day world that he had long celebrated. "When I went to our American history books to learn how our forefathers harrowed the land, I discovered that the historians knew nothing about harrows," he reported. "Yet our country has depended more on harrows than on guns or speeches." Ford contended that "a history, which excluded harrows and all the rest of daily life, was bunk." Homing in on the harrow—an agricultural implement used after plowing a field to help break up clumps of soil, remove weeds, or otherwise help level topsoil before planting seed—Ford found the equipment of the past worth preserving. The harrow and its ilk would debunk American history, leveling it such that "a pewter bowl from the humblest kitchen in the Colonies would be of equal interest with one from that of George Washington." It was not in military conquest or political leaders but the treatment of topsoil and "that thread of communion we can always feel in the presence of relics of our honored ancestors" that Ford asserted the nation's history was enriched and enlivened.[7]

The study of religion has frequently interrogated the fabrication and mediation of the ordinary and extraordinary. "All the relics have one thing in common," Ford told the architect of his new museum, "they are all things used by run-of-the-mill people, not by the elite." He contended that "the soul" or "true spirit of the past" would be found not in the written records of famous treaties or epic battles but in the relics of ordinary kitchens and schoolrooms and farms. His was a history focused on "everyday lives of ordinary folk" who, he repeatedly asserted, had been "overlooked by historians." In the relics of the everyday, Ford developed a history in which the material of the past came alive in the present, "resurrected, so to speak, to a new life beyond the grave." The reliquaries

Ford institutionalized in Edison's name conjured "America" and its past as commonly used but exceptionally realized. In his enshrinement of run-of-the-mill relics he creatively reproduced the sacred inside what historian of religions David Chidester described as "the vagaries of the ordinary and the terror of history." The sacred Ford made was a vernacular Americana, something mundane rendered valuable for its participation in the flow of an exceptionalist national story.[8]

Scholars of material religion tend to emphasize the "genesis of presence" or the hierophaneous eruption of the extraordinary when they approach sacred objects. Ford's own theorization focused on the affective "presence" of "honored ancestors." In this chapter I focus less on how the extraordinary is perceived as a shattering rupture than on how Ford fabricates affective excess *within* the ordinary and the everyday. This requires the simultaneous making and dissolution of distinction—a requirement that the work of incorporation marks. In the industrialist's invocation and inventory of the relic, Ford sacralized his "pioneer past" as a present matter. Artifacts were celebrated as ordinary in elaborate reenactments, accumulated at a massive scale, and consumed in both educational environs and tourist venues. Articulated and assembled as a memento of his modern mission, the relic helped Ford manufacture and mediate American history through rituals of dispossession. He set out to render the past as a practice of material debunking, a way for him to challenge textual interpretation and level the furrows of time. Tracing these practices and ambitions, I contend that Ford reenchanted historical materials through magical purchase. Not disenchanted. Not de-magicked. Ford's run-of-the-mill relics and the American history he said was worth a "tinker's dam" bring to the fore the auto-industrialist's investment in a magical economy of capital possession.

The Magic of Light's Golden Jubilee

Ford began collecting artifacts early in the twentieth century. From the beginning he collected many "Edison relics." Over the years, he acquired and assembled a growing mass of Edisoniana, including several of the inventor's original patents and prototypes. Ford's acquisitions included phonographic materials, an electric pen, telephone transmitter, dynamos, motion picture equipment, typewriters, a vast assortment of laboratory gear and furniture, and eventually an elaborate reconstruction of Edison's entire Menlo Park complex. In 1931, Charles Edison, son of the inventor, even sent Henry Ford a test tube purportedly containing "Edison's last breath," a relic that remains part of Ford's collection.[9]

Yet, it was in advance of Edison's fiftieth anniversary festivities, when the Wizard of Menlo Park was still very much alive, that Ford most extravagantly celebrated his friend. Amid the many corporate-sponsored events planned to honor "The Man Who Lighted the World," the dedication of Ford's new Edison Institute was the crowning occasion, and it was certainly the most lavish. In addition to an elaborate parade organized for Edison in Detroit, Ford invited more than five hundred special guests and dignitaries to celebrate the inventor's anniversary during the dedication of Ford's new museum and village. The President of the United States, Herbert Hoover, and several of his cabinet members made appearances, as did delegations from Japan and Europe, along with dozens of other notables—among them Charles Schwab and John D. Rockefeller Jr., Marie Curie, William Mayo, Orville Wright, Walter Chrysler, Harvey Firestone, Jane Addams, George Eastman, and Will Rodgers. Prince Edward of Wales and President von Hindenburg of Germany sent messages of congratulations. Calling from Berlin, Albert Einstein transmitted a special audio message conducted over the American Telegraph and Telephone Company's transatlantic circuit and broadcast over the radio to listening audiences.[10]

Guests who attended in person were carried into the historic gathering in a refurbished, wood-burning train and were the first visitors to officially tour the sites. Packed into horse-drawn carriages, coaches, hacks, carryalls, phaetons, and buggies, guests promenaded through the muddy streets of Greenfield Village, stopping to take in the newly assembled historical sites along the way—a log cabin, tin-type studio, chapel, one-room schoolhouse, post office, pharmacy, and town hall. Attendees lunched by candlelight at the Clinton Inn and lit ceremonial fires in the hearths at the Logan County courthouse, a recently relocated venue where Abraham Lincoln had reputedly argued several cases when he was practicing law in Illinois. The façade of Ford's yet-unfinished museum nearby was itself designed to be an architectural reproduction of Independence Hall, complete with a Liberty Bell replica. This was also where the evening's formal banquet was later held.[11]

While guests waited at their tables, Edison, Ford, and President Hoover left the candlelit museum and proceeded back out through the rain into Greenfield Village. They, along with an entourage of media types, traipsed through the mud—a unique mire, since Ford had procured seven freight cars full of red New Jersey clay soil to infill the site of the newly reconstructed Menlo Park complex—and made their way into the gas lamp-lit laboratory. "We have reestablished Menlo Park at Dearborn, exactly like the first Menlo Park, even to the trees and shrubs," Ford proclaimed. The celebrated inventor agreed. "By golly if Henry hasn't even moved in the stump of that old elm tree," Edison exclaimed. "I tell you it's just exactly as it was, every bit of it." Ford gathered original buildings, furniture, and decor, and when unavailable, he commissioned replicas. "People will be able to see the exact scene out of which came the electric light and to realize how simply even the greatest things come into being," he explained. Showcasing how the great was wrought in and as the simple, the relics Ford gathered would help reanimate the exacting scenes of Edison's achievement. With Edison cast as "one of the common people . . . who lifted a light to guide us out of darkness," Ford's new Institute reassembled and incorporated together the exceptional and the commonplace as characteristic of his new enterprise in American industry.[12]

To facilitate Edison's Jubilee reenactment, one of Edison's former assistants, Francis Jehl, joined the crew and provided the distinguished inventor with handwritten notes to help guide him through the broadcasted performance. NBC aired the event, and members of Ford's film department captured the scene on celluloid as it unfolded. Radio commentators recounted the jubilant moment in especially grandiloquent tones. Their words resounded through loudspeakers in the museum atrium where Ford's guests eagerly listened in. Millions of others tuned in to the radio broadcast, which some accounts said reached as far as Antarctica. Radio correspondents urged audiences gathered around their receivers at home to turn off their electric lights, listening instead to the dramatization of Edison's reenactment by candlelight or from the glow of their home hearths. "The light is now ready, as it was a half century ago. Will it light? Will it burn?" Graham McNamee, the NBC Blue announcer asked breathlessly, heightening the suspense as only an experienced sports broadcaster could. "Now the group is once more about the old vacuum pump," McNamee rehearsed. "Mr. Edison has two wires in his hand; now he is reaching up to the old lamp; now he is making the connection." At the moment when McNamee proclaimed, "It lights!" listeners everywhere were prompted to switch on their bulbs, participating in the ritual themselves and baptizing the world anew in Edison's incandescent creation. "Light's Golden Jubilee has come to a triumphant climax!" McNamee exclaimed. The 1929 recording of this event remains one of only a few intact recordings of pre-1935 radio in existence today, marking the occasion as a central event in histories of electric light, public relations, and the medium of radio. These public theatrics—those recorded in the Menlo Park complex replica and those practiced at home by the masses listening in—inaugurated the industrialist's new venture and introduced audiences to mass-mediated forms of interactive ritual that would become increasingly important in consumer culture and religious media throughout the twentieth century.[13]

According to newspaper accounts of the Jubilee, as the wires of Edison's invention connected, Ford's industrial empire blazed anew. "Thousands upon thousands of lights flashed up from the Ford land," the *New York Times* reported. "Great golden bulbs, which had been concealed up to the moment of achievement thrust themselves out of the night. Vivid beams of light flashed the sky and dipped to cover the ground with clean white light. The high beacon at the airport flashed into view, its outlines traced in powerful bulbs, and looking at a distance like the strands of a fiery necklace, loosely suspended from the heavens." The reconstructed Menlo Park complex was "completely floodlighted." Guests waiting in Ford's museum participated in the ritual lighting, too. Its "golden lights were turned on" and "the tower seemed sheathed in gold, as the illumination gained volume and strength," while Ford's reconstructed "Liberty bell in the cupola rang out sturdy notes," proclaiming to those gathered inside and to radio audiences around the world "that Edison's light has been born anew." Search lights cut through the dark sky, "filling the night with weird, flashing paths of color." Despite the inclement weather and dangerous flying conditions, two airplanes roared up from the airport with the word "Edison" and the years "'79" and "'29" illuminated under their wings. "One, in white lights, circled high above the hall. The other, coated with red bulbs, drummed in a wider circle over Detroit, where the bells were rung and the whistles blown." Automobile horns around the city roared and cars flashed their headlights in a way that made some "think of some great telephonic switchboard." The entire metro area erupted in celebratory fireworks and sirens pealed across the city. As the enlightened ritual ended, the white and gold lights of the Edison Institute shone brightly, gas lamps and candlelight now replaced by gleaming incandescent bulbs. "This wonderful age of light has just come into magic being," Phillips Carlin, McNamee's on-air co-host proclaimed. Amid this ritualized reenactment, it seems no one could escape the brilliance and "magic being" of these two industrialists and their contributions to an enlightened world.[14]

Illuminating Ritual and the Magic of Ford's Modern

To refer to the Jubilee's reenactment as "ritualized" is an argumentative claim. The Jubilee scenes that Ford organized as well as its multiple mediations in print, film, and radio are instructive for analysis of Ford's historic projects and for critical studies of religion and history. Jonathan Z. Smith has shown that religion cannot be understood without recourse to ritual observance and mythic narrative, "most especially to that dimension of taking-care." It is this "scrupulousness"—an "ethos and ethic of taking-care"—that I draw on here to think about Ford's vow of comprehensive rigor when excavating his "Edison relics." "We took everything but the climate," Ford later boasted. "I believe that the reproduction is exact. It must be exact, for if this is to be a re-creation of the old scenes then there can be no compromise with accuracy. I want the imaginations of those who see history thus concretely presented to start with the thing itself and not be wasted trying to supply missing parts of the scene."[15]

The phenomenological precision and comprehensive presentation of Ford's votive product, his meticulous management of materials, and the exacting choreography of historical space and performative scene that he supplied, also harken to what scholars of religion have studied as mimetic or imitative magic. This category of magic-making is typically linked to James George Frazer, an anthropologist from the early twentieth century, who theorized magic based on its power to work at a distance in exacting imitation and sympathetic influence. "The sympathetic influence exerted on each other by persons or things at a distance is the essence of magic," Frazer wrote in *The Golden Bough*, published seven years prior to the Jubilee event, "whatever doubts science may entertain as to the possibility of action at a distance, magic has none." Following Michael Taussig, I seek to acknowledge the "magical power of replication" and to better understand the "fetishlike power of the copy." To recognize the mimetic magic at work in this jubilant celebration draws renewed attention to the magic of Ford's mass-produced modern. "Inanimate things, as well as plants and animals, may diffuse blessing or bane around them, according to their own intrinsic nature and the skill of the wizard," Frazer theorized. According to Ford, the Edison Institute of Technology was a product of the most industrious wizard: "The inspiration that must come from association with the workshop and equipment of one of the outstanding inventors of all times will influence the future of American research and experimentation." The sympathetic influence exerted through Ford's scrupulously reproduced Menlo Park complex was not just reverential nostalgia or a public memorial for his friend. It was a charmed copy carefully conjured to scrupulously structure more spirited advancements to come.[16]

"To find a man who has not been benefited by Edison and who is not in debt to him, it would be necessary to go deep into the jungle," Ford later wrote. "Wherever civilization exists, there also is Edison." Pronouncing his mentor "our greatest American," Ford said that if the Edison Institute taught even a few children "something of the spirit which made this country, then the labor will not have been in vain." What was that spirit? Ford answered decisively: "The American spirit of endeavor as represented in its fullness by Thomas Alva Edison," which was, he continued, "the real wealth of the nation." The Edison Institute was purposed for nothing less than to inspire, enchant, and recreate a prosperous nation. Turning again to histories of religion, Frazer reminds once more, about the workings of a "public magic," what the anthropologist described as a form of "sorcery" practiced on behalf of a community's "common good." In such instances, "the magician ceases to be merely a private practitioner and becomes to some extent a public functionary." Because a community's welfare depends upon the performance of these magical rites, "the magician rises into a position of much influence and repute and may readily acquire the rank and authority of a chief or king." The wealth and welfare of the nation depended, Ford believed, upon this kind of inspiration, influence, and authority. A guidebook for the Edison Institute confirmed the stimulating power and progressive charm of the Wizard and his Menlo Park compound in Ford's historical village, where it is described as "a tribute of respect and admiration for Edison's life and work" which would "cast the spell of Edisonian inspiration over all who enter their doors." The historical rites Ford was working were not just for him. They were for the community's good. Making relics public and developing living history exhibits offered public magic through which the power of industry could be extended throughout the civilized world. Perhaps beyond that, even "deep into the jungle."[17]

One report of Edison's grand experiment explained how Hoover, Jehl, and Ford, like those listening to the tale beamed around the world, were among those spellbound by the Jubilee's spectacle of magical creation: "Mr. Edison, standing in the same laboratory in which fifty years ago he brought to practical fruition his dream of incandescent light, reconstructed that first lamp. Its glow lighted the faces of the three men watching intently, under the spell of the moment, as though they really were witnessing the birth of the age of light." In this account, the reenactment transported the inventor into a past-present, faux-real dreamscape. The lab and the lamp replicated as part of Ford's new educational institute transformed into the "same" ones Edison had engaged half a century before. The inventor was at once alive and immortalized; his past made present and yet also precisely rendered in futurist vintage through ritual stagecraft. It harkened a nativity scene for enlightened modernity. Three wise men keep guard by night, watching intently as witnesses to the genesis of a newly enlightened age and the rebirth of industry. This ritual curation offers a "temporal tangle," in which past and present, living and the afterlife, resist any simple linear plot.[18]

It would be all too easy to dismiss this kind of event as a public relations stunt with accompanying overwrought journalistic reports. The Jubilee was, indeed, a shining example of early twentieth-century promotional puffery, and Ford had the distinct ability to excite the hype machine. Yet our focus here is on how Ford situated Edison's invention as the origin story of modern industry. To conceive an origin is an historical making that is its own magical maneuver. Taussig placed "origin history" as a form of mimetic magic alongside Frazer's theories of sympathy. Its crucial work occurs through practices of "chanting or whispering or simply just thinking a thing's *origin* [which] gives the ritualist power over it." As reports recounted the origins of Edison's creative achievement and narrated its reenactment as central to Ford's dedication of the Edison Institute, they exercised ritual power. "Trac[ing] the connection through history," Taussig explains, is how ritualists exercise a mimetic power, as "one thing becomes another thing while in some profound sense remaining the (mimetic) same." This power is glimpsed in a "sequence of magical transformations of one thing into another thing while, through the very act of transforming, conserving the notion of an underlying sameness." Origin history conjures through the "formed yet transformed." Among the Cuna Indians that Taussig studies, origin history is commonly linked to forms and figures of female reproduction—birthing, the womb, the Great Mother. Yet, as in this instance of the Jubilee event, ritual leaders were "nearly always male." To recount Edison's inventive scene was a kind of historical wizardry and masculine reproduction. In guidebooks and film productions, in photo-ops and press reports, Ford summoned an origin story for his enduring industrial program. With the aid of reporters and broadcasters, he reproduced the material of an "origin history" that lighted the way for his own modern making—one he said was "worth a tinker's dam."[19]

The magic of modernity, Taussig points out, "puts the power of historicism in a new light." Ford historicizes, marking the centrality of Edison to the existence of industry that ensured both their places in textbooks. Making history is itself a ritual practice of mimetic magic, a way to incant certain subjects repeatedly into being. History does not give us science; it gives us ritual stories. History is "one particular way of being in, and seeing, the world," a mode of thought that declares itself "history" and identifies artifacts and behaviors as component to it. Ford insisted the history that mattered was the one he made and that the past worth preserving was a pioneering one. That past, that history, was a preservation and remaking of enlightened expedition. Despite considerable challenge within the ranks of historians to a concept of history as Ford would have it—because it romanticized, because it did not include all perspectives, because it served a particular outcome, namely, his industrial significance—the appeal of a history with the power to debunk and to reorganize the public good is one that endures, often as a counter to prejudicial presumptions. Complicating this history of history is how

Ford, too, positioned his historical intervention in similar terms. "Mr. Ford felt that much of what we read is prejudicial information," Ernest Liebold, one of Ford's executive secretaries, explained. His boss's real intention in creating the Edison Institute was, Liebold said, "as a means of proving that history as it was written was bunk." Ford did not trust how it was written. This is why enshrining relics became so important. They would sympathetically influence and materially connect Ford's incantations of industrial origin to the brand of American abundance he most wanted to disseminate.[20]

Debunking History

Many commentators, including Ford's secretary, Ernest Liebold, contended that the auto-industrialist's venture into public history and industrial education was largely a response to charges made against him, particularly those issued in the *Chicago Tribune*. In 1916, amid US border disputes with Mexico, the *Chicago Tribune* published an editorial questioning Ford's patriotism and lambasting his apparent policy of refusing to hold jobs for workers enlisted in or recruited by the National Guard after President Woodrow Wilson had mobilized the force to fight the revolutionary general Pancho Villa's raids in the southwest. The report about Ford's refusal to hold workers' jobs was never substantiated, but the longtime pacifist was no fan of military action. So, it may well have seemed an entirely reasonable policy issued on behalf of a longtime antiwar activist and peacemonger.

In the wake of the Peace Ship's public failure, Ford was ready to reclaim his historic power, and he was primed to react to the *Chicago Tribune*'s unattributed editorial, which condemned Ford for his apparent lack of support for US involvement in armed conflict at its southern border. The *Tribune*, then owned by Colonel Robert McCormick, accused Ford of "not believ[ing] in service to the nation in the fashion a soldier must serve it," and insisted that the Ford Motor Company's apparent policy of not holding jobs for National Guardsmen—and, implicitly, Ford's broader anti-war positions—revealed the industrialist to be both "an ignorant idealist" and "an anarchistic enemy of the nation which protects him in his wealth." Shots were thus fired in the long-standing war of publicity, and in that kind of battle, Ford was never pacific. He vehemently denied the report and returned the attack, charging the *Tribune* with libel and asking for $1 million in damages. If the Peace Ship taught him anything, Ford thought that history was what he made, not some lesson of military might rehearsed in argumentative exchange or emerging from interminable political negotiation. To make history—just simple, straightforward, objective history—Ford declared that the world needed something other than books and bombs; it required something more mechanically fitted for his tinkered time.[21]

The *Tribune*'s public invectives against Ford—libelous charges, he insisted—prompted a commitment in the automaker to represent the history of his country as he saw it, against those like McCormick who sought to muddy Ford's good (brand) name and in opposition to those whom he understood to be profiting from warmongering. In the wake of the *Tribune* trial, Ford reportedly informed Liebold that Ford Motor Company was "going to build a museum that's going to show industrial history, and it won't be bunk!" "We'll show the people what actually existed in years gone by and we'll show the actual development of American industry from the earliest days that we can recollect down to the present day." The *writing* of history, from Ford's post–Peace Ship, post–*Tribune* trial perspective, was where the problem lay. Textbooks were especially leading documents in prejudicial presentation, but Ford was convinced that he could offer a truer picture, one materialized in the artifacts of American industry. Better than any interpretive script handed down from historians, the material setting of America's pioneer past would debunk editorial prejudices, harrow the furrowed terrain of the past, and reveal instead a truly *objective* history. "You can tell how a people develop only by seeing what they used and made," Ford explained. "That's how they expressed themselves, not how they were reported in histories, and you know that no two reporters see the same things or tell the same story." Proclaiming positivist possibilities in material form, Ford said the artifacts of history would express a complete and accurate story of America's past without the narrative variances and prejudices of the present. Denying "with emphasis" any "patriotic interest," the auto-industrialist contended that the Edison Institute was "a textbook of human and technical history." Meant "to minister to the student type of mind," Ford set out to construct "an engineer's vision of history."[22]

Ford's history was to be one otherwise "unknown to school textbooks, for it has small reminder of politics," or so he and his supporters claimed. The industrialist had gotten his fill of "politics" in his Peace Ship voyage. "The real revolution was going on quietly in a laboratory," Ford explained, which is why the history he was engineering would feature labs like Edison's but have "practically none of wars." The people and dates taught in the standard textbook, "the whole web and woof of our story as a schoolboy learns it," was not to be rewritten or revised. It would be debunked by the vernacular objects and artifacts that shaped and powered daily life. Imposing events like the Missouri Compromise or the shots fired at Fort Sumter would be "only incidental interruptions" to the arc of ordinary progress "in general living conditions" and "in comfort and taste" as Ford understood and celebrated them. Civic life and civility were part of the scenery of the pioneer past Ford engineered, though they were rendered small and subject to the privatizing power of industrial and agricultural forces. Unlike historians and textbook authors who wrote with all the political prejudices of their time, Ford claimed he had a better, less biased understanding of history's mechanics.[23]

It was an audacious assertion from the man that the *Detroit Jewish Chronicle* called "the world's richest anti-Semite" and "breeder of race hatred," who was responsible for publishing the book that became, in Louis Marshall's words, "the 'Anti-Semites' Bible." Having closed the *Dearborn Independent* in December 1927 and (at least publicly) ended his print media campaign against Jews, Ford turned his attention from written works to what he said were more objective forms of historic mediation. The historical relics he accumulated and the built environs he constructed would, he suggested, better convey his devotion to political neutrality and the primitive Americana he sought to accumulate. Of course, Ford's depoliticized perspective was never so simple as its exceptional assertion. The conflicts and conquests of colonial encounter and imperial advance were never such "incidental interruptions" as Ford and his admirers wanted to imagine. Ford's harrowing approach to history intimated a dangerous flattening of America as an empire and of the United States' role in global power dynamics, as well as the effects Ford had in both. One particularly acute example is Ford's effort to extend his reach into the "almost impenetrable jungle" to extract rubber from Brazil and export Ford's strict Americanism in turn.[24]

Strictly American, at Home and Abroad

Ford initiated his South American excursion around the same time that he began developing the Edison Institute. Just ten days before the Jubilee dedication ceremony, Ford announced his plan to tour South America with Charles Lindbergh in his famous *Spirit of St. Louis* airplane, during which the two men would visit Fordlândia, the Ford Motor Company's newly formed rubber plantation in Brazil. The publicized voyage never happened, but Ford's extractive interests in rubber production continued. "Almost like magic, Ford men created the town of Boa Vista—later named Fordlandia," a Ford radio production narrated. Over the next five years, the Company established two separate plantations on some 2.5 million acres of land in Pará, one of Brazil's more remote regions in the Amazon River basin. Ford's plantation economies were intended to help Ford "free himself from dependence on . . . foreign sources of vitally necessary rubber" and to vertically integrate the Company's increasingly global supply chain. The plantations also offered Ford a civilizing occasion. Describing how "the crack of the axe echoed through the jungle, and a spot of civilization appeared," a Company trade booklet for Brazilian hardwoods emphasized the connection between Ford's extraction and civilization efforts. Bringing his specific brand of prosperity to a region otherwise full of "virgin wilderness" would, he hoped, convert Brazilian workers as much as Brazilian land into Ford products.[25]

The industrial and Americanization efforts Ford implemented in Pará so closely mirrored the projects he initiated in Dearborn that Belterra, one of Ford's plantation communities, earned the nickname "Dearborn in the Jungle." From plant to plantation, what Ford would find, though, was that histories of colonialism, the expectations, experiences, and expertise of local inhabitants, and the ecological particularities of place were decidedly not incidental. Nor could they simply be stamped out through the systems of Ford's industry or his pioneering ambitions. Indeed, Ford's Brazilian project was always more successful as an idea and ideal than as a reality. Ford established an elaborate plantation system, complete with a hospital, dining hall, sanitation systems, church, swimming pools, golf course, sidewalks with fire hydrants, and rows upon rows of clapboard cottages, but neither Fordlândia nor Belterra ever actually managed to produce much rubber, lumber, or other resources for manufacture or sale. Leaf blight, insects, and other ecological and environmental challenges ravaged Ford's tightly packed rows of rubber trees.

Ford's vision of bringing small-town Americana to the Amazon River basin never really worked either. No matter how hard he tried to introduce his own favorite vernacular pastimes—including an open-air dance hall for old-time dancing on the town square, outdoor film screenings of in-house documentaries, public readings of his favorite authors, and various competitive sporting events—Ford's effort to cultivate an Americanized utopia in his image strained against the considerable challenges to his vision he found there. Local cultural practices and expertise among Brazilian rubber tappers pushed back on Ford's Americanization campaigns. Never "incidental interruptions," Ford could also not simply harrow the rough realities of changing Brazilian political administrations, federal/state legal negotiations, tax and tariff disputes, and, increasingly, the reality of impending world war. Indeed, by the time that the United States entered World War II, Ford's rubber interests in Brazil had been effectively nationalized. After the Company removed itself from the region and returned its languishing plantations to the Brazilian government in 1945, Fordlândia became a kind of American ghost town. Ford's efforts abroad—whether on plantations or in peacekeeping—did not allow him to easily render "incidental" the histories he insisted did not matter. Still, he kept working at it, finding progress in the mundanity of Americana material.[26]

The "American" Ford wanted was not to be the cultures or industries, laborers or land, he found upon arrival in Brazil. It had to be made in his image. He insisted that the American history he was helping to harrow was not so much about the violence of the harrow's topping than it was an effort to cultivate the ideal terrain of daily life in America. That ideal was not only presented as a corrective to the partialities of textbook treatments but was also meant to valorize the "strictly American." "We have no Egyptian mummies here, nor any relics of the Battle of Waterloo, nor do we have any curios from Pompeii," Ford asserted, "for everything we have is strictly American." Produced as the emblem of that stricture, Ford was also celebrated publicly as "so typical of his time and kind and country that anywhere, under any circumstances, he would be recognized as an American." Part of what Ford managed to do in his museum and village, which he failed at so spectacularly in his South

American endeavors, was to mass-produce the everyday, the run-of-the-mill, the vernacular, the mundane, himself. And to mark those things a specific brand of American—"as American as Dearborn, Chautauqua, the Eighteenth Amendment, the front porch." The domestic preservation projects Ford undertook contributed to the very myth-making of the business and businessman as American brand, and the lessons he taught there pressed his emblematic Americanism into the narratives recounted about his nationalizing product.[27]

"Henry Ford is creating in his own terms his own epic of and for the American people," a sympathetic reporter wrote. The museum and village were designed to offer Ford's historical object lessons in and through items like the harrow. Indeed, the museum would come to house a substantial collection of these agricultural implements, including some fifteen full-size versions. These and other instruments would help instruct visitors in the "national characteristics" of America because they "formed the characteristics of our people," Ford's guidebooks explained. Unfortunately, Ford worried, the "relics and souvenirs" of that past were "often permitted to decay or disappear." This, he contended, was true for even the "great men" purportedly of national interest. Imagine then what was lost of the humbler. Blaming the state for recognizing such deterioration only "too late" and aiming to salvage the nation's "early surroundings," the Edison Institute was conceived to come to the rescue, preserving the country's material heritage and serving as a venue "to learn the lessons of the past." While Fordlândia became a relic of capital hubris, the Edison Institute thrived through the privatized provision of America's "relics and souvenirs." Offering educational opportunities and economic improvement, it became the reliquary of Ford's debunked American history.[28]

Engineering Abundance

In the years leading up to the Edison Institute's public opening and in subsequent decades, Ford built the structures of a vibrant tourist economy around his historic Institute—an airport, hotel, restaurants, public bathrooms, and souvenir shops. As one historian rightly summarized, Ford "embraced consumption as a tool for preserving cultural traditions he feared modernity was erasing." If Ford was selling souvenirs, food, and lodging, so too was American history an artifact on offer. From its earliest iterations, the Edison Institute was conceived as a project for the broader public. "It is to be an institution of learning for young fellows and old fellows, for everybody who wants to know the greatness of our country and what has made it great," Ford explained. Even before the Edison Institute was technically open to the public, people demanded admission. Just after the dedication ceremony (but still some four years prior to its official opening), Ford received roughly 400–500 daily requests to visit the Institute. Much like the tourists in his factories, Ford was not able to keep out the masses, nor was he really interested in doing so. Calculated early in 1933, some months before the official grand opening of the Institute later that year, non-student visitors totaled approximately a thousand people every day. And Ford was eager to accommodate them. Regular groups of twenty-five embarked for a tour of the Institute's massive grounds every fifteen minutes, guided by Edison Institute students. Among the manual training and domestic instruction students received as part of their "learn-by-doing" schooling, pupils apparently also practiced the burgeoning trade of public relations and served as museum docents. After Ford officially opened the Institute to the public, students from the Greenfield Village high school and the nearby Henry Ford Trade School were recruited as additional tour guides.[29]

The American history that Ford was making was to be understood as progressively improving and growing abundantly. The Institute was a place for visitors to understand and engage this past both up close and in its vastness. Ford told his longtime ghostwriter, Samuel Crowther, that his aim was to "assemble a complete series of every article used or made in America from the days of the first settlers down to the present time." Seeking comprehensiveness in his collecting practices, Ford wanted to educate his public on the "process of evolution" through the array of goods he gathered from settler society. "By looking at the things that people used and the way they lived," Ford contended that his public would gain "a better and truer impression . . . in an hour than could be had from a month of reading." Ford's point was not just that material objects were more effective educators, though he insisted that they were. He calculated that they were also more efficient. Every single item from Ford's vast collection was meant to be put on display. Nothing was to be stored away; all surplus reinvested as capital, all put to work supplying the public with proper instructional materials.[30]

Ford's methods of historical representation consequently required equally vast spaces for display and use. The architect of Ford's museum, Robert Derrick, designed one of the largest industrial museums in the world at the time. Early drawings include an immense showroom floor sandwiched between a full basement for storage and a balcony with additional exhibition space, a design decision Derrick said would help break up the sprawl of the structure. When Ford saw the scale model Derrick had crafted of the building, the automaker exclaimed, "What is this up here? . . . I wouldn't have that [balcony]; there would be people up there, I could come in and they wouldn't be working. I wouldn't have it. I have to see everybody." When Ford glimpsed the basement, he reacted similarly: "I couldn't see those men down there when I came in. You have to do the whole thing over again and put it on one floor with no balconies and no basements." The leveling of Ford's history was built into his museum's design and structured around the industrialist's surveilling approach to labor supervision. Derrick redesigned the structure, its footprint growing to encompass some fourteen acres. The result was an approximately 360,000-square-foot museum building with entry façades and open courts, its main hall connected by five arcades. The central exhibit hall stretched out under an immense ceiling, lighted from above with clerestory windows, and supported by 180 columns encased in steel.[31]

Once finished, Ford initially patterned his collection in chronological order, with pieces arranged into long series, stretching from earliest implements to present-day tools and equipment. This organization was meant to enable the ever-discerning visitor to observe minute changes in technical design and configuration from one item to the next. "One of the eternal truths of this world is that there is nothing permanent in it except change," Ford reportedly explained in reference to the Edison Institute, "but the change is that of growth. To our students and to our visitors we are showing some of the changes which have taken place as generations have improved upon the past." The scope and scale of the museum collection were designed to showcase this generational improvement and abundant growth in minute detail and massive scale. They were also arrayed to help the thinking visitor get ready for the next iteration, to help inspire that next invention and prompt progress in increased abundance. "Don't regard these thousands of inventions, thousands of things which man has made, as just so many material objects," Ford instructed. "You can read in every one of them what the man who made them was thinking—what he was aiming at. A piece of machinery or anything that is made is like a book, if you can read it. It is part of the record of man's spirit." Images of the mammoth exhibit floor show sets of implements lined up in successive rows, positioned in bays between large, concrete columns. The effect was something like Ford's giant open-floor factory design. In this instance, the fabrication of the present product took the form of an evolutionary assembly line forded across historical time and museum space. "Whatever is produced today has something in it of everything that has gone before," Ford suggested. "Even a present-day chair embodies all previous chairs, and if we can show the development of the chair in tangible form, we shall teach better than we can by books." Ford's present production embodied its past, each successive iteration a material reincarnation of what had come before. Grasping "the connection between the past and the present," he explained that the "perceiving visitor" would likewise "project it into the future" or "apply it to his own life in some way."[32]

Ford's aims were not lost on his devoted public. Bruce Blivens, writing for the *New Republic*, described how "the visitor tramps such incredible distances that he yearns for roller skates, or better yet, one of Mr. Ford's own convertible cabriolets with the top down." By Blivens's account, more than 400,000 people did come to the enormous Edison Institute in just one year (1936) alone. "In his museum, Mr. Ford undertakes to tell the story of agriculture, manufacture, and transport from the earliest days down to the present time. He has, in original or duplicate, the most ancient plows, spinning wheels, carriages, steam and gasoline and electric engines." Blivens continued, offering a long inventory of items on display—"an acre of clocks," "a square block of radio sets," several complete "historic railway trains," "famous airplanes," and "a vast procession of automobiles from the earliest times down to the twenty-five-millionth Ford." Blivens's cataloging impulse was a familiar refrain among those who visited the museum, an appreciation of its scope verging into a kind of rote inventory keeping. Ford's was the kind of abundance that seemed to compel an accounting. Other visitors found, in the bounty of the museum, that promise of future innovation Ford promoted. Ralph S. Euler, vice president of Union Trust Company of Pittsburgh, wrote excitedly about his visit: "The ideas that it represents are most significant and valuable as a heritage to the American people. It is simply a beautiful living picture. . . . I could not help but think how we have all been taught that 'necessity is the mother of invention' but that Mr. Ford and his organization—like Mr. Edison—have proven that invention may also be the child of abundance."[33]

Ford made a "beautiful living picture" of the world he thought America was. This picture did not remain only in his holdings. Walt Disney, a repeat visitor to Ford's historical institute, seemed to offer evidence of the effectiveness of Ford's creative impact. Disney toured the museum and village on three separate occasions. During one visit, he brought his daughter with him. In a photo of father and daughter, they each sit atop a bicycle in Ford's grand exhibition hall, posing spiritedly. During that same visit, Disney served as a guest speaker in the Edison Institute's theater, where he sketched an image of his own newly famous industrial creation—Mickey Mouse—for the assembled students. Disney's regular visits to Dearborn were not the only impact Ford had on the artist. In 1941, Disney visited Fordlândia as part of a 1941 promotional tour for the US Office of Inter-American Affairs. Three years later, using film from the Ford Motor Company, Disney produced *The Amazon Awakens*, a documentary about Fordlândia and three other South American cities. But Ford's impact on the artist went far beyond his role in amusing Disney's daughter and helping the artist conceive jungle locales. After Disney's second visit to Ford's Dearborn Institute, as he rode the train back to California, he wrote a memo that echoed the structure of Ford's village setting: "The Main Village . . . is built around a village green or informal park . . . Around the park will be built the town." In addition to Fordlândia, Ford's Michigan-based village helped orient the "Imagineer's" vision toward an Americana history—one Disney later reproduced as his own Main Street U.S.A., the old-timey townscape located inside Disneyland. The small-town aesthetics Ford brought to life in his village of living history quickly came to dominate twentieth-century media and its American mythos for the century to come.[34]

Pioneering the Pastoral

Ford's "early American village" is the central iconography of Ford's Americana. Greenfield Village was to be the place where Ford mobilized the implements of that history into use. It was conceived as "an animated textbook . . . a living, working, institution." As a reliquary of "living" history, the Edison Institute was a kind of historical reincarnation. "I don't like 'dead' museums," Ford told the New Thought author, Ralph Waldo Trine. "Yes, everything will be like life. I don't like stationary exhibits. The old trades and stores and inns will be in operation in our village." Ford worried that an understanding of his forebears could not be fully obtained in books or pictures but, he thought, it "might be done by assembling an early American village here at Dearborn and showing the early crafts as they were actually used day by day." Here again, Ford's historical approach was meant, he said, to improve both pedagogical effectiveness and learning efficiency for even the most unimaginative. "In Mr. Ford's scheme of things," an authorized report on the village explained, "there will be no need for anyone to do any digging to discover the material history of America." Ford would make it all evident. Conceived as a historical scenario come alive, Greenfield Village would reveal "the beginnings of industrial development which has brought us to the present day" and "preserve this for the coming generation by gathering in one typical village these genuine structures of older days, furnished with the actual equipment of the times."[35]

This "typical village" was designed on an imagined New England plan of cultivated landscape and patterned settlement, understood as a village centered on a common green and headed by a community church. Historians have shown such a bucolic vision to be an invention of nineteenth-century imaginations, but it was a vision Ford replicated with all the commitment of an industrialist dedicated to mass-producing the Anglo- in the American. "The buildings will be grouped in a loose way about a green, and the green is primarily an old English institution, transplanted to New England," an early account of Ford's planned village reported. That Ford's vision of his American village of the past was an imagined one was not entirely lost on the industrialist either. He simply understood its romanticized idyll to be a composite creation of some earlier reality, one merely more complete than would have been found in any single instance. Ford's replication was meant to level history in accordance with his own harrowing ambitions. "It will be a cross section of a hundred villages rather than a representation of one village," Ford's ghostwriter explained. Ed Cutler, the man Ford charged with planning the village, similarly explained his employer's approach. Ford's village was, Cutler noted, a utopian project, a no-place of intuition more than an actual representation. "It was your impression," Cutler explained, "it was purely imaginative." If the museum was designed to trace an exacting evolution of technological change, the village was designed to collapse divisions at the cross- section of Ford's imagination. "While antiquarians may make period divisions," one account insisted, "real life does not. Neither will the village be of any one section of the country, for that again would too greatly restrict its scope." The time and place of Ford's textbook of living history was produced in Greenfield Village as simultaneously eternal and particular, historic and utopian, impressionistic and exacting, ancient and modern, Anglo and American.[36]

In addition to Menlo Park, the most commented upon buildings in Ford's village were the Logan County Courthouse and the Martha-Mary Chapel. Structures that surrounded the village green varied over the years, but the purpose was to circle the town center with "public buildings"—a school, courthouse, town hall, post office, general store, hostelry, and chapel. Ford especially revered the Logan County Courthouse for its connection to Abraham Lincoln. When he was casting about for historic structures in advance of the Jubilee celebration, he was reportedly looking specifically for something related to Lincoln, and he found it in Postville, Illinois, the former Logan County seat. The old courthouse had, since 1840, been refurbished many times—as post office, general store, school, jail, and private home. Ford bought the building to restore it to its earlier version. Rightly fearing local uproar, he urged Cutler to get the courthouse to Dearborn as quickly as possible. "That job was one of those hurry up things," Cutler remembered, since there was a local "gang of people getting an injunction against us to stop it." Ford did not pause for their "political" machinations. "By the time they had their legal end of it taken care of," Cutler and his laborers "had the walls and whole thing flattened to the ground and were carting it off."[37]

Reconstructed around Ford's village green, the industrialist soon used the courthouse to house some of his most treasured relics, including the red plush rocker that President Lincoln was reportedly sitting in when he was assassinated. Though further verification of the artifact is impossible given limited acquisition records, Ford's Manager of Guides and Public Relations, William Simonds, promoted the relic regularly and drew special attention to how "the faded rose and gold upholstery at its back is stained yet with his blood." Furniture and other items taken from Lincoln's law office and childhood home were also added to the courthouse. These items were often highlighted on tours and in guidebooks. What was far less often, if ever, mentioned was the Civil War. Instead, as historian Jessie Swigger has traced, guides' scripts "emphasized Lincoln's humble beginnings, his intelligence and congeniality, his work in local politics, and his untimely death." Neither did Simonds mention the war in his review of the Village and its structures, focusing instead on a set of rails said to have been split by the President early in his life. Simonds does briefly note a set of structures positioned near the courthouse: two "slave huts" that Ford had brought to Greenfield Village from the Hermitage Plantation near Savannah, Georgia.[38]

Ford purchased the Georgia plantation in 1934. He had first visited the area with friend and naturalist, John Burroughs, and began acquiring property in the region with the hopes of developing it as a site of agricultural experimentation, including a source of domestic rubber production. The Fords enjoyed the area enough that they decided to build a new vacation home there, refurbishing building materials from the original plantation house and evicting two Black families who had been living in the brick quarters up to that time. Formerly owned by Henry McAlpin, the plantation once was the site of rice cultivation along with related industries (including the making of barrels, cast iron products, cut lumber, and especially extensive brickwork). The prosperous plantation was worked by two hundred enslaved people. Those McAlphin enslaved lived in roughly fifty-two different quarters, similar to the two that Ford brought north to Michigan. Through at least the late 1930s, though, Greenfield Village tour guides regularly skipped these structures. When they did include them in a tour, their scripts told visitors that the "slave huts" were important because they appeared in D. W. Griffith's 1915 film, *The Birth of a Nation.* Early in the following decade, research showed that they were not actually portrayed in the movie, and the scripts were revised to emphasize their connection with the Logan County Courthouse. Painted white in photographs and marketing material for the village, an early Edison Institute guidebook describes the slave quarters as standing "in the shadow of the Courthouse . . . typical in size and furnishings of the slave homes of the old South, and are made of brickbats from the brickyard on the plantation." In joining the slave quarters with the courthouse, both materially and discursively, Ford endeavored to reconstruct and affirm a successfully Reconstructed nation. Lincoln's legal representation ostensibly eclipsed the shaded reality of America's history of slavery, civil war, and ongoing racism. The connection Ford drew between slave quarters and courthouse further demonstrated his project to harrow history's rough terrain, here presenting instead a redeemed nation in gently bucolic forms. The built environment of Ford's village mirrors the portrait rendered in the Ford Motor Company's 1921 film, *Civil War Period*, which was part of the Ford Educational Library series. The film includes a telling title card about the war's close: "The struggle ended; men beat their shields into plowshares and their swords into pruning hooks. The slave was made free; the Union was preserved." After footage about Lincoln's martyrdom, the film reaffirms Ford's vision of historical preservation as a redemptive arc of progress and national unity. "Though the scars may last, the wounds are healed. A nation torn within itself is now made whole again." In Ford's scrupulously harrowed history, a healthy nation was made whole, its civil strife and past practices of enslavement rendered "incidental."[39]

Yet another central feature connecting Ford's Greenfield Village to the Anglo-American heritage the auto-industrialist so heralded was the Martha-Mary Chapel. The structure was positioned at the Village's highest point and was used to orient the village green, an imagined pastoralism here manufactured for Ford's "pioneer past." Deemed by Ford "the most important structure in the village," the red brick chapel was designed by Cutler and based on the plans of a Unitarian church in Bradford, Massachusetts, a nineteenth-century Georgian-style structure that best represented the auto-industrialist's "idea of a New England church." The interior of the building held a pipe organ and "tall-backed, white-painted pews with their mahogany top-rails." The new ecclesiastical structure was named for the mothers of Clara and Henry Ford, respectively, and guidebooks described how "the bricks in the building and the doors are from the girlhood home of Mrs. Ford." Dominating

the village green, the chapel was "non-sectarian in character," and operated by the student guides of the Edison Institute. On Sundays, it held
a brief service with a choir composed of young men from the Institute's
staff and included readings either "from one of the humbler American
poets or one of the world's masterpieces." The liturgy of Ford's chapel
placed the humble and the masterful in kind, and though it was purportedly started "to provide a period of reflection and worship for the
Village on Sunday mornings," it quickly attracted a great many visitors,
"both from those in the Village for the day and from residents of nearby
Dearborn." In fact, by 1940, the Martha-Mary chapel services were being
broadcast nationally on the radio each Sunday, and the chapel quickly
became an increasingly sought-after venue for weddings. Weekday and
Saturday visitors to the Village also toured the chapel, where a student-
organist took personal hymn requests. "Often silent tears creep down
the cheeks of listeners at memories that come flooding back as they hear
once more the soft melodious strains of a dearly loved tune," Simonds
narrated. In sentimental tones and shaded histories, Ford assembled an
Anglo-American past that wedded a pastoral, nonsectarian protestantism with pioneer relics and small-town publics. "This is the only reason
Greenfield Village exists," Ford concluded, "to give a sense of unity with
our people through the generations, and to convey the inspiration of
American genius to our young men. As a nation we have not depended
so much on rare or occasional genius as on the general resourcefulness
of our people." The magical economy of Ford's material abundance was
displayed in and as a typical New England village forded in the soil of
the industrialist's Midwestern frontier and cultivated by "the average
man . . . who by his labor, and loyalty, helped make civilization." Ford's
history harrowed the past as pioneering accomplishment and civilizing
possession. His conveyance of Anglo-American heritage became what
subsequent decades of the good life looked like, smoothed of difference
and heralding a history that never was.[40]

* * *

Ford understood his museum and village to be central to the Edison
Institute's educational endeavors, civilizational projects, and institutionalized ministry. The industrialist's accumulation of artifacts was put on
display to offer a more material and living history for a nation on the

move in the world. His was a museum of actual objects and a prefabri-
cated village that together were meant to serve as didactic tools for the
study and practice of progress by modern man in the speedy era of the
automobile. Amid that pace of progress, one Ford still hoped to quicken
through the inspiration of his pioneering past, Americans were to be
shown "by actual example" how those who came before them shaped
the standards of living presently enjoyed. But looking back at those who
came before was not just a way to appreciate what they had. They would
also "become aware that something solid and vitally valuable in the past
has escaped us—and that we must strive back toward it at all costs."
Being able to "read a coherent story of mankind," Ford said, would
allow Americans to understand that loss and to change it, to "look *forward* and predict what lies ahead." Ford's collections would allow his
public to more effectively and efficiently glimpse the spiraling temporality Ford manufactured in the machinery of past and present. In the
process, American history and the nation's future were forded through
"the pioneer towns and villages of our departed ancestors." Positioning
American history at the intersections of elite and popular, the valuable
and the lost, Ford debunked and harrowed history in mythic terms and
magical economies. In the material array of that primitive America, he
amassed an enlightened industry of modernity.[41]

The auto-industrialist likewise summoned a devoted public of his
own. Over the latter half of his life, as word spread about Ford's collections and his interest in the everyday lives and labors of Americans,
people around the country began to send him things they had made.
They gave him ceramics, walking sticks, vases, woodcuts, sculptures,
dioramas, hand-embroidered pillows, and wall hangings, among many
others. Many of the items depict Ford's likeness in logo, in countenance,
and in cars. Among those sent to the industrialist were two hooked rugs,
each of which featured the face of that now familiar pair of engineer-
inventor-industrialists, Ford and Edison, this time rendered in burlap,
rayon, and silk by a woman named Fay Badden from Bonners Ferry,
Idaho. Badden sent her handmade rugs to Ford in 1935. They remain in
Ford's collection as part of his assembled relics today.[42]

These and other items in the Edison Institute collections took on a
renewed reverence in the wake of Henry Ford's death in 1947. As the
waters of the Rouge River rose and the incandescent bulbs of his Vil-

lage flickered out, Ford passed. But not quite away. Two days after his death, Ford's bodily remains were laid in repose at Greenfield Village. Crowds gathered to see this new relic at Ford's historic institution, before Ford was buried at the nearby Addison Ford Cemetery. In honor of its founder, the Edison Institute of Technology was soon renamed. No longer the Edison Institute, the organization became known as the Henry Ford Museum and Greenfield Village. Years later, after yet another rebranding, it became simply: *The Henry Ford*, an institutionalized reincarnation of the businessman and his American brand.

On the sprawling campus of The Henry Ford, I sat for several weeks in the chilly reading room of the Benson Ford Research Center, calling boxes of Ford's materials from the personal collections and corporate archives now housed inside it. The efficiency of those calls seemed a far cry from the chaotic anteroom that was adjacent to Ford's office at Highland Park which initially housed his collections. Ford's historic assembly—which includes the Research Center, the expansive museum and village that he once imagined as "my Smithsonian Institute," and the multi-venue tourist hub currently promoted in The Henry Ford's marketing campaigns—has been streamlined through archival bureaucratic order. The careful inventories, detailed finding aids, and quickly conveyed boxes that were carefully brought to the table assigned to me each day harkened the brand of efficiency that made Ford famous. Outside the windows of the reading room, crowds of visitors gathered to take in the "relics and souvenirs" that Ford had so carefully tended, along with the voluminous acquisitions The Henry Ford continues to accumulate. No longer directed by the industrialist to display every object in their hold, the vast, factory-like spaces of the museum hall array primary collections alongside its ever-updating, interactive exhibits. An enormous IMAX theater anchors one end of the museum building, and ticketing for The Henry Ford now includes an option to visit Ford's nearby Rouge plant. Most prominently, as its promotional machine describes, are the museum's many hands-on displays, a legacy of Ford's long-lasting, "learn-by-doing" philosophy. When I wandered the galleries at the end of the day, a group of elementary school kids were working along a miniature assembly line, constructing a tiny version of Ford's famous Model T. "If it had not been play," I remembered Ford-executive Charles Sorensen writing, "it would have killed them. They were as men possessed."[43]

The high daily ticket prices convinced me to purchase a membership for my extended research stay. To stretch my legs and escape the chilled conditioning and studied quiet of archival research, I would occasionally wander through the gates of Greenfield Village, joining the masses gathering inside Ford's "beautiful living picture" of Americana industry. The summer sun was warm on the Village's dusty walkways, as we meandered the Ford farm or stopped to watch on-staff artisans demonstrate how to blow glass. Paved avenues called attention to the relatively sparse foliage on main street and its surrounds. The longest lines tended to be for the ice cream shop and the queue to ride in one of the several original Model Ts transporting people on an automotive tour of the Village. Despite Ford's teetotaling, a stagecoach tavern on the Village grounds served cold beers and crisp cocktails to weary tourists. Costumed workers with handlebar mustaches or elaborately braided hair kept tidy under bonnets rode penny-farthings or paraded the Village Green on foot to answer questions, perform music, or tell stories of early American life. Though all the accredited schools from yesteryear are now closed, Ford's public history project remains centered on the aesthetics of an imaginatively palatable past. As I dug into his historical documents and wandered his preservation projects, I wondered at the difference between historical critique and its consumption.

I most clearly found Ford's futurist vision of American do-it-yourself innovation one July week when the suburban Dearborn venue was hosting the fourth annual Makers Faire Detroit. In the sprawling surface parking lots that serviced The Henry Ford, there was a carnival of robotics equipment, 3D printers, cyberpunked musical instruments and hacked synthesizers, a build-your-own-drone center and construct-a-truck modeling exhibit, a life-size Mousetrap game, go-cart track, and elaborate Lego creations. A great many varieties of wheeled vehicles maneuvered around the vast outdoor event space, and inside rows upon rows of computers were set up for the tinkerers, hackers, and inventors that The Henry Ford understood to be its legacy demographic. In this grand event, meant to celebrate and inspire innovations in science, technology, engineering, and mathematics (STEM) fields, I caught an echo of Ford's jubilant dedication. In corporate sponsorship and STEM celebration, I puzzled through Ford's bequest. He urgently sought a more enlightened world, and insisted his public innovate new ways to serve his interests. Is there a way to tinker with, hack, or innovate that inheritance?[44]

Studying Ford's run-of-the-mill relics, situated as they are amid the scenes of the living and the not-quite-past, The Henry Ford and its collections increasingly pressed me toward questions about incorporative power. Ford's industrial system and its magical methods sought to incorporate all into the American standards he supplied. Dedicated at the Jubilee but extending far beyond, I came to understand that the industrialist's concern for historical preservation was indissolubly bound to an image of harrowing redemption and enlightened advance—a view of a pioneer past illuminated and reconstructed, flattened and objectified, for present consumption and future reform.

In the ritualized performance of the Jubilee and in his proliferating run-of-the-mill relics, Ford put on elaborate display his delight in and ambition for the radiance of enlightened settlers of both great and humble origins. His historic projects worked to institutionalize an enlightened interpellation of Ford's consuming publics, of his tourists and students. His historic empire endeavored to enlighten a world through a radiance that Max Horkheimer and Theodore Adorno, writing in the twilight years of Ford's life, referred to as "triumphant calamity." Enlightenment—understood broadly as the advancement of thought and extension of freedom—is a system entangled with masterful domination. "Enlightenment is totalitarian," they write. "Any intellectual resistance it encounters merely increases its strength. The reason is that enlightenment also recognizes itself in the old myths."[45]

The old myths are something that the study of religion knows something about. Both Frazer and Taussig focus on effigies—materials of mythic proportion. Their focus offers an opportunity for methodological reflection of and for my own purposes, too, as I have endeavored to represent Ford in description, citation, and argument. Recall that this book began with its own inaugurating scene of the death of Henry Ford. The effigy is a rendering of critique. Contra Frazer, who suggests an effigy is mostly "analogy . . . taken too literally," with Taussig I recognize that at least sometimes "the magically effective copy is not, so to speak, much of a copy." The effigy, the effectively mimetic image, the representation, the copy that is not a copy, the formed that is transformed, is typically "only a crude outline of the human body, and . . . does not display any likeness to the man." It is (Taussig here is now miming two additional scholars of religion and magic, Marcel Mauss and Henri Humbert) "a very schematic representation, a poorly executed ideogram." It need not, Taussig provokes, be "a faithful copy." Or rather, "what makes up for this lack of similitude, what makes it a 'faithful' copy, indeed a magically powerful copy," is "the material connection."[46]

It is worth considering how, in this book, Ford might likewise be taken as an imperfect ideogram, a crude outline, or critical effigy of that otherwise human form, legal entity, or corporate person. The citational matter of Ford's making—his words, his works—are attached, are footnoted, to more "faithfully" render that copy that is not a copy. The effectiveness is still to be determined, but with Taussig, my point is to notice that this book—*and* I am suggesting history more broadly—might be at least partly understood as an example, experiment, and exercise in what we might elsewhere refer to as a kind of magical realism. Not to hedge or hide. Nor to press endlessly toward relativist or nihilist arguments. But to prompt reconsideration of "our very notion of what it means to be an image of some thing, most especially if we wish not only to express but to manipulate reality by means of its image."[47]

Ford said the writing of history did not matter. I disagree. He said his objects were the real thing. This book is an inquiry into and an endeavor to describe Ford as an historical reality as it was historically shaped by Ford's own historical practices. I do so to begin the work of transforming that reality through critique. It may well take a kind of power often deemed "magic" to effect that kind of change. Mine is one attempt to grapple with some of the materials that have affected that kind of power. But there is danger here. History, its concept and practice, is never innocent. Among the dangers that history hails, there is the potential to too-easily mirror Ford's mimesis, to fall into what Taussig calls "the colonial mirror of production." Rather than debunking, I have sought to show what I saw and how I see. It is with these things in mind that we turn, in the closing chapter, to other assemblages of Ford. Other ways to see, render, and critique, the power organized in his figure and font.[48]

Conclusion

In the spring of 1933, Diego Rivera completed a twenty-seven-panel series of frescoes in the garden courtyard of the Detroit Institute of Arts, entitled *Detroit Industry*. Rivera's depiction of twentieth-century American industry and culture centers on scenes of automotive manufacturing, showcasing what Henry Ford's son, Edsel, described as Rivera's "idea of the spirit of Detroit." The central panels focus on scenes of industrial production modeled on Rivera's observations at Ford's River Rouge plant. Many artists, historians, and scholars of visual culture have offered important readings of this portrait of industrial design. I focus on one small detail, located on a narrow panel on the right side of the courtyard's western wall where Rivera rendered what he considered the prototypical Engineer.[1]

Rivera's Engineer is positioned at the base of the panel in what appears to be the factory's powerhouse, the place where steam was transformed into electrical energy by giant turbines. These machines are shown in Rivera's mural as resembling something like an enormous ear—an organ of sound perception and vibrant discernment as well as an important machine of modern conversion. At a desk nearby, ruler in hand, the Engineer appears to be surveying a portion of a blueprint spread before him—his stopwatch close by to ensure efficient management and the careful tracking of labor time. Rivera's representation of this stern, archetypal figure is reportedly a combined portrait of two imposing and superimposed characters of American industry: Henry Ford and Thomas Edison. While it is less clear in art historical terms what, if any, particular images of these two men Rivera used to render the Engineer's portrait, what has been well documented by other historians and curators is that this detail was, indeed, designed to be a composite image of the Motor King and the Wizard of Menlo Park, the efficient industrialist and phonographic inventor. Though Ford understood the Engineer as a seer of industrial achievement, this small detail in Rivera's mural offers no simple celebration of the Engineer as prophetic persona. Positioned across the doorway from a dove and a prototypical worker in the powerhouse and below a portrait of a hawk and a warplane, Rivera's detail suggests the abiding ambivalence of this oracular figure of industrial engineering. Far from alone in his conception of the Engineer as both a contested and composite creation, other commentators and critics of Ford have likewise wrestled with the never simple force of the auto-industrialist's effect in twentieth-century American manufacturing and beyond. The conjunction of Ford and Edison was for Rivera a way of portraying the capital power of American industrial force and its role in the always ambivalent enlightenment of the world.[2]

Twentieth-century capitalism in America is a massive and massively powerful subject. Both tragically and absurdly so. Historically, that subject has gone by the name of Ford. An individual, an institution, an empire. A man and a brand. Automotive and industrial technology, an American emblem, and a system of political economy. How to approach a subject of such immensity and effect? Must any rendering of Ford—so massively manufactured and reproduced—match the scale of Ford's ambition? If Ford and his story are "about as well known as the Nativity," as one of his many biographers recently wrote, why does he not appear in histories of religion in modern America? And why is Ford's story so often studied and redescribed elsewhere? The research for this book was, in part, an attempt to think through this interrogative disjunction of Ford—as nowhere and everywhere at once.

The approach I took to bring that research to the page was to trace associations in the enormity of Ford's making. But I can imagine other ways into the matter. Historians of religion might, for example, consider changing patterns of church membership and missionary activities in the wake of increased automobile usage. For, as sales of automobiles grew, particularly among those living in the US country-side, patterns of religious worship were also profoundly altered. Some people even combined the two in surprisingly literal ways, as did one Reverend Branford Clarke of Brooklyn, New York, who converted his Model T into a traveling chapel, equipped with stained glass windows, a small organ, and a steeple, all built upon the famous Ford chassis. Alternatively, one might analyze autoworker prayer groups, union activities, or relations between auto companies and churches to better glimpse the range of institutions central to the formation of religion in the automobile age. For instance, Catholic priests, Juan P. Alanis and Juan B. Mijares, worked with Ford Motor Company's Latin American Club and the Mexican Auxiliary of the Society of St. Vincent de Paul to help raise funds for the 1923 establishment of Our Lady of Guadelupe Church, which was the first Mexican Catholic church in the Midwest. Another way into related histories would be to examine the road trip and the "spiritual powers" of highways and other transporting infrastructure as sites of ritual practice or lived religion. One could even examine the growing number of sacrifices to the so-called Modern Moloch, as motorcar fatalities rose on congested urban streets and garnered much attention in newspapers of the day. Or, delve into the religio-racial formations of automotive culture and services among black motorists who relied upon *The Green Book* travelers' guide to help navigate with greater safety and dignity the United States' highly segregated tourist structures and related dangers in Jim Crow America. In what seems shiny and smooth, such a history would instead look for the sharp edges and rough surfaces, clawing out the gristle and sinew of lived reality. While mine did not become that kind of social history, perhaps others can follow these threads into new directions or find their way into related materials for own purposes.[3]

If I have ultimately been less concerned with piercing Ford's own feet of clay or focused less on cutting the automotive giant down to size, it is because the research I did ultimately drew my attention more toward the organizational, institutional, mediated, and relational means that the auto-industrialist and others used to set Ford apart and to prop him up, overcoming resistances to that bracing, and importantly, entice others to join in on or help advance his never-innocent projects. The worry, of course, is that in the study one risks a joining. It seems right to me to question that possibility, even as I continue to hope that the risks of immanent critique are at least in part met by my critique of how Ford has been worked on and worked up into a mythic power of American might and historic occupation.

While many have described Ford's religious engagement in terms of the odd or outlandish, it is clear that Ford's religious ideas were never mere eccentricities. Quite the opposite. His ideas about religion were inextricably interwoven with his larger set of organizational ambitions and imperial projects. Ford's professed connection between industrial and ecclesiastical forms, his "nebulous theories" and rites of production, media claims and historic campaigns, were entangled with and contributed to broader currents circulating in the late nineteenth and early twentieth centuries. This included new temporal measurements and historic preservation, prying social surveys and dangerously common scientific racism, metaphysical experiments and new filmic media, show trials and global conflict. Tracing these kinds of associations in connection with documents from Ford's collections, alongside categories of analysis central to the study of religion in the West, it is possible to glimpse new religious forms engineered by and incorporated at Ford, a brand he set up to be both historic arbiter and archive of surplus value. The fording of institutional structures, manufacturing systems, and industrial labor helped to constitute a particular kind of capital power—one flattened into the historically authorizing cursive script of his name and managed as part of a secularism he supplied in antisemitic terms.

As much as I summarize here my own assemblage, I began this concluding chapter with Rivera's relatively diminutive portrait to notice how others have also sought to assemble Ford and his capital brand. Just one year before Rivera's frescoes were unveiled, Aldous Huxley depicted the auto-industrialist as a figure of consecration and curse, of religious veneration and erotic profanity, of technological reverence and mechanized blasphemy in his book, *Brave New World*. With the replacement of a single letter, Huxley transformed "Lord" to "Ford" in satirical, pedantic tone. Characters regularly herald the automaker, "Our Ford," while making the sign of a T. The honorific of the highest-ranking official in Huxley's novel is "His fordship," and hymns are sung in concert, extolling Ford and his "shining Flivver." Processing in drug-infused soma circuits, at Ford's Day celebrations, in communal songs at Fordson community centers, and in ritual practice at solidarity groups, characters chant his name in quivering, liturgical refrain:

> Orgy-porgy, Ford and fun,
> Kiss the girls and make them One.
> Boys at one with girls at peace;
> Orgy-porgy gives release.

As in sensual rapture, so too do Huxley's characters expound the automaker's name in times of exasperation, casual frustration, or outright despair: "Oh Ford, Ford, Ford!" "Ford, I should like to kill him!" and "for Ford's sake" they shout, murmur, or whimper. Likewise, in Huxley's telling, 1908—the year Ford introduced the Model T to a US market—becomes year zero, the "Year of Our Ford," and the point of departure for all time yet to come, with "A.F." thereby designating the eclipse of the *anno domini* calendar system. Ford is also offered as the measure of cultural advancement in Huxley's new world order, particularly when his characters first embark from their urban center to the pueblos of a far-off frontier, a locale we learned that Ford pictured itself in its own film production, *Pueblo Indians*. Upon encountering the "Indians and half-breeds" and other "absolute savages" on the mesa reservation, Huxley's characters moralize about how "cleanliness is next to fordliness," even as they philosophize about how "these people have never heard of Our Ford . . . they aren't civilized," echoing themes we now know Ford too regularly pronounced upon. Indeed, Ford is Huxley's device through which all time, space, and language is reordered and reconfigured. In *Brave New World*, Ford is positioned as the center around which seemingly contradictory but actually complementary—even constitutive—practices of modernity are enacted, practices Bruno Latour conceived in terms of the doubly asymmetrical processes of mediation and purification, and which we know Ford too manufactured thusly in his factories and communities, in workers' bodies and in historical renderings. Huxley—who is primarily known in the study of religion for his later writings on perennial philosophy—reinscribed in *Brave New World* a modern execution. He simultaneously secularized the Christian Lord in the figure of Ford and sacralized Ford as the Brave New Lord. Ford is rendered, at once, the god of industry and efficiency *and* the formative spirit of fascist totalitarianism, master maker and tyrannical villain, religious icon and secular conceit.[4]

Huxley was not alone in his conception of Ford as a kind of apocalyptic character, archetypically capable of originary creativity and immanent destruction. Vincent Curcio's biography of Henry Ford began by placing him in the eminent company of Johann Guttenberg and Martin Luther, thereby deeming him one of the "few individuals, a very few, whose work and influence are so profound that over time they fundamentally change the ways in which people live." Yet this sense of hagiographic praise for Ford as a force of inventiveness and inspiration quickly gave way, in Curcio's diagnosis, to Ford's darker legacy. "Ask anyone today about Henry Ford," Curcio observed, and "the first, and often the only thing that pops out of their mouths is, 'Oh, he was a terrible Antisemite.' . . . Well, he *was* a terrible Antisemite . . . perhaps more influential than any other Antisemite outside of Nazi Germany, and he needs to take full blame for the repercussions of this fact. Yet he was still, despite this, a man of monumental accomplishment." This conception of Ford as an ambivalent yet monumental, perhaps even millennial, force has guided much interpretation of the automaker. At the close of the twentieth century, *Fortune* magazine named Ford the "Businessman of the Century," laying on thick its own dose of revolutionary rhetoric about the man. Ford's story, the authors said, "is stained already. In his latter years he surrounded himself with goons, spouted ugly anti-Semitic bile, and left his company in terrible shape." But, they countered:

> He was the greatest managerial thinker. No fewer than three of the biggest management brainstorms of the century happened in Ford's head: the idea of the moving assembly line, the idea of paying workers not as little as possible but as much as was fair, and the idea of vertical integration that made Ford's River Rouge plant the chief wonder of the industrial world. The oil industry, the highway-construction industry, nearly universal homeownership—all these things, from Big Oil to Big Macs, can trace their parentage to the Model T Ford. The American Dream itself is inextricably linked to the automobile. The Businessman of the Century was the builder of an industry that transformed the very land we live on, the first to create a mass market as well as the means to satisfy it, as great an entrepreneur as we've ever seen. He was a provincial and a curmudgeon; a man with all the prejudices of his time, who had as well the kind of genius that endures. He is Henry Ford.

If, in *Fortune*'s adjudication, the balance of Ford's inheritance is stained by his latter-day associations and provincial prejudices, they ultimately awarded him a legacy as *the* definitive innovator of and enduring entrepreneurial genius behind an American dream of automotive and bureaucratic power. As we have seen, however, these divergent constructions of Ford are contingent: There is no mass production outside of mass prejudice. There is no organization without demolition, no purchase without dispossession.[5]

One year before *Fortune* awarded its era-defining businessman's award, Broadway memorialized Ford on the stage. In 1998, the musical theater adaptation of E. L. Doctorow's 1974 historical novel, *Ragtime*, was performed to widespread acclaim. Doctorow's narrative, then set to award-winning music, plots the triangulated relations between three, ostensibly archetypal modern American families—a white family from New Rochelle, New York, a Jewish family immigrating to America from Latvia, and a Black family in Harlem. The story unfolds as the three groups simultaneously encounter one another and a host of historical figures, including Booker T. Washington, Emma Goldman, Sigmund Freud, Harry Houdini, J. P. Morgan, and Henry Ford.

Described as one of the men who can't help making America great, standing at "the very apex of the American pyramid . . . like Pharaoh's reincarnate," the automotive industrialist gets his own score in the Broadway musical adaptation. There presented as a kind of ambivalent seer: "See my people, well here's my theory, of what this country is movin' toward. Every worker a cog in motion. Well, that's the notion of Henry Ford," the character intones amid twisting ratchets. Division and deskilling of labor, standardization of production, endless speed-up of time, and the increased singularity of movement are presented in the song as a "genuflection" and "praise [to] the Maker—of the Model T." Picking up the pace, the chorus chants: "Sure amazin' how far some fellas can see. . . . Mass production will sweep the nation, a simple notion. The world's reward!" The auto-industrialist himself adds lyrically, "Even people who ain't too clever can learn to tighten a nut forever, attach one panel, or pull one lever. . . . Grab your goggles." "And," the cast join in, "climb aboard!" In the play, they do. "I'm ready, Lord," cheers the play's protagonist, before driving off in his new car.[6]

In Doctorow's ragged time history, written as the war in Vietnam raged, that earlier era's music seemed to him to provide a somehow less totalizing structure than did Theodore Adorno's critique of that other infamous "jazz" era, the latter which we know Ford, too, found so distasteful. Amid ragtime's improvisational promise, though, it is no mere coincidence that the automobile is the preferred mode of transportation for the harrowing hopes of Doctorow's bourgeois family relations, ethnic assimilation, racialized violence, and mass production, an artifact gifted to the world as if a reward. Doctorow's narrative—and the musical it was adapted into—can be read as a declension story of American diversity, a turn toward the assimilating power of the culture and car industries. In Doctorow's telling, it was not just ragtime that had captivated the nation. So too had the automobile. And it was the car, not the music, that prevailed.

The car, an apparatus engineered for and as power, carried with it social structures and productive practices, ideas and ideals, hailing subjects historically and subjecting them to a history forded in the automotive industry. The musical *Ragtime* vibrates with twentieth-century American desires for the automobile's power to drive "a better day and a better time"; justice and truth are promised by and premised on the ability to purchase "a car full of hope" in order to ride "the wheels of a dream." Rendered in grand registers, the automobile marked the progressive urge and slick efficiency of an optimistic future tensely played against a more divergent, ragged time ahead. If in a rag, the left hand performs a systemic rhythm while the right juxtaposes it with syncopation, this book has sought to tune our ears toward the dominant, if never entirely determining, patterns of the port side. Is there a way to refuse Ford's systemic assembly? Is it possible to ford Ford? Would we even want to if we could, if we should? Or, would we, too, rather climb aboard?[7]

In Samuel Marquis's early interpretation of Ford, the minister laments Ford as improperly assembled. "He has in him the makings of a great man, the parts lying about in more or less disorder," Marquis writes in a tone at once elegiac and anticipatory. "If only he would do in himself that which he has done in his factory!" What would it mean for Ford to be "properly assembled"? In the pages of this book, I have sought to compile descriptions of Ford amid the material and magical aporias of religious study and historical interpretation. To do so, I have endeavored to bring forward as much of Ford's language, as much of the forms and fabrications, mechanics and myths and metaphysics, of and by Ford, as my chapters (and myself) could bear. Having conveyed Ford, it is worth asking anew: What died with Henry Ford in that inaugurating scene of passing that opened this book? Did Ford's temporal regime pass with him? Is Ford's Machine Age history? Is it possible to reassemble religion and history, the secular and labor, in less harrowing, post-forded terms? To answer these questions, scholars of religion in modern America must confront and contend with Ford's already much worked upon making.[8]

ACKNOWLEDGMENTS

I have had an abundance of care and support in the research and writing of this book, and I have studied Ford long enough to know that any such surplus is wrought through significant material and relational assemblage. Any acknowledgment of that reality falls considerably short of the labors of so many, particularly those who intrepidly traverse the intense intersections of the intellectual and personal that so often occupy my work, and me. Whether in caregiving or copyediting, with finding aids and financial aid, in conference hallways and classrooms and in all those track changes, I am enduringly grateful to those who have helped make this book possible. If there are splinters in the hegemonic empire of Ford's capitalizing All, I glimpse them best in our conversations—in thinking with, listening to, and learning from you, each and all.

My research and writing benefited enormously from the generous support of the rich intellectual homes that welcomed me. I am particularly grateful for the lively backing and pedagogical mentorship of Sid Brown, Tam Parker, and Eric Thurman, experienced colleagues who also somehow managed to make me feel immediately welcomed as a comrade. You show me daily, with verve and dignity and good humor, new and better ways (and reasons) to move from the slow and urgent study we do in the quiet of our offices to the socially charged and critically engaged spaces of the classroom and committee meeting and town street, and back again. Discussions with colleagues in neighboring departments and offices have further enriched my thinking. Thanks especially to Stephanie Batkie, Lisa Berner, Kate Cammack, Lucia Dale, Mark Hopwood, Mandi Johnson, Ross Macdonald, Shelley MacLaren, Cassie Meyer, Linnea Minich, Emily Puckette, Woody Register, Betsy Sandlin, Sid Simpson, Clint Smith, Leslie Todd, Lily Thompson, Lauryl Tucker, Keri Watson, Kelly Whitmer, Jessica Wohl, and the late Matt Reynolds. The purpose of our academic work and shared pedagogical practice comes into sharper focus through conversations with you.

Kathryn Lofton, Tisa Wenger, Sally Promey, and Skip Stout were foundational interlocutors and treasured voices of advice as this project moved from dissertation to book, each helping me better grasp its range of possibilities. Judith Weisenfeld not only writes books that inspire, she also graciously served as an outside reader of an early chapter from this project and offered her characteristically expert feedback. The walk and talk we took that breezy May day along the High Line was a true highlight of my graduate studies. I was also fortunate to find dear friends during my time in New Haven. Emily Johnson, Alexandra Kaloyanides, Sarah Koenig, Michelle Morgan, Shari Rabin, and David Walker, you are, together and alone, exemplary minds and dear persons. I am thankful for your kindness as I first began to put words to page and for the critical replies that emerged in our ongoing discussions. The conversations we had then are paradigmatic for me now of what really and truly *shared* thinking can look like, and how profound it can feel. Thanks also to April Benson-Scearce, Molly Greene, Lucia Hulsether, and Tina Post, who generously read early drafts of this project and pressed me to go farther interpretively and argumentatively. To this list of graduate writing partners, I am grateful for spirited arguments and valued connections found with other grad school compatriots over the years—Sonja Anderson, Meredith Baldi, Alex Beasley, Seren Gates Amador, Marko Geslani, Ellen Gough, Christina Harker, Olivia Hillmer, Chris Kramaric, Cody Musselman, Kimberly Pendleton, Joey Plaster, Sasha Restifo, Sara Ronis, Andrew Seal, Devin Singh, Tyler Smith, and Zachary Smith. This project emerged amid the broader thinking I have done with and alongside you all.

So too did study begun years earlier at both NYU and Washburn shape the contours of my questions and the joys of their pursuit, which took me from there to here. Ann Pellegrini, Adam Becker, and Angela Zito introduced me to the study of religion. The chance to study with you and the questions you taught me to broach only transformed my entire life. Jennifer Ball, Gary Forbach, and Jorge Nobo showed me the enduring value of the liberal arts. You modeled a pedagogy of candid critique and serious compassion, a humane and vital posture I continue to strive for in the classrooms in which I am now so fortunate to teach. Thanks also to the students in those classrooms—especially those in classes on American religion, technology, and capitalism—who have, time and again, pressed me to clarify my questions and find new ways to make more transparent and better accessible the work of religious studies. As a fellow traveler in the study of religion, I am grateful for how you remind me about the need and the potential to create new, better, more equitable communities that also resist all those relentless retail schooling types. That work, and the challenge of it, remains. It is my distinct privilege to pursue it with you.

My research and writing were also generously supported over the years by Yale's Beinecke Rare Books and Manuscript Library, its Program in the Study of Antisemitism, and dissertation fellowships from Yale University and David A. Gimbel. Sewanee's Faculty Research Grants and Kennedy Fellowship further supported my work in significant ways. Much of this funding helped facilitate crucial travel to archives, extended research in manuscript collections, and substantive time for focused reading and writing. I am likewise grateful for the wisdom of librarians, archivists, and curators at several institutions: Linda Skolarus and Stephanie Lucas (Benson Ford Research Center), Leslie Edwards and Gina Tecos (Cranbrook Academy Archives), Brent Newman (Edison and Ford Winter Estates), Robert Hughes (Koreshan State Park), Bob Hovansian (Richmond Hill Historical Society), Nancy Kilmartin (Southwest Florida Historical Society), and Bailey Rodger and Mel VandeBurgt (Florida Gulf Coast University Archives and Special Collections). Bart Bealmear, Rebecca Bizonet, Trent Boggass, and Miriam Cady, each of whom I met in connection with my research at The Henry Ford, offered additional conversation and valuable email exchanges about Ford and related subjects.

Isaac Weiner generously invited me to workshop the manuscript for this book early in its formation, and the feedback I received from his students and colleagues at Ohio State, and most importantly and especially from him, convinced me the project was, indeed, worth pursuing beyond the form of the dissertation. Nancy Levene and Courtney Bender have written work that features prominently in my endnotes. They also graciously invited me to write on related subjects for the *Immanent Frame*'s Tenth Anniversary Forum, offering coveted editorial counsel and the chance to sharpen my scholarly voice at precisely the time I most needed it. Papers related to this project were also presented at annual meetings of the American Academy of Religion as well as the

American Religious History and Sensory Cultures of Religion working groups at Yale, the Religions in America Seminar at Columbia, the Faith and Work in the New Economy Symposium at Princeton, and the Berle Symposium for the Center for Corporations, Law, and Society at Seattle University Law School, as well as at faculty research luncheons at Sewanee. In each and every instance, these proved to be formative occasions to refine my arguments, and the feedback I received pressed me always to return to the stakes of their wager.

As I began to finalize the manuscript of this book, I was fortunate to join a roster of exceptional scholars as a fellow of Material and Visual Cultures of Religion (MAVCOR), a multi-cycle program expertly led by Sally Promey and funded in part by the Henry Luce Foundation and Yale University. The conversations that Sally organized as part of the Material Economies of Religion (MERA) project cycle galvanized my thinking, and she and the people she assembled spurred me into truly unexpected directions and new forms of writing. I have and continue to learn much from Judith Brunton, Chip Callahan, Emily Floyd, Paul Johnson, Hillary Kaell, Pamela Klassen, Kathryn Lofton, Lerone Martin, Cody Musselman, Suus van Geuns, David Walker, Judith Weisenfeld, and Lexie Williams, among the great many other creative voices with whom I have been so fortunate to work. Thanks go especially to Alexandra Kaloyanides, a friend and co-conspirator of unrivaled proportions, who made me and my work better with every sentence, every discussion, every text. Writing and working with you on our sprawling MERA project helped me move with more confidence into the close of this one.

Laura Levitt and Tracy Fessenden wrote MERA pieces that made me think anew. They also graciously invited me to submit my manuscript to the North American Religions series, which they so beautifully shepherd with David Harrington Watt and Jennifer Hammer at NYU Press. I am particularly thankful for Jennifer's guidance and foresight. She saw merit in this project from the get-go, and her initial advice, even before the dissertation was complete, helped me better see the project's promise. I am indebted to your expert direction, confident stewardship, careful reading, and timely counsel. Thanks also to the two anonymous readers whose critical evaluations and constructive responses measurably improved the manuscript, and to Veronica Knutson, Brianna Jean, and Alexia Traganas for their editorial assistance.

The study of religion not only shapes my professional life. It has brought me sustaining companionship in the midst of it. David Walker, Alexandra Kaloyanides, and Kathryn Lofton offered needed feedback on chapters of this book as it moved toward publication. Your readings helped me hone the prose, refine my footnotes, and sharpen the scope of this work. Along with Marko Geslani, their critical perspectives and friendship through it all buoyed me through the loneliness of the ladder, the nadirs of pandemic labor, and helped remind me that I could find and make myself anew amid the alienations of early parenthood. On that front, too, profound thanks are due Sarah Ralston-Stark and every one of the gallant teachers at Sewanee Children's Center, who stepped in and up when my little family needed them most. You showed us the kindness of community when I thought it empty. I am grateful, too, for Tanysha Truax, whose gently probing questions and compassionately candid retorts find me amid the mess and prompt me to embrace it. Enduring thanks also to Brenda Badger, who suffers none of my foolishness and asks me to do better. You remind me why I want to and show me how I might.

Finally, to my family: Lexi Amos, my first and constant friend, whose quick mind and fierce feeling reassure me that the world can be good— thank you for being my sister in the deepest sense of the word. I closed the writing of this book in a space Darin Curts tenderly crafted for me, along a path hewed by his hands. It, and you, are a gift whispered in every sway of the trees, cascading in the lavish rush of the fall. In the end, this book is for my first teachers, Dan and Karen Amos, and for my newest, Eme Curts. Thank you for the lessons of you.

ABBREVIATIONS

SSM   Samuel Simpson Marquis Papers, Cranbrook Archives, Bloom-field Hills, Michigan, Acc. 1983–07

THF   The Henry Ford, Benson Ford Research Center, Dearborn, Michigan, www.thehenryford.org.

FMCC   Ford Motor Company Collection, National Archives, College Park, Maryland

NOTES

PREFACE

1 Accounts of Henry Ford's death and funeral are prolific, and the scene of Ford's passing features prominently in each. See, e.g., Baldwin, *Henry Ford and the Jews*, 317; Brinkley, *Wheels for the World*, 515–519; Curcio, *Henry Ford*, 265–268; Lacey, *Ford*, 441–448; Snow, *I Invented the Modern Age*, 335–336; Watts, *People's Tycoon*, 531–533. The "Sage of Dearborn" reference is commonly used throughout biographies of the industrialist. It's not clear where the term originated, but among its early uses was Philip Slomovitz's sardonic use in his 1924 critique. Slomovitz, "Ford and Two Jewish Dailies."

2 Derrida, "Différance," 3–27; Baudelaire, "On the Heroism of Modern Life," 128. Also influencing my thinking and approach here is Foucault's reading of Deleuze's "complex logic" of the "meaning-event," for which death (e.g., "Ford is dead") is posited as the best example. Foucault, "Theatrum Philosophicum," 885–908.

3 Barthes, *Mythologies*, 110; Lofton, "Commonly Modern," 137–144.

4 Marquis, *Henry Ford*, 160–162. Watts's *People's Tycoon* is one of the more recent accounts to reproduce the apparent paradoxes associated with Henry Ford. Among earlier commentators who followed Marquis's interpretive model were Upton Sinclair and Ida Tarbell. Sinclair asked for and received feedback from Marquis on his manuscript about Ford, which was subsequently published by the United Automobile Workers of America as *The Flivver King: A Story of Ford-America* (1937). Tarbell was a college friend of Marquis's, and the two corresponded regularly. Marquis compiled data about Ford for Tarbell, and she asked for feedback on "Making Men at Ford's," which she later published as part of her autobiography, *All in the Day's Work* (1939). See correspondence between Marquis and Sinclair and between Marquis and Tarbell in Boxes 1 and 8, SSM.

5 Durkheim, *Elementary Forms*, 140–182. For a related take on the study of religion with sharp reference to Durkheim, see Lofton, *Consuming Religion*. Though I do not pursue the topic at significant length here, nor do I know of any current studies on the matter, it is worth considering how Durkheim's theorization of the totemic principle drew from histories and practices of corporate trademarks, business slogans, company logos, and the like. I have gestured toward such possibilities when referencing the proximate relations of Durkheim's and Ford's projects chronologically. My point is to call attention to the capitalist context in which Durkheim was writing and the contemporaneous chronology of Durkheim's and

Ford's theorizations of "religion." Additional examination of such contexts and interrelations may help extend critiques of Durkheim's colonial logics, further trace long-standing capital interests embedded in the study of religion, and (as I do here) put Durkheim's theorizing into conversation with less canonical but chronologically contemporaneous ones, including Ford's. For now, my specific point in connecting these two is to observe how Ford and Durkheim share an affinity for the powerful force of assemblage. Lucia Hulsether touches on this in her brief reflection on Durkheim's conception of "worker corporations" in his earlier study on suicide and in her call for additional work "to compare Durkheim's history of the corporation to his history of religion." Hulsether, *Capitalist Humanitarianism*, 89–90, 205n.26–30.

6 Durkheim, *Elementary Forms*, 314; Derrida, "Structure, Sign, and Play." When I invoke the "inaugural" here and elsewhere, I also mean to allude to Michel de Certeau's discussion of the "inaugural scene" of colonial conquest in *Writing of History*, xxv. So, too, my thinking on this is influenced by Derrida's articulation in *Specters of Marx* of an inauguration that is also a spectral return and a question of repetition: "a spectre is always a revenant. One cannot control its comings and goings because it begins by coming back." It is the deferral of appearance, a tracing of iterative associations, the paradoxical temporality of ghostings, the not-quite-corporeal presence, the un/knowingness of mourning, to which Derrida attends in his language of a hauntology and that is pertinent in my thinking about Ford's inaugural orientation and corporate engineering. "What does it mean to follow a ghost? And what if this came down to being followed by it, always persecuted perhaps by the very chase we are leading? Here again what seems to be out front, the future, comes back in advance: from the past, from the back." Derrida, *Specters of Marx*, 10–11.

7 Derrida, "Structure, Sign, and Play."

8 Modern, "An Impossible Film."

9 Durkheim, *Elementary Forms*, 148–149.

10 On Ford as public persona: Lewis, *Public Image of Henry Ford*; Alvarado and Alvarado, *Drawing Conclusions on Henry Ford*; Watts, *People's Tycoon*. On celebrity in the study of religion: Stout, *Divine Dramatist*; Sutton, *Aimee Semple McPherson and the Resurrection of Christian America*; Lofton, *Consuming Religion*; Brehm, *America's Most Famous Catholic*.

11 Law, "Notes on the Theory of the Actor Network"; Latour, *Reassembling the Social*. The notion of animate-inanimate agency organized and ordered as a "network" is useful to me as a way to rethink and critique systemic power. Scholars of religion have, however, begun a valuable historical critique of the conception of "network." See, e.g., Modern, *Neuromatic*. I aim to participate in this critique by contributing to a study of how "system" has been imagined and mechanized historically and theoretically, but I do so while also benefiting from and drawing upon insights gleaned in my reading of systems theories like ANT. Mine is, then, very much an immanent critique of such theories and methods.

INTRODUCTION

1 Marquis, *Henry Ford*, 88.

2 Marquis, *Henry Ford*, 90; "Ford Says He Reads Bible Every Day."

3 Hall, *Lived Religion in America*; Smith, *Imagining Religion*, xi.

4 Marquis, *Henry Ford*, 90–91.

5 On merchandise and consumptive commerce in the study of religion: Valeri, *Heavenly Merchandize*; Kirk, *Wanamaker's Temple*; Rotman, "Brandism vs. Bazaarism"; Moreton, *To Serve God and Wal-Mart*; Sullivan, *Church, State, Corporation*; Long, *Spiritual Merchants*; Johnson and Keller, "The Work of Possession(s)"; Logan, "The Lean Closet." On religion, national mythos, and forms of collectivity, especially the corporation: Moodie, "Retail Religion"; Hulsether, "Buying into the Dream"; McLaughlin et al., "Why Scholars of Religion Must Investigate the Corporate Form"; Weiner, "The Corporately Produced Conscience"; Porterfield, *Corporate Spirit*. On the "business turn" in the study of religion: Porterfield et al., *The Business Turn in American Religious History*; Vaca, *Evangelicals Incorporated*; Hammond, *God's Businessmen*. On the study of religion, media, and technology: Morgan, *The Lure of Images*; Supp-Montgomerie, *When the Medium Was the Mission*; Martin, *Preaching on Wax*; Gitelman, *Scripts, Grooves, and Writing Machines*; Lindsey, *A Communion of Shadows*. On religion, industry, and infrastructure: Dochuk, *Anointed with Oil*; Rudnyckyj, *Spiritual Economies*; Callahan, *Faith and Work in the Kentucky Coal Mines*; Johnson, *A Shopkeepers Millennium*; Walker, *Railroading Religion*; Ellis, "Infrastructure Between Anthropology, Geography, and Religious Studies" and "Infrastructure and American Religion"; Callahan et al., "Allegories of Progress." On religion and political economy: Bartel and Hulsether, "Introduction"; Curts and Kaloyanides, "Characterizing Material Economies of Religion in the Americas"; Rivett and Martin, "A Closing Conversation."

6 Berlant, *Cruel Optimism*.

7 Marquis, *Henry Ford*, 88–89. There remain debates about the veracity of Marquis's claims. Some of the minister's contemporaries saw hypocrisy where the minister brusquely affirmed Ford's moral character. One of the central areas of Ford's biography that continues to provoke questions about his "sincerity" relates to his marital life. Many have written about an extramarital affair between Henry Ford and Evangeline (Eve) Côté Dahlinger. Ford and Eve Dahlinger reportedly had a child together, John Côté Dahlinger, who wrote about his mother's and his own relationship with Ford in *The Secret Life of Henry Ford* (1978). Dahlinger's memoir, along with several oral histories of Ford executives and associates, are the primary sources used by historians who recount the affair. See, e.g., Watts, *People's Tycoon*, 332–341. Some accounts of Henry Ford's death, including Dahlinger's, suggest that Clara Ford or one of the servants at Fair Lane, the Ford's estate, called Eve Dahlinger and that both women were present at the dying man's bedside. In an interview with historian, Robert Lacey, Henry Ford II reportedly confirmed that Eve Dahlinger was present when he and his wife arrived at his grandfather's

deathbed. Lacey, *Ford*, 733, also referenced in Watts, *People's Tycoon*, 532, 571n68. For more on the import of "sincerity" and "scandal" in histories of American religion and culture, see McCrary, *Sincerely Held* and Krivulskaya, "Disgraced" and "On Protestant Sex Scandals."

8 "Ford Says He Reads Bible Every Day"; Bryan, *Henry's Lieutenants*, 206; Letter from Marquis to Rev. O.T. Gifford, 17 April 1916, Box 1, Folder 4, SSM. On Protestant virtue, (dis)establishment, and taste: Wenger, *Religious Freedom*; Promey, "Material Establishment and Public Display"; Dowland, *Family Values and the Rise of the New Christian Right*; Morgan, *Visual Piety*; Douglas, *The Feminization of American Culture*.

9 Samuel Crowther, "Henry Ford and the Jews," p. 10, typescript, Acc. 572, Box 2, Folder 4, THF; Ford, *My Life and Work*, 162, 251; Ford, *The International Jew*.

10 It is customary here to offer a footnote that aims to represent or identify landmark texts in a vast field. There's value to that scholarly custom. It introduces readers otherwise unfamiliar with an area of scholarly specialization to influential texts in the field, and it provides specialists a glimpse into a book's key interlocutors. In this case, that would include: Asad, *Formations of the Secular*; Fessenden, *Culture and Redemption* and "The Problem of the Postsecular"; Anidjar, "Secularism"; Warner, "Secularism" and *Varieties of Secularism in a Secular Age*; Taylor, *A Secular Age*; Scott and Hirschkind, *Powers of the Secular Modern*; Jakobsen and Pellegrini, *Secularisms*; Pellegrini, "Feeling Secular"; Casanova, "The Secular and Secularisms"; Wenger, *We Have a Religion*; Lofton, *Oprah* and *Consuming Religion*; Modern, *Secularism in Antebellum America*; Agrama, *Questioning Secularism*; Mahmood, *Religious Difference in a Secular Age*; and McCrary, *Sincerely Held*. Yet, this scholarly rite can also risk reifying a broader and more dynamic field, canonizing particular texts and potentially reproducing problematic citational politics. I observe this genre of notation because I am implicated in its performance and reproduction. It is worth considering how these risks are consequently managed. Some aim for comprehensiveness—demonstrating expertise in the extensive and proffering inclusion in multiplicity. Witness my citational spill above. But any tumble of references stumbles at full inclusivity since its performance draws boundaries as it inscribes. Consult Levene, "Courses and Canons in the Study of Religion," for further reflection on this practice. Given such dynamics, I might turn to advocacy instead, urging readers toward specific texts, to showcase and articulate "the best" or "the original" in a vast field. Such a performance would, for me, gesture to Asad's *Formations of the Secular*, Anidjar's "Secularism," and Jakobsen and Pellegrini's *Secularisms* as foundational to my specific thinking on the subject, and to Fessenden's *Culture and Redemption*, Pellegrini's "Feeling Secular," Wenger's *We Have a Religion*, and McCrary's *Sincerely Held* as particularly sharp renderings situated at the intersection of secular studies and the area of specialization in which I was most closely trained (American religious history). Notes like this one inevitably serve other purposes, too. My point in acknowledging the specificity of the form and the stakes of its standardization is to draw into

sharper relief the questions that undergird their enaction (and inaction?). Whose work is cited and why? What practices of incorporation happen in the work of such inscriptions? What canon constructed, conveyed, managed, challenged? What "religion" managed and mass-produced? For a critical examination of related citational matters and bibliographic comment in the study of religion: Ali and Serrano, "The Person of the Author."

11 The language of the "religio-racial" that I use here and throughout this book is borrowed from Weisenfeld, *New World A-Coming*. See also the special issue of the *Journal of the American Academy of Religion* 88.2 (2020), in which several scholars build upon and extend Weisenfeld's valuable analytic.

12 Marquis, *Henry Ford*, 89–91.

13 Caterine, "The Haunted Grid"; Adams, *The Education of Henry Adams*; Nadis, *Wonder Shows*; Modern, *Secularism in Antebellum America*; Klassen, *Story of Radio Mind*; Bender, "American Reincarnations" and *New Metaphysicals*; Albanese, *Republic of Mind and Spirit* and *Delight Makers*; Ahlstrom, *Religious History of the American People*.

14 Marquis, *Henry Ford*, 89; Viereck, "I Have Lived Before," 4; "Ford Thinks Ancients Had Planes and Radios." Ford's inquiry into the reincarnation of Shanti Devi is documented in Henry Ford Office Papers, Acc. 285, Box 2141, THF. On Ford's connection to ideas of reincarnation vis-a-vis Theosophy, see: correspondence from Percival Perry, Fair Lane Papers, Acc. 1, Box 114, THF. David Nye reported on Ford's idea that Dorothy Richardson Heber—the granddaughter of one of Henry Ford's cousins—was the reincarnation of Mary Ford, the industrialist's mother. Nye's account is based on two interviews he conducted with Heber. Heber reportedly recounted how Ford spoke openly of his belief, and that the auto-industrialist gave the young girl a theosophical text and invited her to play Ford's mother in a short vignette in an early Ford film. Irving Bacon, the artist and ad-man who was commissioned to paint scenes from Ford's life, was also directed to use Heber as his model for Mary Ford. According to Bacon, Ford reasoned that the young girl cut a perfect resemblance to his mother. Nye, *Henry Ford*, 117–118; Irving Bacon, "Reminiscences," p. 123, Owen W. Bombard Interview Series, Acc. 65, THF.

15 Fair Lane Papers, Acc. 1, Box 115, Folder 1, THF. The description of New Thought's worldview is R. Marie Griffith's. Griffith's study offers a much more complex and detailed examination of New Thought than the intentionally pithy description cited here. Griffith, *Born Again Bodies*. On New Thought, see also: Lofton, *Oprah*; Bowler, *Blessed*; White, *Unsettled Minds*; Satter, *Each Mind a Kingdom*. On "sovereign ritual" and fraternal relation: Logan, *Awkward Rituals*.

16 Marquis, *Henry Ford*, 89. For Ford's remarks about (un)orthodoxy, see "Ford, Denying Hate, Lays War to Jews." On Ford's religious views as eccentricities: Lacey, *Ford*, 7; Watts, *People's Tycoon*, 320. Notable exceptions to this are Nye, *Henry Ford* and Coir, "The Gospel of Work." Few scholars of American religion have considered Ford at all. The primary exception is Albanese, *Republic of Mind and Spirit*. On Ford's expansive approach to religion: Trine, *Power That Wins*, 141–142.

17 Marquis, *Henry Ford*, 89–90.

18 Marquis, *Henry Ford*, 98, 140; "Lecture by Doctor Marquis, Delivered Before the Advisors of the Educational Department," 11 Jan 1917, Box 8, Folder 4, SSM.

19 Marquis, *Henry Ford*, 153–154; Marquis, "The Ford Idea in Education," *A Talk to the National Education Association*, Detroit, pp. 1, 10, Box 8, Folder 7, SSM. On the conjunction of humanist endeavor, Christian commission, pedagogical project, and corporate enterprise: Bowler, *Blessed*, 11–40; Kirk, *Wanamaker's Temple*, 15–16, 88–191; Moreton, "The Soul of Neoliberalism," and *To Serve God and Wal-Mart*; Seales, *Religion Around Bono*; Lorusso, *Spirituality, Corporate Culture, and American Business*; Lofton, *Consuming Religion*; Hulsether, "Buying into the Dream" and *Capitalist Humanitarianism*; Bartel, *Card-Carrying Christians*. On Ford's welfare capitalism and social gospel reform: Drake, "Between Religion and Politics," 332; Meyer, *Five Dollar Day*, 97–98; Watts, *People's Tycoon*, 206.

20 Marquis, *Henry Ford*, 90. On the social gospel: Evans, *The Social Gospel in American Religion*; Curtis, *A Consuming Faith*; Luker, *Social Gospel in Black and White*.

21 Marquis, *Henry Ford*, 92. On assemblage: Slack and Wise, *Culture and Technology*, 149–162; Puar, "I would rather be a cyborg than a goddess" and *Terrorist Assemblages*; Curts, "Temples and Turnpikes."

22 Marquis, *Henry Ford*, 122, 140–141, 144–145, 155–156. On Ford's drive system: Norwood, *Strikebreaking and Intimidation*, 176. On the Service Department's "tyrannical rule": Weiss, "Corporate Security at Ford Motor Company," 18.

23 Norwood, *Strikebreaking and Intimidation*, 171–193; Weiss, "Corporate Security at Ford Motor Company," 22, 24, 27–28; Letter from F.A. Lankin to Marquis, 7 December 1922, Box 1, Folder 6, SSM. On Forditis: Meyer, *Five Dollar Day*, 40–41. On the shift from sociological to service work: Moreton, *To Serve God and Wal-Mart*, 101–108.

24 Marquis, *Henry Ford*, 144, 187; Henry Ford II, "The Challenge of Human Engineering: Mass Production, a Tool for Raising the Standard of Living," An Address Delivered at the Annual Meeting of the Society of Automotive Engineers (Dearborn, MI: Ford Motor Company, 1946).

For his part, Marquis was partly right about Edsel Ford insofar as Edsel was crucial to the establishment of the Ford Foundation in 1935, which not only helped channel private wealth into social philanthropy, but also helped shelter the Ford estate from taxation after Edsel's untimely death in 1943, as his shares were distributed among surviving family members and the Foundation. Edsel Ford's bequest, along with his father's later one, helped Ford Motor Company maintain its private holding as a family-owned business and set the Ford Foundation on a course to become one of the largest philanthropies in the world. Nevins and Hill, *Decline and Rebirth*, 409–421. The broader sweep of Marquis's story is a familiar one in the annals of American religious history. Jeremiads of reform in histories of American religion routinely plot magnanimous religiosity—one centered in a naturalized Christianity and an enlightened understanding of universalized humanity—as redemptive power for God's chosen people. In such narratives, the elect, who momentarily fall from favor because they have forsaken their errand, are not only to be redeemed through a return to their covenantal relation, but are called anew to reform the world they are commissioned to convert. Bercovitch, *American Jeremiad*.

On Henry Ford II and the "rebirth" of the Company in 1945, see Nevins and Hill, *Decline and Rebirth*, 294, 311, 335, 431–435, 442. It is worth noting that other scholars have significantly nuanced such historical interpretations of Ford II as ushering in an era of renewed industrial goodwill, emphasizing instead the bureaucratization of discipline that he implemented as a strategy to tame industrial unions—a historical change characterized as a movement "from coercion to co-optation." This, especially in combination with the Taft-Hartley Act, which was passed in the same year that Henry Ford (the elder) died and not only outlawed mass picketing, wildcat and sympathy strikes, and secondary boycotts but also permitted the passage of new "right-to-work" laws—served to repress many of the more radical voices in the labor movement. Weiss, "Corporate Security at Ford Motor Company," 32–33.

25 Bercovitch, *American Jeremiad*, xxi, 180. While many people have used the phrase "industrial paradise," I specifically draw here on correspondence from a former Ford employee writing to Marquis, Box 1, Folder 6, SSM. Bercovitch's preface to the 2012 anniversary edition of his text usefully reflects on what Bercovitch describes as "the Americanization of dissent" (xxxi). Marquis's contribution to the long tradition of jeremiadic dissent—in which denunciation and wish fulfillment are mobilized together—seems particularly crucial to recognize given the minister's contribution to the Americanization movement of the twentieth century, an aspect of the Education (née Sociological) Department detailed in chapter 2.

26 Bercovitch, *American Jeremiad*, xvii, xxi; Marquis, *Henry Ford*, 38–39.

27 Latour, *We Have Never Been Modern*; Foucault, "What is Enlightenment?"

1. A METAPHYSICS OF MASS PRODUCTION AND FORD'S "GOSPEL OF EFFICIENCY"

1 Ford, *My Life and Work*, 24, 57; Nevins and Hill, *The Times, the Man, the Company*, 58–59; Richards, *Last Billionaire*, 303–304.

2 Thompson, "Time, Work-Discipline and Industrial Capitalism," 89.

3 Stidger, "Henry Ford Says," 83, 240.

4 Lewis, *Public Image of Henry Ford*, 54; Peters, "Calendar, Clock, Tower," 25–42. The historiography of religion and the temporal is extensive and blends into expansive questions about how to distinguish between and understand the relations of terrestrial and heavenly, finite and infinite, temporary and eternal. Studies of religion and time consciousness likewise shift into and scale up powerful distinctions: of earthly and divine authority, ritual habits of monastic life, exacting regimens of human labor, metaphors of divine intelligence, the mental mechanics of phrenological empiricism, sectarian regulations and Sabbath observations, and proliferating associations of market economies, business cycles, ecclesiastical

structures, and liturgical calendars. See, e.g., Aveni, "Time"; Tomlin, *A Divinity for All Persuasions*; McCrossen, *Holy Day, Holiday*; Schmidt, *Consumer Rites*. On religious versus secular histories of time, Weber's *Protestant Ethic and the Spirit of Capitalism* has had an enduring influence, attested to by recent studies seeking to extend, nuance, and critique his account. See, e.g., Valeri, *Heavenly Merchandize* and Koenig, *Providence and the Invention of American History*. Koenig's book, and early conversations with her, have been crucial to my thinking on these subjects.

5 Foucault, "Theatrum Philosophicum," 855–908; Weber, *Sociology of Religion*, 59; "Ford Cars Grow Up by Magic Methods"; Lewis, *Public Image of Henry Ford*, 54; Albanese, *Republic of Mind and Spirit*. See also the special issue on related topics in *Journal of the American Academy of Religion* 75.3 (2007).

6 McCrossen, *Marking Modern Times* and *Holy Day, Holiday*; Henkin, *Postal Age*; Mirola, *Redeeming Time*; Pietsch, *Dispensational Modernism*; Numbers, *The Creationists*; Rees, *Refrigeration Nation*; Susman, *Culture as History*; Dinerstein, "Modernism."

7 Aldrich, "On the Track of Efficiency"; Quigel, "The Business of Selling Efficiency"; Aitken, *Scientific Management in Action*. On the 1885–1886 strikes on the Gould railways and on Debs and the Pullman strike, see respectively Case, "Free Labor on the Southwestern Railroads" and Salvatore, *Eugene V. Debs*.

8 Emerson, *Efficiency as a Basis for Operation and Wages*, 205; Stewart et al., "The Businessman of the Century"; Taylor, *Principles of Scientific Management*, xi–xiii, 38; Hughes, *American Genesis*, 188. The literature on Taylor and Taylorism is voluminous. See, for example, Nye, *America's Assembly Line*, 33–34; Hounshell, *From the American System to Mass Production*, Haber, *Efficiency and Uplift*; Kanigel, *The One Best Way*; and Maier, "Between Taylorism and Technocracy." For a collection of materials published early in the twentieth century intending to describe the new managerial system, see Thompson, *Scientific Management*.

9 Hounshell, *From the American System to Mass Production*, 249–253; Aitkens, *Scientific Management in Action*, 162; Hughes, *American Genesis*, 197–199; Nevins and Hill, *The Times, The Man, The Company*, 466–476; Meyer, *Five Dollar Day*, 11. Scholarship on religion in America has just begun analyzing efficiency as an ideal and organizational project. See, e.g., Wiard, "The Gospel of Efficiency" and Vaca, "Reimagining the Gospel of Efficiency."

10 Ford, "Mass Production," 821. One of Ford's many hands, probably William J. Cameron, a high-level Ford official and one of his most notorious ghostwriters, likely penned the entry. Yet, Ford—auto company and human character—cannot be dissociated from such writings. It is through sources like this that the discursive production of Ford can be traced. For more on Cameron's specific role in the writing of the encyclopedia entry, see Hounshell, *From the American System to Mass Production*, 1. Hounshell also describes how a year before the official encyclopedia appeared in print, Ford's entry was published as a full-page feature under the headline, "Henry Ford Expounds Mass Production: Calls It the Focussing of the Principles of Power, Economy, Continuity and Speed—Tells Why Accurate

Machines Produce the Highest Standard of Quality—Says System Develops the Worker," *New York Times*, September 19, 1926. The newspaper also distributed it through their wire service, accompanied by an editorial on the subject of mass production. On Ford's early advertising slogan: "Ford 'The Universal Car' Sign, 1910–1918," Object ID 66.61.1, THF, www.thehenryford.org.

11 Ford, "Mass Production," 821; G. Briefs, 'Rationalisierung der Arbeit,' in: Industrie- und Handelskammer zu Berlin, *Die Bedeutung der Rationalisierung für das deutsche Wirtschaftsleben* (Berlin, 1928), 41, quoted and translated in Maier, "Between Taylorism and Technocracy," 54 n.65. The phrase, "a great productive machine," is Charles B. Going's, editor of *Engineering Magazine*. Going used the phrase in correspondence with Horace Arnold, who co-authored (with Fay Leone Faurote) *Ford Methods and the Ford Shops* (1915), which was adapted from a series of articles initially serialized in *Engineering Magazine*. For more on Going's phrase: Smith, *Making the Modern*, 31–33. On the relatively slow adoption of the language of "assembly line," particularly in comparison to the widespread use of "mass production," see Nye, *America's Assembly Line*, 42–43.

12 Street, *Abroad at Home*, 95.

13 Arnold and Faurote, *Ford Methods and the Ford Shops*, 103. Henry Ford also described exponential improvements in production time. See *My Life and Work*, 81–83. Andrew Seal has shown that Ford's system was a mathematically and sociopolitically "averaging" one—a process that contributed to the production of a midwestern common that was exported nationally and internationally as part of a broader Americanization program in the twentieth century, a program explored in chapters 2 and 3. Seal, "Almost Century of the Common Man." On the production of the commons and/as mass consumption, see Cohen, *A Consumers' Republic*.

14 Ford, "Mass Production," 821. On method in the study of religion: Lofton, "Methodology of the Modernists" and "Commonly Modern"; Pietsch, *Dispensational Modernism*; Curts, "Shadowy Relations and Shades of Devotion."

15 Ford, "Machinery, the New Messiah," 363–364; Young, "Ford Scans the Economic Scene."

16 Ford, "Mass Production," 821.

17 Denny, "Times Good, Not Bad, Ford Says"; Trine, *Power That Wins*, 14–16.

18 Ford, *My Life and Work*, 2, 73; Snow, *I Invented the Modern Age*, 184, 214, 222.

19 Denny, "Times Good, Not Bad, Ford Says," 1; Viereck, "I Have Lived Before," 4.

20 Bender, "American Reincarnations," 589–614.

21 Benson, *The New Henry Ford*, 326; Oliver Barthel, "Reminiscences," pp. 70–71, Owen W. Bombard Interview Series, Acc. 65, THF; "Reincarnationist"; Smith, *A Short View of Great Questions*, 6, 31–32, 60, 65.

22 Smith, *A Short View of Great Questions*, 26, 68.

23 Viereck, "I Have Lived Before," 4.

24 Viereck, "I Have Lived Before," 4; Trine, *Power That Wins*, 18, 145–147, 181; McCormick, "Ford Scans the Current Tides."

25 Ford, *Edison as I Know Him*, 6; "Mr. Henry Ford and Reincarnation," 10; "Reincarnationist"; Viereck, "I Have Lived Before," 4; Trine, *Power That Wins*, 146; McCormick, "Ford Seeks a New Balance for Industry."

26 Viereck, "I Have Lived Before," 4; "Reincarnationist"; Bowler, *Blessed*, 13–14. For a more extensive treatment of religion and the brain, see Modern, *Neuromatic*.

27 Stidger, "Henry Ford Says," 240; "Reincarnationist"; Trine, *Power That Wins*, 177.

28 Trine, *Power That Wins*, 178, 180; Viereck, "I Have Lived Before," 4. "Ford, Denying Hate, Lays War to Jews"; Smith, "A Magnate and a Mystic Meet."

29 Bender, "American Reincarnations," 595; Rivett, *Science of the Soul*, 5–22, 78; Ford, *Today and Tomorrow*, 265–266; Viereck, "I Have Lived Before," 4; McCormick, "Ford Scans the Current Tides." On related histories of religious investigation and scientific practices, see, e.g., Minkema et al., "Agitations, Convulsions, Leaping, and Loud Talking"; Taves, *Fits, Traces, and Visions*; Promey, *Spiritual Spectacles*; McGarry, *Ghosts of Futures Past*; Modern, *Secularism in Antebellum America*; Grainger, *Church in the Wild*.

30 Henry Ford Office Papers, Acc. 285, Box 2405, THF. In addition to correspondence with Strobach, the Ford archive is littered with things sent to Ford about reincarnation. It is impossible to know precisely how these items were received and understood by Ford, other than to note that they were saved as part of the relics and reliquaries of The Henry Ford, which are themselves discussed at greater length in chapter 4. On story and history as "mapped layers," see Bender, *New Metaphysics*, 121.

31 Albanese, *Republic of Mind and Spirit*, 330–393. For more on Ford's engagement with Indian teachers and traditions, see Smith, "Magnate and Mystic Meet," and T. A. Raman, "The Story of the Spinning Wheel: From Mahatma Gandhi to Henry Ford," Henry Ford Office Papers, Acc. 285, Box 2141, THF. In contrast to Raman's congenial story of the Gandhi-Ford relation, cf. Callender, "Gandhi Dissects the Ford Idea." On Ford and the story about Shanti Devi's reincarnation, see Henry Ford Office Papers, Acc. 285, Box 2141, THF. On Ford's personal secretaries, see Bryan, *Henry's Lieutenants*, 59–66, 169–176.

 Historiographically, claims of religious authority, credulity, and evaluations of the "sincere" and the "fraud" have tended to orient empirically in studies of nineteenth-century performative rituals. See, e.g., Halttunen, *Confidence Men and Painted Women*; Cook, *Arts of Deception*; Sandage, *Born Losers*; Mihm, *A Nation of Counterfeiters*; Maffly-Kipp, "Tracking the Sincere Believer"; McGarry, *Ghosts of Futures Past*; Walker, "The Humbug in American Religion"; Ogden, *Credulity*; McCrary, *Sincerely Held*.

32 Nye, *Henry Ford*, 117–118; Cooper, *Reincarnation*, 75–77; Bacon, "Reminiscences," 123; Bennett, *We Never Called Him Henry*, 165; Mrs. Stanley Ruddiman, "Reminiscences," p. 90, Owen W. Bombard Interview Series, Acc. 65, THF; Brinkley, *Wheels for the World*, 478.

33 Trine, *Power That Wins*, 79, 146, 180; Viereck, "I Have Lived Before," 4; Berlant, *Cruel Optimism*.

Outside the bounds of this examination but worth further exploration is Ford's relationship to the Koreshan Unity group, a communal settlement in Estero, Florida, initially founded in 1894 as "The New Jerusalem" by a New York–born physician named Cyrus Teed, who changed his name to "Koresh" after receiving a divine illumination in 1869. Ford visited the Koreshan Unity settlement in Estero, Florida, several times in 1931, just around the time that his close personal friend and industrial mentor, Thomas Edison, died. I have examined the Koreshan Unity's primary publication of the time, *The Flaming Sword*, but relatively little mention is made of Ford's visits. However, the Koreshan Unity settlement in Florida was near both Ford's and Edison's winter homes in Fort Myers, and Ford sent for "a complete set of Koreshan literature" around 1930. Others have reported that during Ford's time with the Koreshans, he spoke at some length to members, including Henry Silverfriend, one of the original members of Koreshan Unity. Although I have not located records in either the Ford or Koreshan archives to confirm such reports, news accounts report that the two discussed Ford's beliefs in reincarnation along with the Koreshan Unity's theory of a hollow earth. Ford reportedly agreed with Koreshan theories "that everything now here has lived before and that the people that are in the world now always have been but in a different form." The industrialist is also said to have nearly agreed to have his palm read by Silverfriend, an authority on palmistry, but was ultimately dissuaded by his personal secretary, Frank Campsall, who "convinced his employer it might be the better part of wisdom not to have it done." "Ford Believes in Reincarnation But Not So Sure World Is Hollow"; Cepero, "Ford's Link to Koreshan Strengthened." See also, "Ford, Henry—Reincarnation," Archives Vertical File, THF; Publications, 1892–1999, Koreshan Collection, Acc. 02/01/18, Florida Gulf Coast University Special Collections.

34 Ford, "Mass Production," 821; Ford, "Motto," 1; Trine, *Power That Wins*, 60; Ford, *My Life and Work*, 280. On the American System of manufacture, see Hounshell, *From the American System to Mass Production*, 2–4, 8–9, 331–336. On the importance of Ford's product-line standardization and the division of labor, see, e.g., interviews with Charles Morgana of the Briggs Manufacturing Company, Alvan Macauley, President of the Packard Motor Company, and "Memorandum of Conference with Mr. John Lee," in Acc. 96, Box 12, THF.

35 Ford, "Machinery, The New Messiah," 364; Trine, *Power That Wins*, 60, 79; Viereck, "I Have Lived Before," 4; Ford, *Today and Tomorrow*, 79–80.

36 Trine, *Power That Wins*, 141–142. On New Thought, see Lofton, *Oprah*; Bowler, *Blessed*; Griffith, *Born Again Bodies*; White, *Unsettled Minds*; Satter, *Each Mind a Kingdom*; Albanese, *Republic of Mind and Spirit* and *Delight Makers*.

37 Trine, *Power That Wins*, 11–12. When Ford's office bookshelves were catalogued for the corporate archive, several included Trine's work, including two copies of *The Land of Living Men*, three copies of *What All the World's A-Seeking*, five copies of *The Mystical Life of Ours*, one copy of *Thoughts I Met on the Highway*,

one copy of *The Winning of the Best*, one copy of *Every Living Creature: Heart Training through the Animal World*, and one remaining copy of *In Tune with the Infinite*. Records Moved to Engineering Laboratory in 1919 and Non-Automotive Interests and Activities Record Series, Acc. 62, Box 4, THF. Ford was also apparently an avid reader of Allen's books, several of which were also included in Ford's office library. This included four copies of *Through the Gate of the Good*, two copies of *The Way of Peace*, one copy of *The Path of Prosperity*, four copies of *As a Man Thinketh*, four copies of *Entering the Kingdom*, three copies of *Out from the Heart*, three copies of *The Heavenly Life*, and three copies of *Morning and Evening Thoughts*. Acc. 62, Box 4, THF. Ford likewise sent away for twenty-five copies of Fox's book, *Reincarnation*, and twelve copies of its companion text entitled, *Life After Death*. Letters about these purchases were written by Ford's personal secretary, Frank Campbell. According to Campbell's correspondence, the books were to be delivered directly to Ford's estate, Fair Lane. Henry Ford Office Papers, Acc. 285, Box 2285, THF. Percival Perry, the head of Ford Motor Company's English subsidiary, wrote in a letter to Clara Ford about having received two books from Frank Campsall about reincarnation, "which he said Mr. Ford had read," and "both emanate[d] from the Theosophical Movement." Letter from Perry to Clara Ford, 5 January 1945, Fair Lane Papers, Acc. 1, Box 114, THF. Ford was also seemingly conversant with people who were interested in spiritualism. Letters from a George Holley of Loon Lake, NY, mention Ford's and Thomas Edison's interest in a book entitled *Phenomena of Materialization* by Baron Von Notzing, as well as the subject of "psychic phenomena" through the likes of Sir Arthur Conan Doyle and a local Detroit resident, Mr. Newton Annis, both of whom attested to having encountered "genuine materializations" during séance sittings with the Society for Advanced Psychical Research. Nevins and Hill Research Papers, Acc. 572, Box 10, THF. See also three letters from Frank Campsall to Yogi Publishing Society, requesting multiple copies of Atkinson's text, *Reincarnation and the Law of Karma*, dated 20 July 1922, 28 July 1922, and 12 October 1922, Henry Ford Office, Acc. 285, Box 117, THF. Campsall also wrote to Van Nostrand and Company on 18 July 1922 and again on 9 August 1922 about purchasing a copy of Lauren William de Laurence's *Sacred Book of Death, Hindu Spiritism, Soul Transition, and Soul Reincarnation, etc.*; however, the book was out of stock at the time and the company was unable to procure a copy. Nevins and Hill Research Papers, Acc. 572, Box 10, THF. In addition to Atkinson's and de Laurence's texts, Ford's authorized biographers, Nevins and Hill, also noted three additional texts on reincarnation as being influential to the industrialist, including: Annie Basant's *Reincarnation: Its Necessity*, Ursula N. Gestefeld, *Reincarnation or Immortality*, and James Martin Peebles, *Reincarnation, or, the Doctrine of the "Soul's" Successive Embodiments: Examined and Discussed Pro and Con.*

38 Braden, *Spirits of Rebellion*, 450–464; Bender, *New Metaphysicals*, 137; Albanese, *Republic of Mind and Spirit*, 327–329, 429–436; Telegraph from Unity School of

Christianity to Henry Ford's secretary, Frank Campsall, 14 July 1941, Fair Lane Papers, Acc. 1, Box 115, THF.

39 Correspondence from Silent Unity to Henry Ford, Fair Lane Papers, Acc. 1, Box 115, THF. It is also worth noting that it has become an interpretive trope among Ford's many biographers to linger upon the troubled father-son relation of Henry and Edsel Ford. See, for example, Watts, *People's Tycoon*, 513–530; Nevins and Hill, *Decline and Rebirth*, 242–248; Brinkley, *Wheels for the World*, 474–478; Lacey, *Ford*, 151–153, 159, 253–265, 394–398; Lewis, *Public Image of Henry Ford*, 291, 365–374, 406–409. Many of these narratives build directly on critiques made of the automaker by his colleagues, especially Charles Sorensen's *My Forty Years with Ford*, in which Sorensen wrote about the relationship between the elder and younger Fords as moving "with the inevitability of a Greek tragedy" (320). Sorensen argued that Ford's "greatest failure was his treatment of his only son, Edsel. And this treatment may have hastened his son's death" (301).

Ford's contemporaries and later historians alike have offered many explanations for the strained relation. Ford's interest in affirmative prayer practices and his related conceptions about the mind as a powerful healing mechanism have been overlooked in such accounts. It is possible to understand the elder Ford's increasingly strenuous behavior toward Edsel, at least in part, as an articulation of the elder man's metaphysical commitments. The auto-industrialist fought stridently with his own doctors, preferring the treatment of his chiropractor to all others, and recommending those services as a kind of alternative medicine for his son's healing. Sounding idioms of New Thought–inspired mind cure alongside the might of an industrial engineer confident about his ability to issue men toward right practice, Ford reportedly told Sorensen: "If there is anything the matter with Edsel's health . . . he can correct it himself. First he will have to change his way of living. Then, I'll get my chiropractor to work on him" (318). Voicing opposition to his son's medical care, the elder Ford insisted that "if the hospital can't cure him, I'll get rid of the whole bunch" (Sorensen, 318). Given Ford's long-standing and widespread affinity for New Thought idioms and ideas, it is unsurprising that Ford vigorously sought out Silent Unity's prayer ministry as a healing practice for his dying son. What Ford's physician and former employee suggested were "unusual things" said by a "sick man," can be interpreted as counter-claims and implicit arguments against Ford's New Thought commitments (Sorensen, 323–324). In such a context, Ford's urgent declarations and bold assertions reveal his efforts to spur in his son an embodied response of physical healing and energetic renewal through practices of affirmative suggestion and mind power. The relational effects between father and son and the family dynamics observed by contemporaries and later historians may still be lamentable and worth critique, but they are also rendered more understandable and considerably less "unusual." On healing practices, affirmative suggestion, and theories of mind from the perspective of the New Thought movement and its relation to prosperity gospels, later "positive thinking" practices, and other new age spiritualities that emerged in the twentieth century, see Bowler, *Blessed*; Lofton, *Oprah*; and Albanese, *The Delight Makers*.

40 Bone, "A British Editor Learns Henry Ford's Views on War and Work," 9; Ford, *Ford Ideals*, 397–399; Smith, "Magnate and Mystic Meet"; Trine, *Power That Wins*, 14–15, 17, 170, 172.

41 Trine, *Power That Wins*, 181; Ford, *Today and Tomorrow*, 265–266; Denny, "Times Good, Not Bad, Ford Says," 1, 3.

42 Ford, *My Philosophy of Industry*, 92–94; Ford, *My Life and Work*, 280.

43 Chaplin, *Modern Times*; Modern, "Introduction: Duty Now For The Future," 168, 171. It is worth noting that Chaplin's critique of industrial production in this movie was a marked change from his earlier perspective. Some fifteen years before Chaplin's *Modern Times*, the actor remarked: "For a long time capital has held sway and declared that the present order is the only one, but Henry Ford's methods rather disprove that, don't they? He is getting all the business of the country because he is fair. He gives value received for his merchandise, and on the other hand he considers his workers, pays them a fair wage and has made profit-sharing absolutely practicable." Grant, "The Serious Opinions of Charlie Chaplin." Chaplin also visited Ford's Highland Park plant in 1923 and subsequently made the film, *The Circus*, which affectionately features a Ford Model T as a central character in the plot. That earlier film was apparently an all-time favorite of Ford's. I note these aspects of Chaplin's history with Ford to point to the ambivalence of the Tramp's relationship with industrial modernity. Brinkley, *Wheels for the World*, 363–364.

44 "Ford, Denying Hate, Lays War to Jews."

45 Nye, *Henry Ford*, 105.

46 Viereck, "Henry Ford Discusses Education, Food, and Other Things," 1; Trine, *Power That Wins*, 15, 20–22. The phrase about Ford "making men" appears several times historically and historiographically, and is analyzed at length in coming chapters. See, e.g., Marquis, *Henry Ford*, 153–154; Tarbell, "Making Men at Ford's"; Loizides, "'Making Men' at Ford," 109–148.

On the temporalities of capital and the form of the spiral, see Sewell, "The Temporalities of Capitalism," 517–537; Derrida, *The Gift of Death*, 3–35; Latour, *We Have Never Been Modern*, 75. Latour's celebration of the spiral as a polytemporal form might also be usefully contrasted with Max Horkheimer's and Theodore Adorno's description of the relation between progress and regress in *Dialectic of Enlightenment*, which by my reading might look something like a spiral. The point is that, for many theorists of modernity (including Ford), the spiral may shape the temporal form and formal temporality of the modern.

2. "SPIRITUAL HEGEMONY" AND FORD'S RITE-TO-WORK RELIGION

1 "Job Seekers Riot, Storm Ford Plant"; "Men Rioting for Work at Ford Motor Plant"; "Gale Fails to Halt Rush to Ford Plant."

2 "Ten Thousand Men in Rush to Share Ford's Profit Plan"; Ford, *My Life and Work*, 128; "Crowd of Applicants outside Highland Park Plant after Five Dollar Day Announcement, January 1914," Photographic Vertical File Series, Object ID 84.1.1660.P.833.29, THF, www.thehenryford.org.

3 "Job Seekers Riot, Storm Ford Plant"; "Men Rioting for Work at Ford Motor Plant"; "Gale Fails to Halt Rush to Ford Plant."

4 "Job Seekers Riot, Storm Ford Plant"; "Men Rioting for Work at Ford Motor Plant"; "Gale Fails to Halt Rush to Ford Plant." Similar accounts appeared in other news organs, reporting related if somewhat less violent scenes throughout the previous week. See, for example, "10,000 Fight to Get Jobs"; "Mob Seeks Work at Ford Factory"; "Ford Factory Again Stormed by Job Seekers"; "6,000 Mob Ford Works"; "First Payment of Ford's Bonus to Come Friday"; "Workers Get $10,000,000 of Ford's Profits This Year."

5 "Job Seekers Riot, Storm Ford Plant"; "Ten Thousand Men in Rush to Share Ford's Profit Plan."

6 Ford, *My Life and Work*, 120–121. In *Blessed*, Kate Bowler describes how this metaphysical form of the prosperity gospel "disappeared," becoming part of American culture more generally, only to "resurface" in the post–WWII period as "positive thinking." If forms of the prosperity gospel "disappeared" only to "resurface" later, Bowler argues it did so through a "corporate metaphysics." Ford showcases one powerful and influential brand of corporate metaphysics.

7 Gramsci, *Prison Notebooks*, 358; Ford, *My Life and Work*, 264–265; "Building the American Economy," *Ford Sunday Evening Hour*, radio show script, Ford Times and Dealer Publications Department Records, Acc. 474, Box 4, THF; Lee, "The So-Called Profit Sharing System in the Ford Plant," 299; Sorensen, *My Forty Years with Ford*, 54.

8 Smith, *To Take Place*, 103, 109–110.

9 Asad, "Reflections on the Origins of Human Rights."

10 Asad, "Reflections on the Origins of Human Rights"; Becker, *Revival and Awakening*, 34.

11 Lofton, "Corporation as Sect"; McLaughlin et al., "Why Scholars of Religion Must Investigate the Corporate Form"; "The Corporate Form," Exchanges, Forum on *The Immanent Frame*, April/May 2021, https://tif.ssrc.org.

12 In March 1913, the International Workers of the World (IWW) sent organizers to Detroit to help agitate for unionization at Ford. In particular, the IWW spoke out for an eight-hour day policy (Ford, at the time, had a ten-hour working day). Ford soon forbid workers from leaving the plant for lunch, making it more difficult for organizers to connect with employees during the working day. Although the IWW soon began shifting its efforts toward the Studebaker plants in Detroit, Wobbly organizing materials continued referring to Ford as the "Speed-Up King" and, according to Philip S. Foner, it remained "common knowledge" that an IWW strike was planned for Ford's Highland Park plant in early 1914. Russell, "The Coming of the Line,: 41–43; Peterson, *American Automobile Workers*, 108–109;

Esch, *The Color Line and the Assembly Line*, 37–38. In 1913, Ford's turnover rate was estimated to be approximately 370%, which translated into hiring some 52,000 workers to maintain a workforce of about 13,600 and cost the Company more than $1.8 million. Meyer, *Five Dollar Day*, 83–84.

13 "Workers Get $10,000,000 of Ford's Profits This Year"; "Ten Thousand Men in Rush to Share Ford's Profit Plan"; "First Payment of Ford's Bonus to Come Friday"; Mirola, *Redeeming Time*; Carter, *Union Made*; Wilkins and Hill, *American Business Abroad*.

14 The extent to which Ford's plan was actually a profit-sharing program (in contrast to a minimum wage plan, a bonus, or a one-time dividend distribution) was much debated at the time with questions oriented on the promotional use of "profit sharing" in contrast to "bonus" or "dividend." This debate may have been why one Ford executive referred to the Company policy as a "so-called profit sharing system." Lee, "The So-Called Profit Sharing System in the Ford Plant." For more on various journalistic references to the plan, see e.g. "Ten Thousand Men in Rush to Share Ford's Profit Plan"; "Ford Plan Not for His Rivals"; "Would Curb Foundation." In a 1916 study, the US Department of Labor's Bureau of Labor Statistics reported that it was more accurate to refer to Ford's plan as a "bonus plan commonly known as profit sharing" because "it can not be said that there is an immediate relation between the net profits of the business and the amounts distributed to employees under the plan." To be clear, the report only refers to this plan as "Plan No. 2," but a careful analysis of the details of this plan evinces it to be Ford's. Emmet, "Profit Sharing in the United States," 94. Historians have also debated the question, with some concluding the Five Dollar Day was more akin to a minimum wage plan while others insisting it was "undeniably a profit-sharing plan." Meyer, *Five Dollar Day*, 110. These distinctions (profit-sharing vs. bonus vs. dividend) matter as, among other things, markers of differential power relations, fiscal policy, and legal regulations and requirements. I do not intend to uncritically reproduce such confusions, but I have nonetheless elected to maintain the use of the terms "profits" and "profit sharing" in reference to Ford's Five Dollar Day program, primarily because this is what the vast majority of Company documents and press reports use. For statements about the plan's standards, see Bryan, *Henry's Lieutenants*, 207; Ford, *My Life and Work*, 127–128; "Statement of Henry Ford," United States Commission on Industrial Relations, 1915, p. 1, Acc. 62, Box 6, THF.

15 Nevins and Hill report that 90% of the newspaper comment was favorable. Nevins and Hill, *The Times, The Man, The Company*, 534. See also "The Resplendent Ford Gift"; "Ford Factory Again Stormed by Job Seekers"; "Ford's Eyes Opened By Man Who Stole." It was not until at least the late 1920s that the strongest critiques of Ford were issued from the left. Upton Sinclair's later writing on Ford describes how "a furious controversy arose—on the one side labor and the social uplifters, on the other side manufacturers, businessmen, and the newspaper editors who voiced their point of view. The former said that

Henry Ford was a great thinker, a statesman of industry; the latter said that he was a self-advertiser, a man of unsound mind, a menace to the public welfare." Sinclair, *The Flivver King*, 28. For more on early leftist support of Ford, see Roediger, "Americanism and Fordism," 243; Watts, *People's Tycoon*, 192–194; Nye, *America's Assembly*, 98–102.

16 "Henry Ford Explains Why He Gives Away $10,000,000"; Snow, *I Invented the Modern Age*, 215.

17 William Klann, *Reminiscences*, pp. 138, 141, Owen W. Bombard Interview Series, Acc. 65, THF; Meyer, *Five Dollar Day*, 173; "Socialism Urged by Woman in Auto"; "Second I.W.W. in Highland Park"; Russell, "The Coming of the Line," 41. On IWW organizing and religious formation, see Callahan, "Wobbly Religion."

18 Tarbell, "Making Men at Ford's," 4–5. Tarbell's observations and interviews from the Ford plant first appeared in print in a series of magazine articles. Soon thereafter Tarbell decided to compile her research on Ford into a book. It was at this point that she corresponded at length with Marquis, including asking for feedback on the typescript cited here and which survives in the Marquis papers at Cranbrook Academy. While it is not clear how much advice or assistance the Ford executive offered Tarbell directly in response to this particular request, Marquis and Tarbell were college friends who corresponded often. No response from Marquis from this particular round of correspondence appears to have survived, and Tarbell's book on Ford never came to print. However, Tarbell did eventually get much of her writing on Ford published. Her book, *New Ideals in Business* (1917), mostly reprinted many of her earlier magazine articles. More substantively, a generous portion of what Tarbell initially sent Marquis in the "Making Men at Ford's" typescript was included in her autobiography, *All in the Day's Work*. See also Baker, "Editor's Table," 5; Letter from Tarbell to Marquis, 12 May 1916, Box 8, Folder 3, SSM; Letter from Tarbell to Marquis, 20 Jan 1916, Box 1, Folder 4, SSM; Coir, "The Gospel of Work"; Tarbell, "The Golden Rule in Business," 38, 73; Tarbell, *New Ideals in Business*, 127–129, 224–225.

19 Marquis, *Henry Ford*, 153–154; Marquis, *The Man*, 4. See also Box 8, Folder 4, SSM.

20 Lee, "The So-Called Profit Sharing System in the Ford Plant," 299; Nevins and Hill, *The Times, The Man, The Company*, 526.

21 Ford, *My Life and Work*, 93, 127.

22 Ford, *Ford Ideals*, 29–30; "Henry Ford Explains Why He Gives Away $10,000,000"; "Ten Thousand Men in Rush to Share Ford's Profit Plan."

23 Ford, "Why I Believe in Progress," 688. See also Vertical File—Ford, Henry—Philosophy of Business/Industry, 1920s, THF.

24 "Henry Ford Explains Why He Gives Away $10,000,000"; Snow, *I Invented the Modern Age*, 215. The automaker also earned himself the nickname "mad socialist" during this period. Alvarado and Alvarado, *Drawing Conclusions on Henry Ford*, 43. For more on the populist influences of Ford's Five Dollar Day, see Watts, *People's Tycoon*, 182–187.

25 Ford, *My Life and Work*, 116, 121; *365 of Henry Ford's Sayings*; Ford, "Why I Believe In Progress," 689; Gregory, *The Unintended Reformation*, 235–297.

26 Samuel Marquis, YMCA Address, 17 May 1916. Box 8, Folder 4, SSM.

27 Ford, *My Life and Work*, 95, 120; Ford, "Statement of Henry Ford," p. 9, United States Commission on Industrial Relations, 1915, Acc. 62, Box 6, THF.

28 "Henry Ford Explains Why He Gives Away $10,000,000"; *Factory Facts from Ford*, 55. For similar assertions, see *Helpful Hints and Advice to Employes*, 3; "A Brief Account of the Educational Work of the Ford Motor Company," 12 December 1916, Vertical File—Ford Motor Company—Sociological Department, THF.

Despite Ford's disavowal of paternalist institution-building or philanthropic giving, it is worth noting that he did set up many independent vocational and trade schools. Henry and Clara Ford also helped fund institutions like Berry College. It may be that, like all historical subjects, Ford's inconsistency is a product of human complexity or hypocritical pretense. It may also be that the structure of gender relations Ford accepted and relentlessly managed enabled him to admit paternalism when the subjects to care for were young women, since the funds Ford supplied for Berry College were expressly for the "Girls' School." Alternatively or additionally, there may have been some differences between Henry Ford and the Ford Motor Company's approach to allocating funds in contrast to Clara Ford's approach, and indeed, Clara Ford was a crucial figure in the Berry College relation. Even as publicity around the Fords' contributions to Berry College often emphasized its largess, Martha Berry, the School's founder and namesake, emphasized the limitations and drawbacks of their help. She noted that the gift and the buildings the Fords help the College construct had proven to be "a great burden" for two reasons. The first was that other possible donors seemed to think that the school had less need of their contributions after having received the support of the Fords. The second reason was that the new buildings for which Ford earmarked his funds were, in actuality, considerably beyond what the school really needed and could afford, particularly because the elaborate new spaces necessitated more extensive maintenance and upkeep. In correspondence with friends and supporters, Berry explained: "we need help more than ever before, because our expenses are greater than ever before," and acknowledged that the buildings built by Ford "are really more expensive than I should have liked to have had." Berry complained confidentially that in reality she felt the school suffered from the so-called Ford-boom and pleaded for others to acknowledge that Ford's gift was not an endowment. See Letters from Martha Berry to Anna W. Hollenback (22 Jan 1930), Elizabeth Preston (25 Feb 1930), Mary E. Smith (24 Jan 1930), Albert Shaw (22 Jan 1930), and Marion Jackson (18 Jan 1930), *Martha Berry Digital Archive*, https://mbda.berry.edu/. According to an editorial published in the *Atlanta Constitution* at the urging of Martha Berry, Ford's gift to Berry College was in accordance with the industrialist's "insistence that his philanthropies shall not take the form of charities and gratuities, but that they shall be stimulants to emulation and larger endeavors. He plants to produce more. He eschews endowments. . . . Not perceiving or remembering these personal traits of Mr. Ford a mistaken view of his superb contribution of more than a million dollars to the Berry schools has accompanied the publicity of it, and the erroneous view does a wrong to both Mr. Ford and the schools." "A Gift and a Challenge."

29 "A Brief Account of the Educational Work of the Ford Motor Company"; Ford, *My Life and Work*, 128; "Statement of Henry Ford," 1.

30 *Factory Facts from Ford*, 65; *The Ford Industries*, 47; "Ten Thousand Men in Rush to Share Ford's Profit Plan"; Ford, *My Life and Work*, 128.

31 *Factory Facts from Ford*, 57–59.

32 Lee, *The So-Called Profit Sharing System in the Ford Plant*, 302; Ford, "Statement of Henry Ford," 2. After Samuel Marquis took over leadership of the department in 1915, he maintained Lee's approach. See, e.g., Marquis, YMCA Address.

33 "Map of the City of Detroit: Showing Routes, Advisors, and Approximate Number of Employes in Each District," July 1917, Acc. 572, Box 31, THF; *Factory Facts from Ford*, 43; On the role of police and prison officials, see letter from Christopher E. Stein, "Comments by a Probation Office," A.C. Tait, "Human Interest Story, Number Five," A.E. Gruenberg, "The Results of the Ford Profit-Sharing Plan in its Relation to the Police Department" and Gruenberg, "Progress Among Foreigners Since the Proclamation of Profit Sharing Plan," *Profit-Sharing Plan Testimonials*, Acc. 1018, Box 1, THF. W.M. Purves, another member of the Ford Sociological Department, reported that "doctors, lawyers, and business men of the city are willing to cooperate with an investigator at all times." Purves, "The Investigators' Standing with Employees and Others," *Profit-Sharing Plan Testimonials*, Acc. 1018, Box 1, THF. See also Letter from John Gillespie to Marquis (3 Dec 1914) and Letter from James P. Ramsay to Marquis (29 May 1916), Box 1, Folder 3–4, SSM.

34 "Mr. Lee's Talk to the First Group of Investigators," 15 April 1914, *Profit-Sharing Plan Testimonials*, Acc. 1018, Box 1, THF. For more on accounting and surveying practices in American religious history, see Brekus, "Writing as Protestant Practice," 19–34; Bateman, "Making a Righteous Number," 57–85. My early thinking about the religious work of Ford's Sociological Department investigators benefited from conversations with Shari Rabin, whose study of statistics and demography offers a valuable comparison to Ford's corporate missions and religious reckoning. Rabin, "Let Us Endeavor to Count Them Up." On the value of preaching to the choir in histories of evangelical conversion, see Pellegrini, "Signaling Through the Flames."

35 Bryan, *Henry's Lieutenants*, 206. For a lucid overview of Marquis's social gospel bona fides before, during, and after his time with Ford, see Coir, "The Gospel of Work."

36 "The Ford Idea in Education," Box 8, Folder 7, SSM; "Hints to the Investigator," Box 8, Folder 6, SSM.

37 "Henry Ford Explains Why He Gives Away $10,000,000."

38 Wisehart, "Henry Ford Talks to Young Men," 158; Albion, *Quotable Henry Ford*, 60; Douglas, *Purity and Danger*, 7. Historians of religion have ably demonstrated that concern about dirt and other apparent personal and social pollutants were of central import to the manifold moral reformers and missionaries of Ford's day and beyond. See, for example, Klassen, *Spirits of Protestantism*; Promey, "Hearts and Stones"; Callahan et al., "Allegories of Progress"; Fessenden, *Culture and Redemption*, 137–160; Albanese, *A Republic of Mind and Spirit*, 171, 396; Griffith, *Born Again Bodies*; Rosen, *Preaching Eugenics*; Satter, *Each Mind a Kingdom*; Curtis, *A Consuming Faith*; Winston, *Red Hot and Righteous*; Abzug, *Cosmos Crumbling*, 19–20; 163–182; Hutchison, *Errand to the World*, 107–108.

39 Ford, "Looking Under the Human Hood," 10; Callahan et al., "Allegories of Progress."

40 Marquis, *The Man*, 2–4; Ford, "Looking Under the Human Hood," 10. Ford regularly published or reissued short talks, pamphlets, and booklets to distribute throughout the Company. Marquis's "Talk" was published as a Company imprint in 1912, approximately two years prior to the implementation of the Ford profit-sharing plan and its attendant sociological initiatives.

41 Gramsci, "Americanism and Fordism," 285.

42 *Helpful Hints and Advice to Employes*, 7–8, 13; *Factory Facts from Ford*, 49.

43 "Ford Sociological Work," 81–82; "A Brief Account of the Educational Work of the Ford Motor Company," 11–12; Ford, *My Life and Work*, 187; Ford, *To You*, 2. For statements about "existing" versus "living": A.E. Gruenberg, "Human Interest Story, Number 12" and caption to picture number 425, *Profit-Sharing Plan Testimonials*, Acc. 1018, Box 1, THF.

44 Ford, *My Life and Work*, 129; Lewchuk, "Men and Monotony," 843–845; Tone, *Business of Benevolence*, 140–181.

45 Ford, "Machinery, The New Messiah," 363; Ford, *My Life and Work*, 123. Also quoted in May, "The Historical Problem of the Family Wage," 414.

46 Ford, *Today and Tomorrow*, 151, 154–155.

47 "Ford Sociological Work: The Making of Men and Homes," 81, 83; *Factory Facts from Ford*, 51.

48 "Ford Says He Reads Bible Every Day"; Ford, *The Case Against the Little White Slaver*, 77. On Ford as Prohibitionist, see correspondence about Ford Motor Company employees working with Jason H. Davis, Federal Prohibition Director, Royal E. Decker, Field Head and Asst. Director, John R. McDonald, Group Chief of Federal Prohibition Agents, and Louis Chamberlain, Federal Prohibition Agent. Acc. 572, Box 27, THF. Highland Park, where Ford's factory was located, also passed a resolution in 1916 supporting the passage of a state dry law. "Suburb, Goes on Record for Prohibition."

49 Brown, "Henry Ford Says, 'There Is Always Room for More,'" 154; Shaw, "Reminiscences," pp. 45–46, 49–50, Owen W. Bombard Interview Series, Acc. 65, THF; Barton, "It Would Be Fun to Start Over Again," 8. Although Ford also experimented with cornstalks and watermelon, Ford's most successful and prolific

engagement with industrialized agriculture was his promotion of soy-based products—from salad dressing, soy milk, and feed for livestock to textiles for men's suits and oils and plastics for automobile parts. When used for foodstuffs, the industrialist advocated for soy as a "scientifically controlled" product of both the carefully sanitized laboratory and modern manufactory, and argued for its cultivation as a way to better address limitations of the global food supply. Ford News Bureau, Untitled press release and "Saga of the Soybean," Acc. 536, Box 119, Press Releases-Uncategorized, THF; "I Believe in Reincarnation."

50 Norman Beasley, "The Commonest Thing We Do, We Know Least About: An Interview with Henry Ford Upon a Subject of Great Importance to Everyone," *Redbook Magazine*, n.d., Vertical File—Ford, Henry—Philosophy of Life, THF; Ralph Welles Keeler, *The Physical Life in Spiritual Conquest*, Henry Ford Imprints, Acc. 1023, Box 4, THF.

51 *Factory Facts from Ford*, 41.

52 Beasley, "Keep Interested and Stay Fit," 52; *Factory Facts from Ford*, 14; *Helpful Hints and Advice to Employes*, 17; "Henry Ford Explains Why He Gives Away $10,000,000"; Samuel Marquis, "The Factory Doctor," 12 Jun 1916, Box 8, Folder 4, SSM.

53 H.S. Ablewhite, "Reminiscences," 95, Owen W. Bombard Interview Series, Acc. 65, THF; Feld, "Salvage Teaches Ford Ship-Breaking Trade"; *The Ford Industries*, 40–41; Stengs, "Sacred Waste"; Chidester, "The Accidental, Ambivalent, and Useless Sacred"; Paine, "Sacred Waste"; "Characterizing Material Economies of Religion in the Americas," special issue of *MAVCOR Journal* (fall 2022), https://mavcor.yale.edu.

54 *The Ford Industries*, 41; Ford, *My Life and Work*, 3, 107; Egon Erwin Kisch, "At Ford's Place in Detroit," *Paradies Amerika* (Berlin: Aufbau-Verlag, GmbH, 1929/1994), which is translated from German and quoted in full in Skaff, "Ambivalence and Cigarettes," 119–131. On Ford's changing employment policies regarding disabled workers: Rose, *No Right to Be Idle* and cf. Meyer, *Five Dollar Day*, 99.

55 Ford, *My Life and Work*, 184.

56 Ford and Samuel Crowther, "Henry Ford Looks at Industry," *The American Automobile*, December 1929, Vertical File—Ford, Henry—Philosophy of Business/Industry, 1920s, THF; Loizides, "'Making Men' at Ford," 116; Bates, *The Making of Black Detroit*, 51–53. Racist stereotypes about ethnic and racial capabilities were institutionalized and incorporated in many ways during this time. In addition to entrance exams, corporations were known to make use of other techniques developed within the emerging social scientific fields. For instance, in the 1920s, the Central Tube Company in Pennsylvania charted ethnic groups with different kinds of jobs and working conditions, suggesting that "the best ethnic groups for either 'hot and wet' and 'hot and dry' jobs are (in no particular order) Hungarians, Austrians, Russians, Black Americans, and Chinese." Writing in 1940, Lloyd H. Bailer also described conversations with industry officials who "stated that Negroes can stand more heat and have better stamina on arduous jobs." Notably,

the sentiment was not uncommon, but it was also not universal. The analyst noted that others "point out that the above reasoning is reversed in causation. Negroes are found in the hot and arduous jobs because they can secure nothing else, not because they are by nature better fitted to endure these conditions." Foote et al., "Arbitraging a Discriminatory Labor Market," 529–530.

57 Foote et al., "Arbitraging a Discriminatory Labor Market," 494, 510, 519, 524.

58 Bates, *The Making of Black Detroit*, 51; Ford, *My Life and Work*, 5, 10, 257, 278.

59 Loizides, "'Making Men' at Ford," 114; Bates, *The Making of Black Detroit*, 51–52; Esch, *The Color Line and the Assembly Line*.

60 Loizides, "'Making Men' at Ford," 114; Bates, *The Making of Black Detroit*, 51–52; Esch, *The Color Line and the Assembly Line*; Nevins and Hill, *Expansion and Challenge*, 540.

61 "Human Interest Stories," "Mr. Lee's Talk to the First Group of Investigators," and "'The Investigators' Standing with Employees and Others," *Profit-Sharing Plan Testimonials*, Acc. 1018, Box 1, THF. A copy of this book can also be found in Box 8, SSM. On North Americans' missionary efforts, see Hutchison, *Errand to the World*; Klassen, *Spirits of Protestantism*; McAlister, *The Kingdom of God Has No Borders*; Curtis, *Holy Humanitarians*; Kaell, *Christian Globalism at Home*; Kaloyanides, *Baptizing Burma*; Hulsether, *Capitalist Humanitarianism*.

62 Weisenfeld, *New World A-Coming*; Meyer, *Five Dollar Day*, 153–156; "Human Interest Story, Number Nine," (by F.W. Andrews) and "Human Interest Story, Number Thirty-Eight," (by M.G. Torossian), *Profit-Sharing Plan Testimonials*, Acc. 1018, Box 1, THF. Roediger, *The Wages of Whiteness* and *Working Toward Whiteness*; Roediger and Esch, *The Production of Difference*; Esch, *The Color Line and the Assembly Line*. On the construction of whiteness in the late nineteenth- and early twentieth centuries, see, e.g., Jacobson, *Special Sorrows* and *Whiteness of a Different Color* and *Barbarian Virtues*; Painter, *History of White People*; Dees, "Whiteness."

63 Human Interest Story, Number Nine," (by F.W. Andrews) and "Human Interest Story, Number Thirty-Eight," (by M.G. Torossian), *Profit-Sharing Plan Testimonials*, Acc. 1018, Box 1, THF. Meyer, *Five Dollar Day*, 154.

Little else is known about Kectcheli, but based upon the specificity of Torossian's testimony in regard to the worker's fez and trousers, it might well be possible that Kectcheli was once or had been for a time a member of the Moorish Science Temple (MST), whose members were well-known throughout the city at the time for proudly donning harem pants and turbans or fezzes. Indeed, as Judith Weisenfeld writes in her study of the MST, "the red fez became trademark attire for male members of the MST" (*New World-A-Coming*, 122). Weisenfeld's study of the religio-racial functions of fashion and dress among MST members reveals how the special significance of wearing a fez went far beyond a marker of membership, serving as a central way that members claimed a connection to ancient wisdom, internalized and performed a new sense of sacred history, geography, and identity, and publicly and proudly embraced one's

Moorish American religio-racial self-fashioning. MST members were enjoined theologically and culturally to wear their fez proudly and, in turn, be blessed by Allah. While some members did receive special dispensations for things like military service, a decision to entirely "put aside" such ritual garb, as the Ford investigator reported, would have been a significant transformation for a MST member, indeed. Weisenfeld, *New World A-Coming*, 120–124.

64 "A Brief Account of the Educational Work of the Ford Motor Company," 10–11; Arnold and Faurote, *Ford Methods and the Ford Shops*, 56–59; *Factory Facts from Ford*, 51, 53; "Better Workmen and Citizens," *Ford Times* (Feb 1917): 315–317, 319; Shaw, "Reminiscences," 26–27, 31, 35–38, 46; *Helpful Hints and Advice to Employes*, 31–32; Watts, *People's Tycoon*, 213.

65 "Better Workmen and Citizens," 315–318.

66 "A Brief Account of the Educational Work of the Ford Motor Company," 10; "A Motto Wrought in Education," 407, 409; "Better Workmen and Citizens," 318. For more on Americanization efforts during this period, see e.g., Bogardus, *Essentials of Americanization* (1919), which attested to the racial program of Americanization and argued for the importance of an "average American" centered on ideals governed by the "Pilgrim Fathers" of colonial and US history. The same year, *Ladies Home Journal* published an article by Esther Everett Lape, "Putting America into Your Village," which urged "native Americans" to take up "Americanization as a job instead of debating it as a problem," and insisted upon sanitation as central to that work. Lape's article was preceded by an "official letter of endorsement from the U.S. Secretary of the Interior, Franklin K. Lane." In the same magazine issue, Mary Graham Bonner authored a story, entitled "A Real Piece of Americanization: Why Mr. Angelo Patri's School Has a Running Start in a National Task," about an Americanization program in the Bronx.

67 "The Making of New Americans," 151–152; "A Motto Wrought in Education," 409. For published letters written by Ford English School graduates, see "The Ford School," 1, along with several letters that were included in Part IV of the Sociological Department testimonials book, pages 172–185 (some of which were, ironically, translated from other languages). See *Profit Sharing Plan Testimonials*, Acc. 1018, Box 1, THF.

68 According to one tally by the Company, in 1913, before the introduction of the Five Dollar Day at the Highland Park plant, more than 50,000 workers quit, requiring Ford to hire 52,445 new laborers just to maintain a workforce of approximately 14,000. One year into the new profit-sharing plan, the Company hired just over 14,000 men to keep a significantly larger workforce of about 20,000. During the following year (1915), corporate reports counted only 2,931 workers who had left their jobs. Marquis, YMCA Address, 4–5l; Lewchuk, "Men and Monotony," 824–856.

69 Several of Ford's certificates of membership in the Masonic brotherhood, honorary election as a brother in Zion Lodge, No. 1, and conferral of multiple craft degrees are located in Ford's personal papers. Fair Lane Papers, Acc. 1, Folder 13, Box 193, THF. See also Nye, *Henry Ford*, 96; Lacey, *Ford*, 7.

70 Bennett, *We Never Called Him Henry*, 125; Albanese, *Republic of Mind and Spirit*, 51–52, 124–136; Logan, *Awkward Rituals*, 21–48. Forms of Masonry were certainly far more diverse than the elite white men that Ford and his ilk represent. Though rarely recognized as "true" Freemasonry by white Masons, communities excluded from such brotherhoods along with other white civic associations—including Black, female, and indigenous communities—also used Masonic traditions as a site of self-fashioning, mutual aid, and resistance to and collective action against white, Protestant settler colonial practices. Prince Hall Masons are among the most well-known of these groups. Hackett, *That Religion in Which All Men Agree*.

71 Logan, *Awkward Rituals*, 23, 31–33, 48. If Harry Bennett, the rough-and-ready strongman who later headed up Ford's Service Department, is to be believed, Freemasonry was one way that Ford publicly signaled his anti-Catholic credentials. According to Bennett, Ford was initially displeased about his eldest grandson and namesake, Henry Ford II, converting to Catholicism under the guidance of the famous television bishop, Fulton Sheen, prior to Ford II's marriage to his first wife, Anne McDonnell. However, the Company founder grew especially angry when news reporter and radio commentator Walter Winchell suggested that the elder Ford might also convert to Catholicism. In Bennett's telling, Ford responded to Winchell's charge by delving more deeply and intentionally into Freemasonry. When leaving to perform initiation rites at the Masonic Temple in Detroit, Ford reportedly told Bennett cheerfully, "I'm going down to take care of Winchell," and, at least in Bennett's words, "once Mr. Ford was a thirty-third-degree Mason, he felt better about the whole thing." Bennett, *We Never Called Him Henry*, 126. Consideration of Masonic initiation rites offers one way to understand Ford's turn toward Freemasonry in the wake of Winchell's charge. In contrast to the wrong ritualism of Henry Ford II's Catholic conversion, Ford asserted his advanced civility in Masonic degree.

72 Burroughs's final trip was in 1920 when he invited the group to the Catskills and his famous Slabsides retreat. The octogenarian died the following spring. Press coverage really amped up during the years 1921 and 1924 when Presidents Warren G. Harding and Calvin Coolidge, respectively, joined the Vagabonds on their excursions. Despite Ford's complaints about the camping trips attracting too much attention, he initiated the first major publicity stop during the group's 1919 trip by autographing the cornerstone of a new Ford plant in Troy, New York, an event that drew significant crowds and reporters. For the same trip, Ford also outfitted the Model Ts they used to better accommodate supplies for their increasingly lavish caravan, including cooking supplies for both Ford's and Firestone's chefs who accompanied the group. During a subsequent trip, one truck was outfitted with a refrigerator and another hauled a piano, along with a large dining table. According to Burroughs, the group was "a luxuriously equipped expedition going forth to seek discomfort." Ford, *My Life and Work*, 240; Burroughs, "Our Vacation Days of 1918," Book Collection, Object ID: 64.167.13.32, THF, www.thehenryford.org. *Into the Wild*, exhibit at Edison and Ford Winter Estates, Fort Myers, FL; Watts,

People's Tycoon, 259–265. "Thomas Sato on 'Vagabonds' Camping Trip, Maryland 1921," Photographic Vertical Files Series, Object ID: 84.1.1660.P.34.1921.218, THF, www.thehenryford.org; Firestone, *Men and Rubber*, 188–237. On muscular Christianity, see Putney, *Muscular Christianity*.

73 *Fair Lane: The House and Gardens*; Wianecki, "When America's Titans Went Road-Tripping Together." On nostalgia and the ambivalent relationship between technology and nature, see Marx, *Machine in the Garden*.

74 Ford, *My Life and Work*, 239; Nye, *Henry Ford*, 106.

75 Emerson, *English Traits*, 50–78; Baldwin, *Henry Ford and the Jews*, 47; Painter, *History of White People*, 151, 165–189.

76 Importantly, Link's project demonstrates that the emerging discourse of "Fordism" appealed not only to the increasingly popular fascist forces of the far right in both Weimer and Nazi Germany, but also to those on the left, including significant leaders in Soviet Russia. This is among Link's crucial contributions to historiography on Fordism and one to which my own research in Ford's archive confirms. As the following chapter considers in greater length, Ford appealed to crusaders across the nation and around the globe, which Link describes as illiberal or postliberal radicals (both left and right), based in part on the form of producerism that Ford personified and institutionalized. This notion of a populist form of prosperity routed through industrial producerism, which Ford advanced, is central to the concepts of a rite-to-work religion and supersessionary secularism that I describe in this and the following chapter. Link, *Forging a Global Fordism*, 65–68, passim. On Gottl's notion of Fordism as "white socialism," see also Nolan, *Visions of Modernity*, 57.

77 Gramsci, "Americanism and Fordism," 285; Lears, "The Concept of Cultural Hegemony." My thinking here is further influenced by questions posed in a different register by Berlant in *Cruel Optimism*. Berlant interrogates the promises and attachments that have worn on us if not entirely worn us out—those cruelly optimistic desires that are actually obstacles to our flourishing—including attachments to capitalism's promises of growth and abundance, among other things.

78 The language of "ordinary and extraordinary" power echoes Catherine Albanese's "short description of religion," which has been influential in my thinking. However, I am less interested in reproducing Albanese's "working definition" than I am in acknowledging how Ford helps us better understand how such a powerful orientation has been put to work historically. Albanese, *America*, 6.

79 Gramsci, *Prison Notebooks*, 358.

80 Bourne, "Trans-national America."

3. CAPITAL SERVICE AND FORD'S SUPERSESSIONARY SECULARISM

1 "The Unveiling of Henry Ford," 102.

2 Latour, *We Have Never Been Modern*, 10–12.

3 By some accounts, the proposal of a European excursion was first offered in jest by Lochner. But Ford, always attuned to breezy simplicity and promotional possi-

bility, was taken with the idea. Many in the planning committee opposed the idea at the outset. This narrative of Ford's peace planning at the intersections of irony, opposition, and idealism offers a snapshot of how the event played out. See, e.g., Nevins and Hill, *Expansion and Challenge*, 28–29; Lewis, *Public Image of Henry Ford*, 79–80; Alvarado and Alvarado, *Drawing Conclusions on Henry Ford*, 48–49, 51; Brinkley, *Wheels for the World*, 194–198.

4 "The Ford Excursion"; "Peace Hysteria"; Alvarado and Alvarado, *Drawing Conclusions on Henry Ford*, 45–75 (especially 56–57).

5 Lewis, *Public Image of Henry Ford*, 80; Watts, *People's Tycoon*, 232; Alvarado and Alvarado, *Drawing Conclusions on Henry Ford*, 54–55, 69.

6 Brinkley, *Wheels for the World*, 198. For more on the peace talks after Ford's departure, see Lochner, "The Neutral Conference for Continuous Mediation at Stockholm," 238–241.

7 "Ford Explains Attacks." Some in the press later suggested that Schwimmer was not only largely accountable for the failure of the peace project but also responsible for Ford's increasingly virulent antisemitism. The attribution too quickly ascribes to Ford's own narrative of the voyage. What is more, Ford had issued a number of public diatribes against Jewish people prior to the Peace Ship debacle. For example, more than seven months before Ford announced his commission of *Oscar II*, he proclaimed his anti-war position in a populist accent that signaled antisemitic connotations common in his day. "Moneylenders and munitions makers cause wars," he claimed, "if Europe had spent money on peace machinery—such as tractors—instead of armaments there would have been no war . . . The warmongerers urging military preparedness in America are Wall Street bankers . . . I am opposed to war in every sense of the word" (Baldwin, *Henry Ford and the Jews*, 48). For her part, Schwimmer appealed to Ford years later, asking him to help clear her name in the press, as she struggled to survive economically and to obtain US citizenship. It is not clear whether her letters and personal appeals through friends ever reached Henry Ford. Ford's secretary, Ernest Liebold, flatly and repeatedly refused to help her in any way. Baldwin, *Henry Ford and the Jews*, 161, 247–249. For additional, extended accounts of the Peace Ship excursion, see also Brinkley, *Wheels for the World*, 194–198; Alvarado and Alvarado, *Drawing Conclusions on Henry Ford*, 65–75; Watts, *People's Tycoon*, 226–235, 383; Baldwin, *Henry Ford and the Jews*, 54–66; Nevins and Hill, *Expansion and Challenge*, 26–54; Lewis, *Public Image of Henry Ford*, 78–92.

8 "Ford Explains Attacks."

9 Ford, *International Jew*, 39–40. The movie industry was a favorite site of critique against Jews for Ford. In the second volume of *The International Jew*, an entire chapter was given over to "Jewish Supremacy in the Motion Picture World," and is emphasized again in his chapter on "Jewish Control of the American Theater." Ford, *Jewish Activities in the United States*, 89–99, 127–136.

10 Zito, "Religion Is Media." The newspaper's circulation fluctuated widely from some 26,000 to well over 650,000. The effect of Ford's antisemitic articles in the

paper has been a matter of considerable debate. Some Ford employees insisted that the articles increased circulation. Others have pointed toward informal boycotts during times of low circulation to suggest the opposite. David Lewis has studied the circulation records of the *Dearborn Independent* in significant detail, along with distribution of its various spin-offs, including *The International Jew.* He concluded that the articles may have boosted sales for short periods of time but "had little lasting effect" (141). Lewis instead found the circulation changes to be partly a result of changing economic circumstances in the country more broadly and partly a result of experimental subscription campaigns on behalf of Ford Motor Company. Solicitation of subscriptions for the newspaper were a matter of considerable distributional creativity, including direct sales from newsstands and by agents of the Dearborn Publishing Company as well as through quota requirements for Ford dealers and even sales through schools and churches. Ford dealers often resented their role in the venture and sometimes rolled annual subscription prices into the cost of the automobiles they were in business to sell, though it was a practice that the Company cautioned against. There are many letters in the Ford archives from both disgruntled dealers and annoyed car buyers. Lewis, *Public Image of Henry Ford*, 135–159; Acc. 572, Boxes 2, 6, 8, and 10, Acc. 62, Box 52, Acc. 1, Box 122; Acc. 536, Boxes 117–118, THF.

11 "Dodges Sue Henry Ford"; "Ford Denies Recklessness"; "Henry Ford on Stand."

12 "Dodges Sue Henry Ford"; "Newspaper Specials"; *Dodge v. Ford.*

13 "Ford Makes Reply to Suit Brought by Dodge Brothers"; Nevins and Hill, *Expansion and Challenge*, 97; Ford, *My Life and Work*, 162; *Dodge v. Ford* at 505.

14 "Building the American Economy," *Ford Sunday Evening Hour*, radio show script, Acc. 474, Box 4, THF; "Transcription of *Dodge v. Ford*: Cross-Examination of Henry Ford," 532, 544; Ford, *My Life and Work*, 162, 265; Nevins and Hill, *Expansion and Challenge*, 99–100.

15 *Dodge v. Ford* at 508; "Ford Must Declare $19,275,385 Dividend"; "Henry Ford Beaten in $60,000,000 Suit"; "Ford Loses Dodge Bros. Profit Suit"; "Ford's Plans Are Held Up"; Vargas, "*Dodge v. Ford Motor Co.* at 100."

16 "Ford's Plans Are Held Up"; *Dodge v. Ford* at 507; Vargas, "*Dodge v. Ford Motor Co.* at 100"; Stout, "Why We Should Stop Teaching *Dodge v. Ford*"; Unkovic, "When *Dodge v. Ford* meets Ben & Jerry's"; "Ford Must Declare $19,275,385 Dividend"; Nevins and Hill, *Expansion and Challenge*, 104. On the controversy of *Dodge v. Ford*'s commentary as dicta, see Stout, "Why We Should Stop Teaching *Dodge v. Ford*," 163–176; Macey, "A Close Read of an Excellent Commentary on *Dodge v. Ford*"; Henderson, "Everything Old in New Again"; Vargas, "*Dodge v. Ford Motor Co.* at 100," fn28.

17 Ford, *My Life and Work*, 162; Nevins and Hill, *Expansion and Challenge*, 111–113. Ford remained privately held by the family until 1956, some nine years after Henry Ford died.

18 Meyer, *Five Dollar Day*; Norwood, *Strikebreaking and Intimidation*, 171–193; Esch, *The Color Line and the Assembly Line*, 51–116. For one manager's account of

Forditis and the general fear and nervousness provoked by the Company's labor regime, see "Reminiscences of Logan Miller," pp. 16, 18–22, 42–44, Owen W. Bombard Interview Series, Acc. 65, THF.

19 Norwood, *Strikebreaking and Intimidation*, 171, 187; Esch, *The Color Line and the Assembly Line*, 65, 84.

20 McLaughlin et al., "Why Scholars of Religion Must Investigate the Corporate Form," 15.

21 Moreton, *To Serve God and Wal-Mart*; Kruse, *One Nation Under God*; Grem, *Blessings of Business*; Hammond, *God's Businessmen*; Kirk, *Wanamaker's Temple*; Dochuk, *Anointed with Oil*.

22 Ford, *My Life and Work*, 161–162.

23 Ford, *My Life and Work*, 161, 163–164.

24 Ford, *My Life and Work*, 164, 193–194; Albion, *Quotable Henry Ford*, 56; "Henry Ford Discusses the Wage."

25 "Ford Decries Debt of Credit System."

26 Ford, *My Life and Work*, 140, 194.

27 Ford, *Today and Tomorrow*, 14; Ford, *My Life and Work*, 140, 241–242.

28 The primary and most thoroughgoing exception to the otherwise unanalyzed connection between "service" and "work" in Ford's production is Link, *Forging Global Fordism*.

29 Lewis, *Public Image of Henry Ford*, 135; Nevins and Hill, *Expansion and Challenge*, 124; Bryan, *Beyond the Model T*, 101.

30 The *Protocols* was a text that claimed to be an ancient transcript of teachings for Jews about how to enslave non-Jewish populations and plot a new world order, free of Christianity. This notorious fabrication, a text first published in Russian in the late nineteenth century, apparently came to Ford's attention through Ernest Liebold. Beginning in the 1920s, boycotts and public denouncements of Ford's antisemitic articles occurred regularly. President Harding advised Ford to stop publishing his articles, and in 1923, both Clara Ford's and Edsel Ford's names were removed from the paper's front page. A year later, the controversial nature of the publication was further heightened when a freelance journalist named Robert Morgan wrote an article about farming cooperatives in California. In it he referred to these cooperatives as a Jewish monopoly scheme organized in connection with "international banking rings" and "Jewish international bankers." The article identified Aaron Sapiro as the man heading up these "Jewish combinations" and suggested that Sapiro was attempting to put non-Jewish wheat farmers out of business. Sapiro sued Ford for libel, and the case went to trial in federal court in March 1927. The case was ultimately ordered a mistrial and was settled out of court. Central to that settlement was Ford's agreement to issue a public apology to Sapiro and for the antisemitic statements of his newspaper. For more on the trial and its consequences, see Woeste, *Henry Ford's War on Jews and the Legal Battle Against Hate Speech*.

31 Ford, *Ford Ideals*, 5–6. For more on the production of "Mr. Ford's Page," see Fred Black, "Reminiscences," p. 15, Owen W. Bombard Interview Series, Acc. 65, THF.

32 Ford, *Ford Ideals*, 5–6, 144–148.

33 Lewis, *Public Image of Henry Ford*, 114.

34 *Ford Animated Weekly*, FC-3–6, FC-40–41, FMCC; Lewis, *Public Image of Henry Ford*, 114–115.

35 *Ford Educational Weekly*, FC-2461, 2465–2467, 2478–2484, FMCC; Lewis, *Public Image of Henry Ford*, 115. For more on Ford's early film production: Johnson, *Rhetoric, Inc*; Grieveson, "The Work of Film in the Age of Fordist Mechanization" and "Visualizing Industrial Citizenship," 107–123. Two catalog guides to the Ford film collections at the National Archives have also been published; see Bray, *Guide to the Ford Film Collection in the National Archives* and Stewart, *Henry Ford's Moving Picture Show*.

36 Grieveson, "Work of Film in the Age of Fordist Mechanization," 28. Ford's concern about the Jazz Age was not only expressed in his film production. Ford similarly sought to counter such trends through print production on music and dance. One year before Ford closed the Dearborn Publishing Company, he published a book on "old-fashioned" dance with musical scores, instructions, and calls for the floor manager, as a way to help popularize dances like the quadrille, lancer, minuet, square, and contra dances. These kinds of dances, Ford said (in contrast to the Charleston and its ilk), constituted "the Art of Dancing at its traditional best," with "rhythm of movement, beauty of pattern, the spirit of play, and grace of deportment." Ford sought to initiate a "revival" of these "traditional" and "old-fashioned" dances in a style that "best fits with the American temperament." Ford also suggested a racialized connection to "northern peoples" in this text. Henry and Clara Ford, *"Good Morning,"* 9.

37 Grieveson, "Work of Film in the Age of Fordist Mechanization," 28n19; *Ford Educational Library*, FC-194, FC-483, FC-495, FC-2426, FC-2483, FMCC. Based on my research, Ford's use and reuse of previous film for this new series can be seen, e.g., in footage on the manufacturing practices of the meatpacking industry, which were compiled in a *Ford Educational Weekly* (1919) titled "Cutting Up," and then used again in another Ford Educational Library production, as number 29 in the series, "Industrial Geography of United States," under the title "Meat Packing." This latter film is not dated, but I estimate that it was produced between two and three years later (c.1922). *Ford Educational Library*, FC-192–193, and *Ford Educational Weekly*, FC-2465, FMCC.

38 *Ford Educational Library*, FC-198, FMCC.

39 *Ford Educational Library*, FC-486, FMCC.

40 For more on these publications and translations, see correspondence between Ford's secretary, Ernest Liebold, and the automaker's ghostwriter, Samuel Crowther, in Acc. 572, Box 4, THF.

41 Central to the reading practices Baldwin identifies are Ford's engagement with William Holmes McGuffey's school readers. Baldwin also places Orlando J. Smith's book, *A Short View of Great Questions*, as formative to Ford's antisemitism. Baldwin, *Henry Ford and the Jews*, 1–19.

42 Masuzawa, *The Invention of World Religions*; Chidester, *Savage Systems*.

43 For more on questions of religion, race, and nation, as constructed in talk about religious freedom, see Wenger, *Religious Freedom*. On legal structures (namely statutes about libel and/versus hate speech) as they relate to group rights in this period and to Henry Ford specifically, see Woeste, *Henry Ford's War on Jews and the Legal Battle against Hate Speech*. On the discursive history of religious freedom, see, e.g., Jakobsen and Pellegrini, *Love the Sin* and *Secularisms*; Sullivan, *The Impossibility of Religious Freedom*, Wenger, *We Have a Religion*; Sehat, *The Myth of American Religious Freedom*; Hurd, *Beyond Religious Freedom*; McCrary, *Sincerely Held*.

44 Samuel Crowther, "Henry Ford and the Jews," pp. 1–3, typescript, Acc. 572, Box 2, THF. The other books published with this same title are Lee, *Henry Ford and the Jews* (1980) and Baldwin, *Henry Ford and the Jews* (2001).

45 Crowther, "Henry Ford and the Jews," 3–6.

46 Crowther, "Henry Ford and the Jews," 8–10; Ford, *My Life and Work*, 251.

47 Crowther, "Henry Ford and the Jews," 8. For more on Ford's connections to Nazi Germany, see, e.g., Link, *Forging Global Fordism*, 51–89, 131–171, passim; Baldwin, *Henry Ford and the Jews*, 172–191, passim; Lewis, *Public Image of Henry Ford*, 135–159; Brinkley, *Wheels for the World*, 263, 448–451; Watts, *People's Tycoon*, 376–397.

48 Link, "Rethinking the Ford-Nazi Connection," 136, 139, 150; Link, *Forging Global Fordism*, 55, 68.

4. HARROWING HISTORY AND FORD'S RUN-OF-THE-MILL RELICS

1 Freeberg, *The Age of Edison*, 306; Tye, *The Father of Spin*, 64–67; Lewis, *Public Image of Henry Ford*, 224–225; Hamilton, "The Ford Museum," 773. On "jubilee" as a stabilizing force and way to reproduce existing forms of sovereignty in a political economy: Singh, "Debt Cancellation as Sovereign Crisis Management."

2 Ford, *Edison as I Know Him*, 13–14, 26.

3 "Edison Re-Creates His Electric Lamp as Hoover Leads in Tribute to Him."

4 "Edison Re-Creates His Electric Lamp as Hoover Leads in Tribute to Him"; *Looking Forward Through the Past*, pp. 2–3, Acc. 1023, Henry Ford Imprints, Box 4, THF; Wheeler, "Fight to Disarm His Life Work, Henry Ford Vows"; Barnard, "Ford Builds a Unique Museum."

5 "Our Schools and What They Stand For," *Herald* 7.7 (26 April 1940): 1, Periodical Collection, Object ID: 2015.0.45.1, THF www.thehenryford.org; Upward, *A Home for Our Heritage*, 77–78; *Looking Forward Through the Past*, 18, 40–41; Woolf, "Mr. Ford Shows His Museum"; "Ford Cars Grow Up by Magic Methods"; Lewis, *Public Image of Henry Ford*, 54. On Ford's reproduction of Victorian ideology about "separate spheres": May, "The Historical Problem of the Family Wage"; Loizides, "Families and Gender Relations at Ford"; Watts, *People's Tycoon*, 296–317.

Classroom space in actual school buildings at Greenfield Village was supplemented with spaces in other buildings, including the Town Hall, the Clinton Inn, and several of the homes on the site. On Ford and the educational field:

Swigger, *"History is Bunk,"* 49–50; Wik, *Henry Ford and Grass-Roots America,* 203. In addition to the McGuffey School, Ford later added a log cabin purported to be the birthplace of William Holmes McGuffey, who was an educational icon for the auto-industrialist. "McGuffey belongs in the calendar of our national prophets," a Ford executive pronounced during a radio broadcast of the *Ford Sunday Evening Hour.* "He is honored at Dearborn because moral principles became educational essentials under his system." Among the inaugural documents of Ford's collection were McGuffey's *Eclectic Readers.* Ford eventually gathered over 450 copies and 145 different editions of McGuffey's texts. In addition to this, Ford collected many other McGuffey "relics," including a replica of the man's study table from Miami University of Ohio. Early McGuffey manuscripts and letters were among the earliest artifacts archived in Ford's museum. Cameron, "McGuffey Readers"; Upward, *A Home for Our Heritage,* 2.

6 *Looking Forward Through the Past,* 40–41; Ford excavated several items from Edison's New Jersey laboratory in 1928 and gathered them together as part of his "Menlo Park Relics." Among those that remain in Ford's collection: a light bulb, laboratory vial, bicycle lamp, multiple pipes, fragments of cooking and condiment vessels, a jug, as well as fragments of unknown use. See Object IDs: 29.3018.300 through 29.3018.309, THF, www.thehenryford.org. This is to note only an exceedingly small portion of the material initially excavated. Ford's guide, which was distributed to guests at the Jubilee, reported that excavation at the original New Jersey location "yielded enough equipment and other relics to fill a large-sized room" and included "a great many of the electric bulbs used prior to the successful experiment." For additional use of the language of relic by Ford and his observers, see: "Edison Laboratory Relics from Menlo Park, New Jersey, on Display in Greenfield Village, October 27, 1929" (Object ID: P.188.42281) and "'Mute Relics' Sign Used in Greenfield Village on an Early Exhibit Case Outside Menlo Park Laboratory" (Object ID: 29.3018.299), Edison Institute Records, THF, www.thehenryford.org; Henry A. Haigh, "Important Historical Relics Lately Added to the Ford Collections at Dearborn," *Michigan History Magazine* (Summer-Autumn), 1937, Acc. 6, Edsel B. Ford Office Papers, Object ID: 64.167.6.31, THF, www.thehenryford.org. On relic as a concept in the study of religion: Schopen, "Relic," 256–268. On the sacred status of relics and their secularization: Barnett, *Sacred Relics.* Reasons some observers offered for Ford's historical preservation projects referred to emotional exuberance and unenlightened absurdity. See, e.g., Selden, "Ford Renews the Past for a Machine Age." Ford's confidents also sought to counter such critiques. See, e.g., Crowther, "Henry Ford's Village of Yesterday." Other scholars have approached similar concerns about the colonial heritage of analytic categories in the study of religion. Notable is the work scholars have done to de/construct the concept of "fetish" as it was produced and wielded in frontier zones: Latour, "Fetish-Factish," 42–49; Meyer, "An Author Meets Her Critics," 205–254.

7 Van Vlissingen, "History is Bunk"; Barnard, "Ford Builds a Unique Museum"; *Looking Forward Through the Past,* 41.

8 Bryan, *Henry's Attic*, 17; Barnard, "Ford Builds a Unique Museum"; Chidester, "Reflections on Imitation," 151. On "presence" in the study of religion: Orsi, *History and Presence*; Meyer, "An Author Meets Her Critics." I have benefited in my thinking from Pamela Klassen's sharp and generous response to Meyer's work and have offered my own related critiques amid an enduring appreciation for both Orsi's and Meyer's contributions. "Comments by Pamela Klassen"; Curts, "What 'in the world' Is Theory?" and "Review of *History and Presence* by Robert A. Orsi."

9 Swigger, *'History is Bunk'*; "Edison's Last Breath," Test Tube, 1931, Object ID 51.13.51.3. THF, www.thehenryford.org. Notably, the Edison Institute was not Ford's first historical project. It was an elaboration upon and extension of earlier collecting and preservation practices. Among the most prolific of these early iterations was his purchase and development of the Wayside Inn and its surrounds in Sudbury, Massachusetts, which served as an historical showcase and "working model" for Ford's later preservation efforts in Dearborn. One historian has suggested that the Wayside Inn area was a "pilot project," inaugurating an era of American preservation efforts (e.g., Colonial Williamsburg) and one that "profoundly affected historical guardianship in the United States" since it was "the first place where an individual, possessing all the money needed, set out to restore and put on display not just one famous building, but a sizeable, functioning community of homes, farms, schools, craft industries, chapel, and village tavern—with the purpose, as Ford stated, 'to show how our forefathers lived and to bring to mind what kind of people they were.'" Butterfield, "Henry Ford, the Wayside Inn, and the Problem of 'History is Bunk,'" 60, 65–66.

10 "Edison Re-Creates His Electric Lamp"; Simonds, *Henry Ford and Greenfield Village*, 141–142; Watts, *People's Tycoon*, 401–402. On Edison's nickname, see advertisements from Edison phonograph distributors, including East Liverpool, Ohio, *Evening Review*, January 15, 1917. After Edison's death, the nickname stuck. See, e.g., John Black's "The Man Who Lighted the World," published in various newspapers by way of *Bell Syndicate*.

11 Simonds, *Henry Ford and Greenfield Village*, 139–140, 155; Ford, *Edison as I Know Him*, 11, 51; "Edison Young Again as He Relives Past in Old Laboratory"; Swigger, "History is Bunk," 40–41; *Guidebook for the Edison Institute Museum and Greenfield Village*, 8.

12 Bryan, *Henry's Attic*, 17; "Edison Re-Creates His Electric Lamp"; "Edison Young Again"; Ford, *Edison as I Know Him*, 50; Program for Dinner in Honor of Thomas Alva Edison, Light's Golden Jubilee, 21 October 1929, Object ID: EI.52.2, Edison Institute Records, THF, www.thehenryford.org.

13 "Edison Re-Creates His Electric Lamp"; Watts, *People's Tycoon*, 402; O'Dell, "Light's Golden Jubilee." On religion, media events, and ritual participation, see: Hoover and Clark, *Practicing Religion in the Age of the Media*; Hangen, *Redeeming the Dial*; Walton, *Watch This*; Frederick, *Colored Television*. On Ford's use of radio in the years following the Jubilee broadcast: Fones-Wolf, "Creating a Favorable Business Climate," 221–255.

14 Associated Court Reporters, "Stenographic Report of Proceedings of Light's Golden Jubilee at Dearborn, Michigan, October 21, 1929," Light's Golden Jubilee Records, Object ID: EI.52.32, THF, www.thehenryford.org; "Edison Re-Creates His Electric Lamp."

15 Smith, *Things Said/Things Done*, 2, 6, 16; Ford, *Edison as I Know Him*, 22, 51; Taylor, *The Archive and the Repertoire*, 13, 28–29; *Looking Forward Through the Past*, 24–28.

16 Taussig, *Mimesis and Alterity*, xiv, 2, 22, 45–48, 54–59; Frazer, *The Golden Bough*, 22, 32; Associated Court Reporters, "Stenographic Report of Proceedings of Light's Golden Jubilee at Dearborn, Michigan, October 21, 1929." The magic of modernity to which I refer also draws on Bruno Latour's notion of modernity's double asymmetricality. Latour's study not only helpfully points to the Janus face of the modern but also describes how "modernity was not an illusion, but an active performing." The Jubilee performance helped activate and animate anew the modern project Ford sought to preserve and replicate. Latour, *We Have Never Been Modern*, 144. My thinking on modernity is further influenced by scholars of American religious history who have taken up related concerns about the dual temporality of modern production in past-making practices. These histories have tended to orient on groups who sought to reform the present through a return to the so-called primitive church or apostolic order. Similar themes have likewise been taken up in studies of the Pentecostal movements of the twentieth century as well as the shared modernity of the so-called Fundamentalist-Modernist Controversy. See, e.g., Butler et al., *Religion in American Life*, 201–210; Wacker, *Heaven Below*; Lofton, "The Perpetual Primitive in African American Religious Historiography," 171–191; Lofton, "Commonly Modern," 137–144.

17 Ford, *Edison as I Know Him*, 50, 57, 61; Frazer, *Golden Bough*, 54–55; *Guidebook for the Edison Institute Museum and Greenfield Village*, 6.

18 "Hoover, Ford, and Nation Honor Edison"; Schneider, *Performing Remains*, 8–11.

19 Taussig, *Mimesis and Alterity*, 113, 116, 125; Wheeler, "Fight to Disarm His Life Work."

20 Taussig, *Mimesis and Alterity*, 113; Levene, "Sources of History," 93; Ernest Liebold, "Reminiscences," part 2, p. 890, Owen W. Bombard Interview Series, Acc. 65, THF. On "history" in the study of religion, see also: Smith, *Imagining Religion*, 19–35; Levene, "Courses and Canons in the Study of Religion"; Lofton, "Why Religion is Hard for Historians"; Lofton, "Religious History as Religious Studies"; Walker, "The Humbug in American Religion."

21 "Ford is an Anarchist." The Ford-*Tribune* trial would become one of the era's ever-proliferating "trials of the century." It like others of the era (especially the Scopes Trial) had all the tropes of a show trial that one has come to expect—including the rural setting, massive media presence, divergent casting of folksy everyman (Ford) and urbane sophisticate (McCormick), sensational courtroom testimony, and the headline-grabbing verdict (in which Ford won but was awarded only six cents, total). Ford's performance renewed his folksy persona as a man of the

people with an awe-shucks kind of understanding and a straight-talkin' style. For more on the trial, see Watts, *People's Tycoon*, 266–269 as well as correspondence sent to Ford in Acc. 62, Box 5, THF.

22 Liebold, *Reminiscences*, part 2, 890; McCormick, "Ford Seeks a New Balance for Industry"; *Guidebook for the Edison Institute Museum and Greenfield Village*, 5.

A brief etymological review of the word "bunk" is helpful in contextualizing Ford's use. The term was a form of slang newly popular in the United States in the twentieth century and was adopted as a synonym for "humbug" or "nonsense." An abbreviation of a longer set of related colloquialisms from the nineteenth century, it harkened to the earlier term, "Buncombe" (later spelled "bunkum"). Buncombe is the name of a county in North Carolina, and the phrase "to Buncombe" or "to make a speech for Buncombe" emerged amid debate in the Sixteenth U.S. Congress about whether to officially admit the state of Missouri as a free or slave state. The meeting had been a long and drawn-out affair, so when Felix Walker, the member from Buncombe, rose to speak, his fellow congressmen begged him to stop so they could call for a vote. Walker insisted on making a prolonged speech, proclaiming that the people of his district expected as much and that he was duty-bound "to make a speech for Buncombe." The event soon became proverbial, and was adopted as a kind of Washingtonian expression (not unlike how, later in the century, attaching "-gate" to any scandal harkened to that seemingly originary one, Watergate). The new phrase took several forms—to talk to or speak for Bunkum; to pass for Buncombe; or to make a bid for Buncombe. By the mid-nineteenth century, it had become a common saying in reference to unnecessary, nonsensical speaking and, especially, as political clap-trap, a "political speaking or action not from conviction, but in order to gain the favour of electors, or make a show of patriotism, or zeal." Drawing upon this etymological ancestry while helping reinvent its enunciation, Ford's comment about history as "more or less bunk" brings with it an idiomatic innovation and implicit critique, rendered through his contrarian response to military preparedness. In Ford's assertion, history too often carried with it a tradition of pandering patriotism, something the industrialist endeavored to eschew in his gestures toward speech suffused in more straight-talking populist candor. According to the *Oxford English Dictionary*, Henry Ford's use of the word in 1916 is among the earliest usages of the term, and is catalogued in the OED as its second iteration, listed after the dictionary's citation of G. Ade's 1900 use of the term from *More Fables*: "He surmised that the Bunk was about to be Handed to him." *Oxford English Dictionary*, s.v.v "bunk" and "Buncombe / Bunkum."

23 Barnard, "Ford Builds a Unique Museum"; McCormick, "Ford Scans the Current Tides."

24 Woeste, *Henry Ford's War on Jews and the Legal Battle Against Hate Speech*, 261, 298; *Statement by Henry Ford: Regarding Charges Against Jews Made in His*

Publication; "Ford Summer Hour," Program for Sunday, August 24, 1941, General Personal Records Series, Object ID: 64.167.23.58, THF, www.thehenryford.org.

25 "Ford Summer Hour," Object ID: 64.167.23.58, THF, thehenryford.org; *A Dependable Supply of Distinctive Brazilian Hardwoods: From the Ford Plantation in the Amazon Jungle* (New York: Cooney, Eckstein and Company, Inc, 1933), p, 2, Acc. 38, Charles E. Sorensen Office Files and Personal Records, Object ID: 64.167.38.5, THF, thehenryford.org.

26 Curts, "Fordlândia." For more on Ford's Brazilian plantations and rubber interests: Galey, "Industrialist in the Wilderness," 261–289; Grandin, *Fordlandia*; Wilkins and Hill, *American Business Abroad*; Wolfe, *Autos and Progress*.

27 Upward, *A Home for Our Heritage*, 11; McCormick, "Ford Seeks a New Balance for Industry."

28 Barnard, "Ford Builds a Unique Museum"; Leo E. Landis, "Harrows and Much More: An Uncommon Collection of Common Things," *The Henry Ford*, January 2004, www.thehenryford.org. Ford's agricultural implements, including especially his collection of plows and harrows, were frequently commented upon. See, for example, "Old Plows Added to Ford's Relics"; *Guidebook for the Edison Institute Museum and Greenfield Village*, 10.

29 Swigger, *"History is Bunk,"* 68; Upward, *A Home for Our Heritage*, 93; Simonds, *Henry Ford and Greenfield Village*, 148–149. According to Charles R. Smith Jr., one of the young guides for the Edison Institute in its early years, he was "paid in tomatoes" while working on the farm in the village. During his time as a guide in the museum, Smith noted that in addition to guiding visitors through the space, students also helped service the machinery Ford acquired, helping bring them in, clean them, and get them "put in working order." Smith also worked in the village, mainly in either the post office or the carding mill areas. Upward, *A Home for Our Heritage*, 74–77.

30 Crowther, "Henry Ford's Village of Yesterday"; Kaempffert, "The Mussolini of Highland Park." Crowther's authorized rendering, including entire phrases, was replicated in Barnard's later article, "Ford Builds a Unique Museum." See also: Ford, *Today and Tomorrow*, 225; Bryan, *Clara*, 203; Lacey, *Ford*, 239.

31 Upward, *Home for Our Heritage*, 50; Simonds, *Henry Ford and Greenfield Village*, 155.

32 Woolf, "Mr. Ford Shows His Museum"; Van Vlissingen, "The Idea Behind Greenfield."

33 Blivens, "Mr. Ford Collects"; Letter from Ralph S. Euler to Charles T. Newton, Box 1, Charles Tyler Newton Papers, Bentley Historical Library, University of Michigan.

34 "What Our Schools Are Doing," 2, 12; "Walt Disney Shows Harriet Bennett How to Draw Mickey Mouse during a Visit to Henry Ford Museum" (12 April 1940), Photograph Vertical File Series, Object ID: P.188.27455, THF, www.thehenryford.org; "Signed portrait of Walt Disney posing in Greenfield Village Tintype Studio" (12 April 1940), Greenfield Village Tintype Studio Photographs, Object

ID: 91.0.44.51, THF, www.thehenryford.org; "Walt Disney on High-Wheel Safety Bicycle, with Daughter in Henry Ford Museum" (20 August 1943), General Photographs Series, Object ID: P.833.78482.5, THF, www.thehenryford.org; "Tintype of Walt Disney and Ward Kimball at Greenfield Village Tintype Studio" (23 August 1948), Greenfield Village Tintype Studio Photographs, Object ID: 91.0.44.52, THF, www.thehenryford.org; Cynthia Reed Miller, "Walt Disney Visits Henry Ford's Greenfield Village," *The Henry Ford Pic of the Month*, September 2005, www.thehenryford.org; Grandin, *Fordlandia*. On Disney and Ford, see also: Watts, *The Magic Kingdom*, 157–158; Gabler, *Walt Disney*, 186, 332; Berkowitz, *Mass Appeal*, 140–141; Smoodin, *Disney Discourse*, 3. On Disney and his populist politics and educational projects: Clague, "Playing in 'Toon'"; Watts, "Walt Disney."

35 Crowther, "Henry Ford's Village of Yesterdays"; Van Vlissingen, "The Idea Behind Greenfield"; Trine, *Power That Wins*, 31–32.

36 Wortham-Galvin, "The Fabrication of Place in America"; Crowther, "Henry Ford's Village of Yesterday"; Wood, *The New England Village*, 2; Wood, "'Build, Therefore, Your Own World'"; Swigger, *"History is Bunk,"* 39–40; Watts, *People's Tycoon*, 411; Upward, *A Home for Our Heritage*, 26.

37 Simonds, *Henry Ford and Greenfield Village*, 199; Swigger, *"History is Bunk,"* 46–48; Upward, *A Home for Our Heritage*, 43. Postville's citizens were not the only Americans who found Ford's extraction of local historic buildings upsetting. For other instances of outrage at Ford's extraction practices, see, e.g., Letter from Liebold to Lloyd E. Warren, 26 December 1929, Acc. 572, Box 4, THF; "Assails Ford Plan to Buy Virginia Site"; "Hint that Ford Seeks Bridge Splits County"; "Cape Cod Resents Ford Taking Mill." For more on Cutler's process of dismantling and rebuilding historic structures, including help by laborers from local Ford factories, see Upward, *A Home for Our Heritage*, 108.

38 Simonds, *Henry Ford and Greenfield Village*, 204; *Guidebook for the Edison Institute Museum and Greenfield Village*, 33–34; Swigger, *"History is Bunk,"* 85. On the Lincoln Rocker: "With Liberty and Justice for All" Exhibit, Object ID: 29.1451.1, THF, www.thehenryford.org.

39 Swigger, *"History is Bunk,"* 58–59, 85–86; "Hermitage Slave Quarters," originally built ca. 1820, on exhibit at Greenfield Village in Porches and Parlors District, Object ID: 34.779.1, THF, www.thehenryford.org; *Guidebook for the Edison Institute Museum and Greenfield Village*, 34; "Civil War Period," *Ford Educational Library*, FC-295, FMCC. More recent interpretations and marketing materials of these structures emphasize how rarely brick was used for housing enslaved workers and that the Hermitage Plantation used brick "because brick-making was an important industry" on the plantation. Michelle Andonian, "Hermitage Slave Quarters in Greenfield Village, September 2007," Object ID: 2008.171.640, THF, www.thehenryford.org.

40 Simonds, *Henry Ford and Greenfield Village*, 200–201; Swigger, *"History is Bunk,"* 47, 73; *Guidebook for the Edison Institute Museum and Greenfield Village*, 32; Upward, *A Home for Our Heritage*, 91; Van Vlissingen, "The Idea Behind Greenfield."

After the chapel was constructed, Ford ordered five other replicas of it to be constructed in various places around the country. Upward, *A Home for Our Heritage*, 45. According to one reporter, Ford's preference for Georgian style was "because it combines architectural characteristics of both the Northern and Southern Colonies." Barnard, "Ford Builds a Unique Museum."

41 Van Vlissingen, "The Idea Behind Greenfield"; *Looking Forward Through the Past*, 42–44.

42 "Portrait Rug of Henry Ford," 1935, Object ID: 35.100.1; "Portrait Rug of Thomas Edison," 1935, Object ID: 35.100.2, THF, www.thehenryford.org. For additional items sent to Ford, now included in collections at The Henry Ford, see, e.g., "Diorama Featuring Henry Ford and Ford Automobile," c1935 (Object ID: 00.1510.176); "Diorama Featuring Seven Stages of the Cross, Gift to Henry Ford," c1940 (Object ID: 00.1510.177); "Appliqued Wall Hanging, Birthday Gift to Henry Ford," c1939 (Object ID: 00.1510.37); "American Pride Quilt by Zemma Haynes Taylor," 1932–1933 (Object ID: 33.361.1); "Cameo Portrait of Henry Ford in Presentation Case," c1920–1940 (Object ID: 00.1510.174); "Bedcover with V-8 Symbol, Gift to Henry Ford," c1930–1940 (Object ID: 00.1510.43); "Carved Portrait of Henry Ford," 1926 (Object ID: 27.312.1); "Embroidered Pillow, Gift to Henry Ford," c1925–1935 (Object ID: 00.1510.25); "Hand Carved Shelf Clock, Gift to Henry Ford," 1928 (Object ID: 30.742.1); "Handmade Scrollwork Frame with Portrait of Henry Ford," 1938 (Object ID: 00.1510.17); "Hooked Rug, Gift to Henry Ford," 1927 (Object ID: 27.308.1); "Hand Carved Walking Stick Presented to Henry Ford," 1928 (Object ID: 00.1510.20); "Miniature Plow Created from Rifle, Presented to Henry Ford," 1917 (Object ID: 17.1.1); "Heart Shaped Pillow, 'The Ford is the Heart of the Automobile World,' Christmas Gift to Henry Ford," 1930 (Object ID: 00.1510.26.1); "Tapestry Portrait, Gift to Henry Ford," c1920–1940 (Object ID: 00.1510.31); "Shadow Box, Birthday Gift to Henry Ford," 1930 (Object ID: 2000.0.47.1); "Portrait of Henry Ford in Sculptural Folk Art Frame," c1920–1940 (Object ID: 91.0.46.1); "Needlework Portrait of Henry Ford," c1930–1940 (Object ID: 00.1540.1); "Painting on Turtle Shell, Presented to Henry Ford," 1933 (Object ID: 33.93.1), THF, www.thehenryford.org.

43 Sorensen, *My Forty Years with Ford*, 54.

44 My observations draw upon my visit to the Maker Faire in July 2013. The Henry Ford announced in January 2022 that it would be discontinuing its sponsorship of Maker Faire Detroit and cancelled the 2022 Civil War Remembrance event, typically held on Memorial Day weekend, which included live reenactments by nearly 1,000 soldiers, musicians, and other actors and staff. Both events had been suspended during the previous two years due to the COVID-19 pandemic. Later in 2022, The Henry Ford announced that it would be officially retiring the Civil War Remembrance program for "operational" reasons. Hightower, "The Henry Ford Ends Maker Faire Detroit, Pauses Civil War Reenactment"; Benavides-Colón, "Henry Ford Museum Retires Civil War Remembrance Program."

45 Horkheimer and Adorno, *Dialectic of Enlightenment*, 1, 3–4, 18. Concepts of secular enlightenment and religious spirit have long been joined together and expressed both in the trope of light and in scenarios of actual illumination. See, e.g., Becker, *Revival and Awakening*, 7; Schivelbusch, *Disenchanted Night*, 4, 28; Stolow and Meyer, "Enlightening Religion"; Koslofsky, "Offshoring the Invisible World?"

46 Taussig, *Mimesis and Alterity*, 49, 51–52, 57.

47 Taussig, *Mimesis and Alterity*, 57.

48 Taussig, *Mimesis and Alterity*, 66–67.

CONCLUSION

1 "*Detroit Industry*: The Murals of Diego Rivera," *National Public Radio* (22 Apr 2009), www.npr.org. For readings of the mural: Smith, *Making the Modern*, 199–246; Staudenmaier, "Two Technocrats, Two Rouges," 2–28; Kozloff, "The Rivera Frescoes of Modern Industry at The Detroit Institute of Arts," 58–63.

2 "The *Detroit Industry* Murals, Detroit Institute of Arts," United States Department of the Interior, National Parks Service, National Register of Historic Places Registration Form, NPS Form 10–900, OMB No. 1024–0018, Rev. 8–86, p. 7. See also Smith, *Making the Modern*, 231.

3 Heitmann, *The Automobile in American Life*, 87–91; Coale, "Influence of the Automobile on the City Church," 80–82; "Assistant Missionary in Albay," 519; "Ford Chapel is the Latest," *Fordson Farmer* (Oct 1922), Object ID P.O.3961, THF, www.thehenryford.org; Vargas, "Life and Community in the 'Wonderful City of the Magic Motor'," 59–60; Callahan, "Highway," and "Wobbly Religion," 335–355; *Across the Continent Twice in Three Weeks with a Model A Ford in Midwinter* (1927); *Around the World in an Automobile* (1907); Bedell, *Modern Gypsies* (1924); Copeland, *Overland by Auto in 1913* (1981); Fisher, *A Woman's World Tour in a Motor* (1911); Fitzgerald, *Cruise of the Rolling Junk* (1924); Furniss, *Automobile Tourist Book of New England* (1912); Van de Water, *The Family Flivvers to Frisco* (1927); "Nation Roused Against Motor Killings"; "Sacrifices to the Modern Moloch"; Roman Mars, "Episode 76: The Modern Moloch" *99% Invisible: A Tiny Radio Show about Design with Roman Mars* (4 April 2013), http://99percentinvisible.org. The archives of The Henry Ford include two copies of *The Negro Motorist Green Book*, one from 1937 and another from 1949. See Book Collection, Object ID: 92.150.9685 and Research Center Travel Literature Collection, Object ID: 87.135.1736, THF. See also press releases issued from John W. Thompson about "Christian faith and fellowship" meetings at Ford's Rouge plant and photographs of "rosary services" used by Ford's News Department, in Public Relations Research Library Catalogued Releases, Acc. 536, Box 88, Ford Motor Company Archives, THF.

4 Huxley, *Brave New World*, 23, 25, 29, 33–34, 44, 52, 54, 80–86, 90, 92, 110, 122, 153, 187, 191, 212–213, passim; Latour, *We Have Never Been Modern*, 10–12.

5 Curcio, *Henry Ford*, xiii–ix; Stewart et al., "The Businessman of the Century."

6 Brian Stokes Mitchell, Larry Daggett, and Ragtime Ensemble, vocal performance of "Henry Ford," cast recording, lyrics by Lynn Ahrens, music by Stephen Flaherty, recorded on April 28, 1998, Masterworks Broadway, compact disc.

7 Audra McDonald and Brian Stokes Mitchell, vocal performance of "Wheels of a Dream," cast recording, lyrics by Lynn Ahrens, music by Stephen Flaherty, recorded on April 28, 1998, Masterworks Broadway, compact disc.

8 Marquis, *Henry Ford*, 166. I drew methodological inspiration for this particular aspect of my "assemblage" approach from Harding, *The Book of Jerry Falwell*, and Lofton, *Oprah*, 14–15. See also Curts, "Temples and Turnpikes."

SELECTED BIBLIOGRAPHY

ARCHIVES AND MANUSCRIPT COLLECTIONS

Bentley Historical Library, University of Michigan, Ann Arbor, Michigan
    Charles Tyler Newton Papers, Americanization Committee of Detroit Papers
Cranbrook Academy Archives, Bloomfield Hills, Michigan
    Samuel Simpson Marquis Papers (Acc. 1983–07, Series I: Personal; Series VI: Ford
        Motor Company Welfare Department)
Florida Gulf Coast University Archives and Special Collections, Fort Myers, Florida.
    Acc. 02/01/18, Koreshan Collection, Publications 1892–1999
The Henry Ford, Benson Ford Research Center, Dearborn, Michigan, www.thehenry-
    ford.org
    Fair Lane Papers (Acc. 1), Edsel B. Ford Office Papers (Acc. 6), General Personal
        Record Series/Henry Ford Office Records (Acc. 23), Charles E. Sorensen Re-
        cords Series (Acc. 38), Records Moved to Engineering Laboratory in 1919 and
        Non-Automotive Interests and Activities Record Series (Acc. 62), Oral History
        Papers/Owen Bombard Interview Series (Acc. 65), John F. Dodge Estate Trust
        Lawsuit Collections (Acc. 96), Sociological Department Procedure Manuals
        (Acc. 280), Henry Ford Office Papers (Ac. 285), Ford Times and Dealer Pub-
        lication Department Records (Acc. 474), Press Releases Subseries (Acc. 536),
        Nevins and Hill Research, Original Documents and Notes (Acc. 572), Ford
        Motor Company Non-Serial Publication Collections (Acc. 951), Administra-
        tive Records Series (Acc. 1018), Henry Ford Imprints and Reprints Collection
        (Acc. 1023), Photograph Vertical Series (Acc. 1660), Vertical Files
National Archives, College Park, Maryland
    Ford Motor Company Collection

PUBLISHED SOURCES

365 of Henry Ford's Sayings. New York: P.M. Martin, 1923.
"6,000 Mob Ford Works." *New York Times*, January 10, 1914.
"10,000 Fight to Get Jobs: Form Line at 3 A.M. in Hope of Sharing Ford Millions."
    Washington Post, January 7, 1914.
Abzug, Robert H. *Cosmos Crumbling: American Reform and the Religious Imagination*.
    New York: Oxford University Press, 1994.
Across the Continent Twice in Three Weeks with a Model A Ford in Midwinter. Detroit,
    MI: Ford Motor Company, 1927.

Adams, Henry. *The Education of Henry Adams.* New York: Modern Library, 1946.

Agrama, Hussein Ali. *Questioning Secularism: Islam, Sovereignty, and the Rule of Law in Modern Egypt.* Chicago: University of Chicago Press, 2012.

Ahlstrom, Sydney E. *A Religious History of the American People.* 1972. New Haven, CT: Yale University Press, 2004.

Aitken, Hugh G. J. *Scientific Management in Action: Taylorism at Watertown Arsenal, 1908–1915.* 1960. Princeton, NJ: Princeton University Press, 1985.

Albanese, Catherine L. *America: Religions and Religion.* Fourth Edition. Belmont, CA: Thomson Wadsworth, 2007.

———. *Republic of Mind and Spirit: A Cultural History of American Metaphysical Religion.* New Haven, CT: Yale University Press, 2007.

———. *The Delight Makers: Anglo-American Metaphysical Religion and the Pursuit of Happiness.* Chicago: University of Chicago Press, 2023.

Albion, Michele Wehrwein, ed. *The Quotable Henry Ford.* Gainesville: University Press of Florida, 2013.

Aldrich, Mark. "On the Track of Efficiency: Scientific Management Comes to Railroad Shops, 1900–1930." *Business History Review* 84 (2010): 501–526.

Ali, Kecia and Lolo Serrano. "The Person of the Author: Constructing Gendered Scholars in Religious Studies Book Reviews." *Journal of the American Academy of Religion* 90.3 (2022): 554–578.

Alvarado, Rudolph and Sonya Alvarado. *Drawing Conclusions on Henry Ford.* Ann Arbor: University of Michigan Press, 2001.

Anidjar, Gil. "Secularism." *Critical Inquiry* 33, no. 1 (2006): 52–77.

Arnold, Horace Lucien and Fay Leone Faurote. *Ford Methods and the Ford Shops.* New York: The Engineering Magazine Company, 1915.

Around the World in an Automobile. New York: McLoughlin Brothers, 1907.

Asad, Talal. *Formations of the Secular: Christianity, Islam, Modernity.* Stanford, CA: Stanford University Press, 2003.

———. "Reflections on the Origins of Human Rights." Berkeley Center for Religion, Peace, and World Affairs, Georgetown University, July 17, 2013, www.youtube.com/watch?v=Vd7P6bUKAWs.

"Assails Ford Plan to Buy Virginia Site: Washington Society of Alexandria Feels State Has Been Affronted." *New York Times,* November 25, 1929.

"Assistant Missionary in Albay." *Ford Times* 9, no. 11 (1916): 519.

Aveni, Anthony F. "Time." In *Critical Terms for Religious Studies,* edited by Mark C. Taylor, 314–333. Chicago: University of Chicago Press, 1998.

Baker, Ray Stannard. "Editor's Table." *American Magazine,* February 1915.

Baldwin, Neil. *Henry Ford and the Jews: The Mass Production of Hate.* New York: Public Affairs, 2001.

Barnard, Eunice Fuller. "Ford Builds a Unique Museum." *New York Times,* April 5, 1931.

Barnett, Teresa. *Sacred Relics: Pieces of the Past in Nineteenth-Century America.* Chicago: University of Chicago Press, 2013.

Bartel, Rebecca C. *Card-Carrying Christians: Debt and the Making of Free-Market Spirituality in Colombia*. Oakland: University of California Press, 2021.

Bartel, Rebecca C. and Lucia Hulsether. "Introduction." Classifying Capital: A Roundtable. *Journal of the American Academy of Religion* 87.3 (2019): 581–595.

Barthes, Roland. *Mythologies*. 1972. New York: Hill and Wang, 2001.

Barton, Bruce. "It Would Be Fun to Start Over Again." *American Magazine* 91 (April 1921): 7–9, 121–124.

Bateman, Bradley W. "Making a Righteous Number: Social Surveys, the Men and Religion Forward Movement, and Quantification in American Economics." *History of Political Economy* 33 (2001): 57–85.

Bates, Beth Tompkins. *The Making of Black Detroit in the Age of Henry Ford*. Chapel Hill: University of North Carolina Press, 2012.

Baudelaire, Charles. "On the Heroism of Modern Life." Salon of 1846. In *Mirror of Art: Critical Studies by Baudelaire*, transl. Jonathan Mayne. Garden City, NY: Doubleday and Company, 1956.

Beasley, Norman. "Keep Interested and Stay Fit: An Intimate Interview with Henry Ford." *Psychology: Health, Happiness, Success* 1, no. 7 (November 1923): 7–9.

Becker, Adam. *Revival and Awakening: American Evangelical Missionaries in Iran and the Origins of Assyrian Nationalism*. Chicago: University of Chicago Press, 2015.

Bedell, Mary Crehore. *Modern Gypsies; The Story of a Twelve Thousand Mile Motor Camping Trip Encircling the United States*. New York: Brentano's, 1924.

Benavides-Colón, Amelia. "Henry Ford Museum Retires Civil War Remembrance Program." *Detroit News*, September 28, 2022.

Bender, Courtney. "American Reincarnations: What the Many Lives of Past Lives Tell Us about Contemporary Spiritual Practice." *Journal of the American Academy of Religion* 75, no. 3 (2007): 589–614.

———. *The New Metaphysicals: Spirituality and the American Religious Imagination*. Chicago: University of Chicago Press, 2010.

Bennett, Harry, with Paul Marcus. *We Never Called Him Henry*. New York: Fawcett Publications, 1951.

Benson, Allan. *The New Henry Ford*. New York: Funk and Wagnalls Company, 1923.

Bercovitch, Sacvan. *American Jeremiad*. Anniversary Edition. Madison: University of Wisconsin Press, 2012.

Berkowitz, Edward. *Mass Appeal: The Formative Age of the Movies, Radio, and TV*. New York: Cambridge University Press, 2010.

Berlant, Lauren. *Cruel Optimism*. Durham, NC: Duke University Press, 2011.

"Better Workmen and Citizens." *Ford Times*, February 1917.

Black, John. "The Man Who Lighted the World." *Monroe News-Star*, November 9, 1931.

———. "The Man Who Lighted the World." *San Bernardino County Sun*, November 9, 1931.

Blivens, Bruce. "Mr. Ford Collects." *The New Republic*, April 28, 1937.

Bogardus, Emory S. *Essentials of Americanization*. Los Angeles: University of California Press, 1919.

Bone, James. "A British Editor Learns Henry Ford's Views on War and Work." *Baltimore Sun*, November 17, 1940.

Bonner, Mary Graham. "A Real Piece of Americanization: Why Mr. Angelo Patri's School Has a Running Start in a National Task." *Ladies Home Journal* 36 (November 1919): 83, 130.

Bourne, Randolph S. "Trans-national America." *The Atlantic*, July 1916.

Bowler, Kate. *Blessed: A History of the American Prosperity Gospel*. New York: Oxford University Press, 2013.

Braden, Charles Samuel. *Spirits in Rebellion: The Rise and Development of New Thought*. Dallas, TX: Southern Methodist University Press, 1963.

Bray, Mayfield. *Guide to the Ford Film Collection in the National Archives*. Washington, DC: National Archives and Records Service, General Services Administration, 1970.

Brehm, Stephanie N. *America's Most Famous Catholic (According to Himself): Stephen Colbert and American Religion in the Twenty-First Century*. New York: Fordham University Press, 2019.

Brekus, Catherine A. "Writing as Protestant Practice: Devotional Diaries in Early New England." In *Practicing Protestants: Histories of Christian Life in America, 1630–1965*, edited by Laurie Maffly-Kipp, Leigh E. Schmidt, and Mark Valeri, 235–278. Baltimore, MD: Johns Hopkins University Press, 2006.

Brinkley, Douglas. *Wheels for the World: Henry Ford, His Company, and a Century of Progress, 1903–2003*. New York: Viking Penguin, 2003.

Brown, Raymond. "Henry Ford Says, 'There Is Always Room for More.'" *Popular Science Monthly* 106, no. 2 (February 1925): 37–39, 149–150, 152, 154.

Bryan, Ford R. *Henry's Lieutenants*. Detroit, MI: Wayne State University Press, 1993.

———. *Henry's Attic: Some Fascinating Gifts to Henry Ford and His Museum*. Ed. Sarah Evans. Detroit, MI: Wayne State University Press, 1995.

———. *Beyond the Model T: The Other Ventures of Henry Ford*. Detroit, MI: Wayne State University Press, 1997.

———. *Clara: Mrs. Henry Ford*. Detroit, MI: Wayne State University Press, 2001.

Butler, Jon, Grant Wacker, and Randall Balmer. *Religion in American Life: A Short History*. New York: Oxford University Press, 2003.

Butterfield, Roger. "Henry Ford, the Wayside Inn, and the Problem of 'History is Bunk.'" *Proceeding of the Massachusetts Historical Society*, Third Series 77 (1965): 53–66.

Callahan, Richard J. Jr. *Faith and Work in the Kentucky Coal Mines: Subject to Dust*. Bloomington: Indiana University Press, 2008.

———. "Highway." *freq.uenci.es: a collaborative genealogy of spirituality*, ed. Kathryn Lofton and John Lardas Modern. The Immanent Frame, Social Science Research Council, December 7, 2011, http://frequencies.ssrc.org.

———. "Wobbly Religion: Tactical Formations of Religious Idioms and Space in the Industrial Capitalist City." *Journal of the American Academy of Religion* 90.2 (2022): 335–355.

Callahan, Richard J. Jr., Kathryn Lofton, and Chad E. Seales. "Allegories of Progress: Industrial Religion in the United States." *Journal of the American Academy of Religion* 78, no. 1 (2010): 1–39.

Callender, Harold. "Gandhi Dissects the Ford Idea." *New York Times*, November 8, 1931.

Cameron, William J. "McGuffey Readers." *Ford Sunday Evening Hour*, March 17, 1935.

"Cape Cod Resents Ford Taking Mill; Officials and Business Groups Protest His Plan to Remove Landmark to Dearborn." *New York Times*, November 11, 1935.

Carter, Heath W. *Union Made: Working People and the Rise of Social Christianity in Chicago.* New York: Oxford University Press, 2015.

Casanova, José. "The Secular and Secularisms." *Social Research* 76, no. 4 (2009): 1049–1066.

Case, Theresa Ann. "Free Labor on the Southwestern Railroads: The 1885–1886 Gould System Strikes." PhD diss., University of Texas at Austin, 2002.

Caterine, Darryl. "The Haunted Grid: Nature, Electricity, and Indian Spirits in the American Metaphysical Tradition." *Journal of the American Academy of Religion* 82, no. 2 (2014): 371–397.

Cepero, Christina. "Ford's Link to Koreshan Strengthened." *News Press*, December 23, 2005.

Chaplan, Charles. *Modern Times.* Film. Charles Chaplin Productions, United Artists, 1936.

Chidester, David. *Savage Systems: Colonialism and Comparative Religion in Southern Africa.* Charlottesville: University Press of Virginia, 1996.

——. "Reflections on Imitation: Ethnographic Knowledge, Popular Culture, and Capitalist Economy." *Etnofoor* 22, no. 2 (2010): 139–153.

——. "The Accidental, Ambivalent, and Useless Sacred." *Material Religion* 10, no. 2 (2014): 239–240.

Clague, Mark. "Playing in 'Toon: Walt Disney's *Fantasia* (1940) and the Imagineering of Classical Music." *American Music* 22, no. 1 (2004): 91–109.

Coale, James J. "Influence of the Automobile on the City Church." *Annals of the American Academy of Political Science* 116 (1924): 80–82.

Cohen, Lizabeth. *A Consumers' Republic: The Politics of Mass Consumption in Postwar America.* New York: Vintage Books, 2003.

Coir, Mark. "The Gospel of Work: Henry Ford, Samuel Marquis, and the Five Dollar Day." In *The Model T Reconsidered: Proceedings from the World of the Model T Conference*, edited by Judith E. Endelman, 41–60. Dearborn, MI: The Henry Ford, 2008.

Cook, James W. *Arts of Deception: Playing with Fraud in the Age of Barnum.* Cambridge, MA: Harvard University Press, 2001.

Cooper, Irving S. *Reincarnation, The Hope of the World.* Los Angeles: Theosophical Publishing House, 1920.

Copeland, Estella M. *Overland by Auto in 1913: Diary of a Family Tour from California to Indiana.* Indianapolis: Indiana Historical Society Publications, 1981.

Crowther, Samuel. "Henry Ford's Village of Yesterday." *Ladies Home Journal* 45, no. 9 (September 1928): 10–11, 116, 118.

Curcio, Vincent. *Henry Ford*. New York,: Oxford University Press, 2013.

Curtis, Heather D. *Holy Humanitarians: American Evangelicals and Global Aid*. Cambridge, MA: Harvard University Press, 2018.

Curtis, Susan. *A Consuming Faith: The Social Gospel and Modern American Culture*. Columbia: University of Missouri Press, 2001.

Curts, Kati. "Shadowy Relations and Shades of Devotion." In *Sensational Religion: Sensory Cultures in Material Practice*, edited by Sally M. Promey, 113–133. New Haven, CT: Yale University Press, 2014.

———. "What 'in the world' Is Theory?" *Religious Studies Project* (July 3, 2014), www.religiousstudiesproject.com.

———. "Temples and Turnpikes in the 'World of Tomorrow': Religious Assemblage and Automobility at the 1939 New York World's Fair." *Journal of the American Academy of Religion* 83, no. 3 (2015): 722–729.

———. "Fordlândia." In *America in the World, 1776 to the Present: Dictionary of American History, Supplement*, edited by Edward J. Blum, Cara Burnidge, Emily Conroy-Krutz, and David Kinkela, 368–369. New York: Charles Scribner's Sons, 2016.

———. "Review of *History and Presence* by Robert A. Orsi." *Journal of Religion* 99.2 (2019): 254–256.

Curts, Kati and Alexandra Kaloyanides. "Characterizing Material Economies of Religion in the Americas: An Introduction." Essay, *MAVCOR Journal* 6, no. 3 (2022), doi: 10.22332/mav.ess.2022.8.

Dahlinger, John Côté. *The Secret Life of Henry Ford*. Indianapolis, IN: Bobbs-Merrill, 1978.

De Certeau, Michel. *The Writing of History*. New York: Columbia University Press, 1988.

Dees, Sarah. "Whiteness." In *Dictionary of American History, Supplement: America in the World, 1776 to the Present*, edited by Edward Blum, Cara L. Burnidge, Emily Conroy-Krutz, and David Kinkela, 1092–1097. New York: Charles Scribner's Sons, 2016.

Denny, Harold N. "Times Good, Not Bad, Ford Says: Sees the Dawn of a Bright Future." *New York Times*, February 1, 1933.

Derrida, Jacques. "Structure, Sign, and Play in the Discourse of the Human Sciences." In *Writing and Difference*, translated by Alan Bass, 351–370. Chicago: University of Chicago Press, 1978.

———. "Différance." In *Margins of Philosophy*, translated by Alan Bass, 1–28. Chicago: University of Chicago Press, 1982.

———. *Specters of Marx: The State of the Debt, the Work of Mourning, and the New International*, translated by Peggy Kamuf. New York: Routledge, 1993/1994.

———. *The Gift of Death and Literature in Secret*, 1999, translated by David Wills. Chicago: University of Chicago Press, 2008.

Dinerstein, Joel. "Modernism." In *Companion to American Cultural History*, edited by Karen Halttunen, 198–213. Hoboken, NJ: Wiley-Blackwell, 2008.

Dochuk, Darren. *Anointed with Oil: How Christianity and Crude Made Modern America*. New York: Basic Books, 2019.

"Dodges Sue Henry Ford: Stockholders Object to 'Reckless Expenditures' of Company's Assets." *New York Times*, November 3, 1916.

Dodge v. Ford Motor Company, 204 Mich 459, 170 N.W. 668 (Mich. 1919).

Douglas, Ann. *The Feminization of American Culture*. New York: MacMillan, 1996.

Douglas, Mary. *Purity and Danger: An Analysis of Concepts of Pollution and Taboo*. New York: Routledge Classics, 1966/2002.

Dowland, Seth. *Family Values and the Rise of the New Christian Right*. Philadelphia: University of Pennsylvania Press, 2015.

Drake, Janine Giordano. "Between Religion and Politics: The Working Class Religious Religious Left, 1880–1920." PhD diss., University of Illinois at Urbana-Champaign, 2014.

Durkheim, Émile. *The Elementary Forms of Religious Life*, 1912. New York: Oxford University Press, 2001.

"Edison Re-Creates His Electric Lamp as Hoover Leads in Tribute to Him." *New York Times*, October 22, 1929.

"Edison Young Again as He Relives Past in Old Laboratory." *New York Times*, October 21, 1929.

Ellis, Isaiah. "Infrastructure Between Anthropology, Geography, and Religious Studies." In *Routledge Handbook of Religion and Cities*, edited by Katie Day and Elise M. Edwards, 94–104. New York: Routledge, 2021.

———. "Infrastructure and American Religion: Sites, Methods, and Theories for a Changing Field," *Religious Compass* 17, no. 8 (2023), https://doi.org/10.1111/rec3.12475.

Emerson, Harrington. *Efficiency as a Basis for Operation and Wages*, 1908. New York: The Engineering Magazine, 1911.

Emerson, Ralph Waldo. "Race." In *English Traits*, 50–78. Boston: Phillips, Sampson, and Company, 1856.

Emmet, Boris. "Profit Sharing in the United States." 1916, *Bulletin of the United States Bureau of Labor Statistics* 208.13, US Department of Labor, Bureau of Labor Statistics. Washington, DC: Government Printing Office, 1917.

Esch, Elizabeth. *The Color Line and the Assembly Line: Managing Race in the Ford Empire*. Berkeley: University of California Press, 2018.

Evans, Christopher H. *The Social Gospel in American Religion: A History*. New York: New York University Press, 2017.

Factory Facts from Ford. Detroit, MI: Ford Motor Company, 1915.

Fair Lane: The House and Gardens. Ford Motor Company, Archives Bulletin, no. 3. Dearborn, MI: Henry Ford Archives, 1955.

Feld, Rose C. "Salvage Teaches Ford Ship-Breaking Trade: Methods for Converting Waste to Usefulness Employed in Auto Plant Apply to Vessels Bought from Government." *New York Times*, October 4, 1925.

Fessenden, Tracy. *Culture and Redemption: Religion, the Secular, and American Literature*. Princeton, NJ: Princeton University Press, 2007.

———. "The Problem of the Postsecular." *American Literary History* 26, no. 1 (2014): 154–167.

Firestone, Harvey S., with Samuel Crowther. *Men and Rubber: The Story of Business*. Garden City, NY: Doubleday, Page, and Company, 1926.

"First Payment of Ford's Bonus to Come Friday: Profit Sharing Scheme Goes in Effect Four Days Earlier." *Detroit Free Press*, January 10, 1914.

Fisher, Harriet White. *A Woman's World Tour in a Motor*. Philadelphia, PA: J. B. Lippincott Company, 1911.

Fitzgerald, F. Scott. *Cruise of the Rolling Junk*. Bloomfield Hills, MI: Bruccoli Clark, 1924/1974.

Fones-Wolf, Elizabeth. "Creating a Favorable Business Climate: Corporations and Radio Broadcasting, 1934 to 1954." *Business History Review* 73, no. 2 (1999): 221–255.

Foote, Christopher L., Warren C. Whately, and Gavin Wright. "Arbitraging a Discriminatory Labor Market: Black Workers at the Ford Motor Company, 1918–1947." *Journal of Labor Economics* 21, no. 3 (2003): 493–532.

Ford, Henry, in collaboration with Samuel Crowther. *My Life and Work*. Garden City, NY: Doubleday, Page, and Company, 1923.

———. *Today and Tomorrow*. Garden City, NY: Doubleday, Page, and Company, 1926.

———. *Edison as I Know Him*. New York: Cosmopolitan Book Corporation, 1930.

Ford, Henry. *The Case Against the Little White Slaver*. Vol. 1–4. Detroit, MI: Henry Ford, 1916.

———. *To You*. Cork, Ireland: Henry Ford and Son, Ltd., 1917.

———. *The International Jew: The World's Foremost Problem*. Dearborn, MI: Dearborn Publishing Company, 1920.

———. *Jewish Activities in the United States: Volume II of The International Jew, A Second Selection of Articles from The Dearborn Independent*. Dearborn, MI: Dearborn Publishing Company, 1921.

———. *Ford Ideals: Being a Selection from "Mr. Ford's Page" in The Dearborn Independent*. Dearborn, MI: Dearborn Publishing Company, 1922.

———. "Motto." *Ford News* 5, no. 19 (August 1, 1925).

———. "Mass Production." *Encyclopedia Britannica*. 13th ed. New York: Encyclopedia Britannica Company, 1926.

———. "Machinery, the New Messiah: An Authorized Interview," with Fay Leone Faurote. *The Forum* (March 1928): 359–364.

———. "Why I Believe in Progress." *The Forum*, November 1928.

———. *My Philosophy of Industry: An Authorized Interview*, with Fay Leone Faurote. New York: Coward-McCann, 1929.

———. "Looking Under the Human Hood, As Told to William L. Stidger." *Rotarian* (January 1947): 9–11.

Ford, Henry and Clara Ford. *"Good Morning": After a Sleep of Twenty-Five Years, Old-Fashioned Dancing Is Being Revived*. Dearborn, MI: Dearborn Publishing Company, 1926.

The Ford Industries: Facts About The Ford Motor Company and Its Subsidiaries. Detroit, MI: Ford Motor Company, 1925.

"Ford Believes in Reincarnation But Not So Sure World Is Hollow." *Fort Myers Press*, March 29, 1931.

"Ford Cars Grow Up by Magic Methods." *New York Sun*, March 1, 1914.

"Ford Decries Debt of Credit System." *New York Times*, June 20, 1926.

"Ford Denies Recklessness: Asserts He Cannot Hurt the Dodges Without Injuring Himself." *New York Times*, November 5, 1916.

"Ford, Denying Hate, Lays War to Jews: Asserts They Are the Greatest Victims of a Money System that Is All Wrong." *New York Times*, October 29, 1922.

"The Ford Excursion." *Eugene Morning Register*. December 4, 1915.

"Ford Explains Attacks: Caused by Statements Made to Him by Jews on Peace Trip." *New York Times*, December 5, 1921.

"Ford's Eyes Opened By Man Who Stole." *The Labor World*, January 31, 1914.

"Ford Factory Again Stormed by Job Seekers." *Detroit Free Press*, January 8, 1914.

"Ford Is an Anarchist." *Chicago Tribune*, June 23, 1916.

"Ford Loses Dodge Bros. Profit Suit: Judge Hosmer Orders 50 Per Cent Division of $59,000,000 Dividends." *Detroit News*, October 31, 1917.

"Ford Makes Reply to Suit Brought by Dodge Brothers." *Detroit News*, November 4, 1916.

"Ford Must Declare $19,275,385 Dividend: Court Decides Money Spent for Blast Furnace Project Must Be Refunded to Stockholders." *New York Times*, December 6, 1914.

"Ford Plan Not for His Rivals." *New York Sun*, January 9, 1914.

"Ford Says He Reads Bible Every Day: Keeps One in Every Room of His House—Likens Religion to Electricity." *New York Times*, July 25, 1929.

"The Ford School." *The Ford Man* 1, no. 3 (November 1917): 1.

"Ford Sociological Work: The Making of Men and Homes." *Ford Times*, November 1941.

"Ford Thinks Ancients Had Planes and Radios: Declares Intelligent People Have Inhabited this Globe 'Millions of Times.'" *New York Times*, December 18, 1928.

"Ford's Plans Are Held Up: Court Decides to Hear Further Testimony in Dodge Brothers' Suit." *New York Times*, December 10, 1916.

Foucault, Michel. "Theatrum Philosophicum." *Critique* 282 (1970): 885–908.

———. "What Is Enlightenment?" In *The Foucault Reader*, edited by Paul Rabinow, 32–50. New York: Pantheon Books, 1984.

Frazer, James George. *The Golden Bough: A Study in Magic and Religion*, 1922. New York: Cosimo Classics, 2009.

Frederick, Marla. *Colored Television: American Religion Gone Global*. Stanford, CA: Stanford University Press, 2015.

Freeberg, Ernest. *The Age of Edison: Electric Light and the Invention of Modern America*. New York: Penguin Press, 2013.

Furniss, William E. *Automobile Tourist Book of New England: Throwing Light on Inexpensive Tours On and Off the Beaten Path*. Boston: Tourist Publication Company, 1912.

Gabler, Neal. *Walt Disney: The Triumph of the American Imagination*. New York: Vintage Books, 2006.

"Gale Fails to Halt Rush to Ford Plant: Policemen Injured When Attempting to Check Mob of Ten Thousand." *Washington Times*, January 12, 1914.

Galey, John. "Industrialist in the Wilderness: Henry Ford's Amazon Venture." *Journal of Interamerican Studies and World Affairs* 21, no. 2 (1979): 261–289.

"A Gift and a Challenge." *Atlanta Constitution*, January 26, 1930.

Gitelman, Lisa. *Scripts, Grooves, and Writing Machines: Representing Technology in the Edison Era*. Stanford, CA: Stanford University Press, 2000.

Grainger, Brett Malcolm. *Church in the Wild: Evangelicals in Antebellum America*. Cambridge, MA: Harvard University Press, 2019.

Gramsci, Antonio. "Americanism and Fordism." In *Selections from the Prison Notebooks*, edited and translated by Quintin Hoare and Geoffrey Nowell Smith, 277–320. New York: International Publishers Company, 1971.

———. *Prison Notebooks, vol. 1*. New York: Columbia University Press, 1975/1992.

Grandin, Greg. *Fordlandia: The Rise and Fall of Henry Ford's Forgotten Jungle City*. New York: Metropolitan Books, 2009.

Grant, Jane. "The Serious Opinions of Charlie Chaplin." *New York Times*, September 18, 1921.

Gregory, Brad S. *The Unintended Reformation: How a Religious Revolution Secularized Society*. Cambridge, MA: Harvard University Press, 2012.

Grem, Darren. *The Blessings of Business: How Corporations Shaped Conservative Christianity*. New York: Oxford University Press, 2016.

Grieveson, Lee. "The Work of Film in the Age of Fordist Mechanization." *Cinema Journal* 51, no. 3 (2012): 25–51.

———. "Visualizing Industrial Citizenship." In *Learning with the Lights Off: Educational Film in the United States*, edited by Devin Orgeron, Marsha Orgeron, and Dan Streible, 107–123. New York: Oxford University Press, 2012.

Griffith, R. Marie. *Born Again Bodies: Flesh and Spirit in American Christianity*. Berkeley: University of California Press, 2004.

Guidebook for the Edison Institute Museum and Greenfield Village. Dearborn, MI: Ford Motor Company, 1937.

Haber, Samuel. *Efficiency and Uplift: Scientific Management in the Progressive Era, 1880–1920*. Chicago: University of Chicago Press, 1964.

Hackett, David G. *That Religion in Which All Men Agree: Freemasonry in American Culture*. Berkele: University of California Press, 2014.

Hall, David D. *Lived Religion in America: Toward a History of Practice*. Princeton, NJ: Princeton University Press, 1997.

Halttunen, Karen. *Confidence Men and Painted Women: A Study of Middle-Class Culture in America, 1830–1870*. New Haven, CT: Yale University Press, 1986.

Hamilton, J. G. DeRulhac. "The Ford Museum." *American Historical Review* 36, no. 4 (1931): 772–775.

Hammond, Sarah Ruth. *God's Businessmen: Entrepreneurial Evangelicals in Depression and War*. Chicago: University of Chicago Press, 2017.

Hangen, Tona J. *Redeeming the Dial: Radio, Religion, and Popular Culture in America*. Chapel Hill: University of North Carolina Press, 2003.

Harding, Susan Friend. *The Book of Jerry Falwell: Fundamentalist Language and Politics*. Princeton, NJ: Princeton University Press, 2000.

Heitmann, John. *The Automobile and American Life*. Jefferson, NC: McFarland & Company, 2009.

Helpful Hints and Advice to Employes, to help them grasp the opportunities which are presented to them by the Ford Profit-Sharing Plan. Detroit, MI: Ford Motor Company, 1915.

Henderson, M. Todd. "Everything Old in New Again: Lessons from *Dodge v. Ford Motor Company*." John M. Olin Program in Law and Economics Working Paper No. 373, 2007.

Henkin, David. *The Postal Age: The Emergence of Modern Communications in Nineteenth-Century America*. Chicago: University of Chicago Press, 2006.

"Henry Ford Beaten in $60,000,000 Suit: Dodge Brothers Win Action for Disbursement of Dividends—Ford to Appeal." *New York Times*, November 1, 1917.

"Henry Ford Discusses the Wage." *State Service: The New York State Magazine* (February 1919): 34.

"Henry Ford Explains Why He Gives Away $10,000,000: Declares That He Is Dividing Profits with His Employees." *New York Times*, January 11, 1914.

"Henry Ford Expounds Mass Production: Calls It the Focussing of the Principles of Power, Economy, Continuity, and Speed—Tells Why Accurate Machines Produce the Highest Standard of Quality—Says System Develops the Worker." *New York Times*, September 19, 1926.

"Henry Ford on Stand: Says His Plans, If Executed, Would Revolutionize Automobile Trade." *New York Times*, November 15, 1916.

Hightower, Brendel. "The Henry Ford Ends Maker Faire Detroit, Pauses Civil War Reenactment." *Detroit Free Press*, January 19, 2022.

"Hint that Ford Seeks Bridge Splits County." *New York Times*, April 2, 1931.

"Hoover, Ford, and Nation Honor Edison." *Daily Republican*, October 22, 1929.

Hoover, Stewart and Lynn Schofield Clark. *Practicing Religion in the Age of the Media: Explorations in Media, Religion and Culture*. New York: Columbia University Press, 2002.

Horkheimer, Max and Theodore Adorno. *Dialectic of Enlightenment: Philosophical Fragments*. Stanford, CA: Stanford University Press, 1987/2002.

Hounshell, David. *From the American System to Mass Production, 1800–1932: The Development of Manufacturing Technology in the United States*. Baltimore, MD: Johns Hopkins University Press, 1984.

Hughes, Thomas. *American Genesis: A Century of Invention and Technological Enthusiasm, 1870–1970*. Chicago: University of Chicago Press, 1989.

Hulsether, Lucia. "Buying into the Dream: The Religion of Racial Capitalism in Coca-Cola's World." *Public Culture* 30, no. 3 (2018): 483–508.

———. *Capitalist Humanitarianism*. Durham, NC: Duke University Press, 2023.

Hurd, Elizabeth Shakman. *Beyond Religious Freedom: The New Global Politics of Religion*. Princeton, NJ: Princeton University Press, 2015.

Hutchison, William R. *Errand to the World: American Protestant Thought and Foreign Missions*. Chicago: University of Chicago Press, 1987.

Huxley, Aldous. *Brave New World*, 1932. New York: Perennial Classics, 1998.

"'I Believe in Reincarnation'—Henry Ford: But My Dutch Mother Is in My Orderly Workshops." *Milwaukee Sentinel*, August 5, 1928.

Jacobson, Matthew Frye. *Special Sorrows: The Diasporic Imagination of Irish, Polish, and Jewish Immigrants in the United States*. Cambridge, MA: Harvard University Press, 1995.

———. *Whiteness of a Different Color: European Immigrants and the Alchemy of Race*. Cambridge, MA: Harvard University Press, 1999.

———. *Barbarian Virtues: The United States Encounters Foreign Peoples at Home and Abroad, 1876–1917*. New York: Hill and Wang, 2000.

Jakobsen, Janet R. and Ann Pellegrini. *Love the Sin: Sexual Regulation and the Limits of Religious Tolerance*. New York: New York University Press, 2003.

Jakobsen, Janet R. and Ann Pellegrini, eds. *Secularisms*. Durham, NC: Duke University Press, 2008.

"Job Seekers Riot, Storm Ford Plant." *New York Times*, January 12, 1914.

Johnson, Paul Christopher and Mary Keller. "The Work of Possession(s)." *Culture and Society* 7, no. 2 (2006): 111–122.

Johnson, Paul E. *A Shopkeepers Millennium: Society and Revivals in Rochester, New York, 1815–1837*. New York: Hill and Wang, 1978/2004.

Johnson, Timothy. *Rhetoric, Inc: Ford's Filmmaking and the Rise of Corporatism*. College Park: Pennsylvania State University Press, 2021.

Kaell, Hillary. *Christian Globalism at Home: Child Sponsorship in the United States*. Princeton, NJ: Princeton University Press, 2020.

Kaempffert, Waldemar. "The Mussolini of Highland Park." *New York Times*, January 8, 1928.

Kaloyanides, Alexandra. *Baptizing Burma: Religious Change in the Last Buddhist Kingdom*. New York: Columbia University Press, 2023.

Kanigel, Robert. *The One Best Way: Frederick Winslow Taylor and the Enigma of Efficiency*. New York: Viking, 1997.

Kirk, Nicole. *Wanamaker's Temple: The Business of Religion in an Iconic Department Store*. New York: New York University Press, 2018.

Klassen, Pamela. *Spirits of Protestantism: Medicine, Healing, and Liberal Christianity*. Berkeley: University of California Press, 2011.

————. "Comments by Pamela Klassen." *Religion and Society: Advances in Research* 5 (2014): 231–235.

————. *The Story of Radio Mind: A Missionary's Journal on Indigenous Land.* Chicago: University of Chicago Press, 2018.

Koenig, Sarah. *Providence and the Invention of American History.* New Haven, CT: Yale University Press, 2021.

Koslofsky, Craig. "Offshoring the Invisible World?: American Ghosts, Witches, and Demons in the Early Enlightenment." *Critical Research on Religion* 9, no. 2 (2021): 126–141.

Kozloff, Max. "The Rivera Frescoes of Modern Industry at The Detroit Institute of Arts: Proletarian Art Under Capitalist Patronage." *Artforum* 12 (1973): 58–63.

Krivulskaya, Suzanna. "Disgraced: How Sex Scandals Transformed American Protestantism, 1832–1988." PhD diss., University of Notre Dame, 2019.

————. "On Protestant Sex Scandals." *New Books Network,* October 3, 2022, www.newbooksnetwork.com.

Kruse, Kevin. *One Nation Under God: How Corporate American Invented Christian America.* New York: Basic Books, 2015.

Lacey, Robert. *Ford: The Men and the Machine.* Boston: Little, Brown, and Company, 1986.

Lape, Esther Everett. "Putting America into Your Village." *Ladies' Home Journal,* November 1919.

Latour, Bruno. *We Have Never Been Modern,* translated by Catherine Porter. Cambridge, MA: Harvard University Press, 1993.

————. *Reassembling the Social: An Introduction to Actor-Network Theory.* New York: Oxford University Press, 2005.

————. "Fetish-Factish." *Material Religion* 7.1 (2011): 42–49.

Law, John. "Notes on the Theory of the Actor Network: Ordering, Strategy, and Heterogeneity." *Systems Practice* 5 (1992): 379–393.

Lears, T. J. Jackson. "The Concept of Cultural Hegemony: Problems and Possibilities." *American Historical Review* 90, no. 3 (June 1985): 567–593.

Lee, Albert. *Henry Ford and the Jews.* New York: Stein and Day, 1980.

Lee, John R. "The So-Called Profit Sharing System in the Ford Plant." *Annals of the American Academy of Political and Social Science* 65, no. 1 (May 1916): 297–310.

Levene, Nancy. "Sources of History: Myth and Image." *Journal of the American Academy of Religion* 74, no. 1 (2006): 79–101.

————. "Courses and Canons in the Study of Religion (With Continual Reference to Jonathan Z. Smith)." *Journal of the American Academy of Religion* 80, no. 4 (2012): 998–1024.

Lewchuk, Wayne A. "Men and Monotony: Fraternalism as Managerial Strategy at the Ford Motor Company." *Journal of Economic History* 53, no. 4 (1993): 824–856.

Lewis, David L. *The Public Image of Henry Ford: An American Folk Hero and His Company.* Detroit, MI: Wayne State University Press, 1976.

Lindsey, Rachel. *A Communion of Shadows: Religion and Photography in Nineteenth-Century America*. Chapel Hill: University of North Carolina Press, 2017.

Link, Stefan. "Rethinking the Ford-Nazi Connection." *Bulletin of the GHI* 49 (2011): 135–150.

———. *Forging a Global Fordism: Nazi Germany, Soviet Russia, and the Contest over the Industrial Order*. Princeton, NJ: Princeton University Press, 2020.

Lochner, Louis. "The Neutral Conference for Continuous Mediation at Stockholm." *Advocate for Peace* 78, no. 8 (1916): 238–241.

Lofton, Kathryn. "The Methodology of the Modernists: Process in American Protestantism." *Church History* 75, no. 2 (2006): 374–402.

———. "The Perpetual Primitive in African American Religious Historiography." In *The New Black Gods: Arthur Huff Fauset and the Study of African American Religions*, edited by Edward E. Curtis IV and Danielle Brune Sigler, 171–191. Bloomington: Indiana University Press, 2009.

———. *Oprah: The Gospel of an Icon*. Berkeley: University of California Press, 2011.

———. "Religious History as Religious Studies." *Religion* 42, no. 3 (2012): 383–394.

———. "Commonly Modern: Rethinking the Modernist-Fundamentalist Controversies." *Church History* 83, no. 1 (2014): 137–144.

———. "Corporation as Sect: Religious Freedom in the United States." *The Immanent Frame* Social Science Research Council, January 20, 2015, https://tif.ssrc.org.

———. *Consuming Religion*. Chicago: University of Chicago Press, 2017.

———. "Why Religion Is Hard for Historians (and How It Can Be Easier)." *Modern American History* 3, no. 1 (2020): 69–86.

Logan, Dana W. "The Lean Closet: Asceticism in Postindustrial Consumer Culture." *Journal of the American Academy of Religion* 85, no. 3 (2017): 600–628.

———. *Awkward Rituals: Sensations of Governance in Protestant America*. Chicago: University of Chicago Press, 2022.

Loizides, Georgios Paris. "'Making Men' at Ford: Ethnicity, Race, and Americanization During the Progressive Period." *Michigan Sociological Review* 21 (2007): 109–148.

———. "Families and Gender Relations at Ford." *Michigan Sociological Review* 25 (2011): 19–32.

Long, Carolyn Morrow. *Spiritual Merchants: Religion, Magic, and Commerce*. Knoxville: University of Tennessee Press, 2001.

Lorusso, James Dennis. *Spirituality, Corporate Culture, and American Business: The Neoliberal Ethic and the Spirit of Global Capital*. New York: Bloomsbury Academic, 2017.

Luker, Ralph E. *The Social Gospel in Black and White: American Racial Reform, 1885–1912*. Chapel Hill: University of North Carolina Press, 1991.

Macey, Jonathan R. "A Close Read of an Excellent Commentary on *Dodge v. Ford*." *Virginia Law and Business Review* 3, no. 1 (2008): 177–190.

Maffly-Kipp, Laurie F. "Tracking the Sincere Believer: 'Authentic' Religion and the Enduring Legacy of Joseph Smith Jr." In *Joseph Smith Jr.: Reappraisals after Two*

Centuries, edited by Reid L. Neilson and Terryl L. Givens, 175–188. New York: Oxford University Press, 2009.

Mahmood, Saba. *Religious Difference in a Secular Age: A Minority Report*. Princeton, NJ: Princeton University Press, 2015.

Maier, Charles S. "Between Taylorism and Technocracy: European Ideologies and the Vision of Industrial Productivity in the 1920s." *Journal of Contemporary History* 5, no. 2 (1970): 27–61.

"The Making of New Americans." *Ford Times* (November 1916): 150–152.

Marquis, Samuel S. *The Man: A Talk by Samuel S. Marquis, On the Scientific Self-Management of a One Man-Power Three-Cylinder Engine*. Dearborn, MI: Ford Motor Company, 1912.

———. *Henry Ford: An Interpretation*. Boston: Little, Brown, and Company, 1923.

Martin, Lerone A. *Preaching on Wax: The Phonograph and the Shaping of Modern African American Religion*. New York: New York University Press, 2014.

Marx, Leo. *The Machine in the Garden: Technology and the Pastoral Ideal in America*. New York: Oxford University Press, 1964.

Masuzawa, Tomoko. *The Invention of World Religions: Or, How European Universalism Was Preserved in the Language of Pluralism*. Chicago: University of Chicago Press, 2005.

May, Martha. "The Historical Problem of the Family Wage: The Ford Motor Company and the Five Dollar Day." *Feminist Studies* 8, no. 2 (1982): 399–424.

McAlister, Melani. *The Kingdom of God Has No Borders: A Global History of American Evangelicals*. New York: Oxford University Press, 2018.

McCormick, Anne O'Hare. "Ford Seeks a New Balance for Industry." *New York Times*, May 29, 1932.

———. "Ford Scans the Current Tides: Opposed to Spread of Government and Unconvinced by New Social Concepts." *New York Times*, October 21, 1934.

McCrary, Charles. *Sincerely Held: American Secularism and Its Believers*. Chicago: University of Chicago Press, 2022.

McCrossen, Alexis. *Holy Day, Holiday: The American Sunday*. Ithaca, NY: Cornell University Press, 2001.

———. *Marking Modern Times: A History of Clocks, Watches, and Other Timekeepers in American Life*. Chicago: University of Chicago Press, 2013.

McGarry, Molly. *Ghosts of Futures Past: Spiritualism and the Culture Politics of Nineteenth-Century America*. Berkeley: University of California Press, 2012.

McLaughlin, Levi, Aike P. Rots, Jolyon Baraka Thomas, and Chika Watanabe. "Why Scholars of Religion Must Investigate the Corporate Form." *Journal of the American Academy of Religion* 88, no. 3 (2020): 693–725.

"Men Rioting for Work at Ford Motor Plant." *Atlanta Constitution*, January 13, 1914.

Meyer, Birgit. "An Author Meets Her Critics: Around Birgit Meyer's 'Mediation and the Genesis of Presence: Toward a Material Approach to Religion.'" *Religion and Society: Advances in Research* 5 (2014): 205–254.

Meyer, Stephen, III. *The Five Dollar Day: Labor Management and Social Control in the Ford Motor Company, 1908–1921*. Albany: State University of New York Press, 1981.

Mihm, Stephen. *A Nation of Counterfeiters: Capitalists, Con Men, and the Making of the United States*. Cambridge, MA: Harvard University Press, 2007.

Minkema, Kenneth P., Catherine A. Brekus, and Harry S. Stout. "Agitations, Convulsions, Leaping, and Loud Talking: The 'Experiences of Sarah Pierpont Edwards.'" *William and Mary Quarterly* 78, no. 3 (2021): 491–536.

Mirola, William A. *Redeeming Time: Protestantism and Chicago's Eight-Hour Movement, 1866–1912*. Urbana: University of Illinois Press, 2015.

"Mob Seeks Work at Ford Factory." *Washington Times*, January 7, 1914.

Modern, John Lardas. *Secularism in Antebellum America*. Chicago: University of Chicago Press, 2011.

———. "An Impossible Film: Commentary on *Blood*." *Syndicate Theology*, February 25, 2015, https://syndicate.network.

———. "Introduction: Duty Now For The Future," Forum: Monstrosity. *J19: The Journal of Nineteenth-Century Americanists* 3, no. 1 (2015): 165–173.

———. *Neuromatic: Or, A Particular History of Religion and the Brain*. Chicago: University of Chicago Press, 2021.

Moodie, Deonnie. "Retail Religion: Hinduism for a Neoliberal Age." *Journal of the American Academy of Religion* 89, no. 3 (2021): 863–884.

Moreton, Bethany. "The Soul of Neoliberalism." *Social Text* 25, no. 3 (2007): 103–125.

———. *To Serve God and Wal-Mart: The Making of Christian Free Enterprise*. Cambridge, MA: Harvard University Press, 2009.

Morgan, David. *Visual Piety: A History and Theory of Popular Religious Images*. Berkeley: University of California Press, 1998.

———. *The Lure of Images: A History of Religion and Visual Media in America*. New York: Routledge, 2007.

"A Motto Wrought in Education." *Ford Times* (April 1916): 406–409.

"Mr. Henry Ford and Reincarnation." *The Scotsman*, November 19, 1928.

Nadis, Fred. *Wonder Shows: Performing Science, Magic, and Religion in America*. New Brunswick, NJ: Rutgers University Press, 2005.

"Nation Roused Against Motor Killings: Secretary Hoover's Conference Will Suggest Many Ways to Check the Alarming Increase in Automobile Fatalities—Studying Huge Problem." *New York Times*, November 23, 1924.

Nevins, Allan and Ernest Hill. *Ford: The Times, the Man, the Company*. New York: Charles Scribner's Sons, 1954.

———. *Ford: Expansion and Challenge, 1915–1933*. New York: Charles Scribner's Sons, 1957.

———. *Ford: Decline and Rebirth, 1933–1962*. New York: Charles Scribner's Sons, 1962.

"Newspaper Specials." *Wall Street Journal*, November 4, 1916.

Nolan, Mary. *Visions of Modernity: American Business and the Modernization of Germany*. New York: Oxford University Press, 1994.

Norwood, Stephen. *Strikebreaking and Intimidation: Mercenaries and Masculinity in Twentieth-Century America*. Chapel Hill: University of North Carolina Press, 2002.

Numbers, Ronald L. *The Creationists: From Scientific Creationism to Intelligent Design*. Expanded edition. Cambridge, MA: Harvard University Press, 2006.

Nye, David E. *America's Assembly Line*. Cambridge, MA: MIT Press, 2013.

———. *Henry Ford: Ignorant Idealist*. Port Washington, NY: Kennikat Press, 1979.

O'Dell, Cary. "Light's Golden Jubilee (October 21, 1929)," pp. 1–2, National Registry Addition, National Recording Preservation Board, 2005, Motion Picture, Broadcast and Recording Division, Library of Congress, www.loc.gov.

Ogden, Emily. *Credulity: A Cultural History of US Mesmerism*. Chicago: University of Chicago Press, 2018.

"Old Plows Added to Ford's Relics." *New York Times*, February 21, 1926.

Orsi, Robert A. *History and Presence*. Cambridge, MA: Belknap Press of Harvard University Press, 2016.

Paine, Crispin. "Sacred Waste." *Material Religion* 10, no. 2 (2014): 241–243.

Painter, Nell Irvin. *The History of White People*. New York: W.W. Norton, 2010.

"Peace Hysteria." *Wichita Daily Eagle*, December 1, 1915.

Pellegrini, Ann. "Feeling Secular." *Women and Performance* 19, no. 2 (2009): 205–218.

———. "'Signaling Through the Flames': Hell House Performance and Structures of Religious Feeling." *American Quarterly* 59, no. 3 (2007): 911–935.

Peters, John Durham. "Calendar, Clock, Tower." In *Deus in Machina: Religion, Technology, and the Things in Between*, edited by Jeremy Stolow, 25–42. New York: Fordham University Press, 2012.

Peterson, Joyce Shaw. *American Automobile Workers, 1900–1933*. Albany: State University of New York Press, 1987.

Pietsch, Brendan M. *Dispensational Modernism*. New York: Oxford University Press, 2015.

Porterfield, Amanda, Darren Grem, and John Corrigan, eds. *The Business Turn in American Religious History*. New York: Oxford University Press, 2017.

Porterfield, Amanda. *Corporate Spirit: Religion and the Rise of the Modern Corporation*. New York: Oxford University Press, 2018.

Promey, Sally M. "Hearts and Stones: Material Transformations and the Stuff of Christian Practice in the United States." In *American Christianities: A History of Dominance and Diversity*, edited by Catherine A. Brekus and W. Clark Gilpin, 183–213. Chapel Hill: University of North Carolina Press, 2011.

———. "Material Establishment and Public Display." Mediations. *MAVCOR Journal* (2016), doi: 10.22332/con.med.2016.2.

———. *Spiritual Spectacles: Visions and Image in Mid-Nineteenth-Century Shakerism*. Bloomington: Indiana University Press, 1993.

Puar, Jasbir. "'I would rather be a cyborg than a goddess': Becoming-Intersectional in Assemblage Theory." *philoSOPHIA* 2, no. 1 (2012): 49–66.

———. *Terrorist Assemblages: Homonationalism in Queer Times*. Durham, NC: Duke University Press, 2017.

Putney, Clifford. *Muscular Christianity: Manhood and Sports in Protestant America, 1880–1920*. Cambridge, MA: Harvard University Press, 2001.

Quigel, James P. Jr. "The Business of Selling Efficiency: Harrington Emerson and the Emerson Efficiency Engineers, 1900–1930." PhD diss., Pennsylvania State University, 1992.

Rabin, Shari. "'Let Us Endeavor to Count Them Up': The Nineteenth-Century Origins of American Jewish Demography." *American Jewish History* 101, no. 4 (2017): 419–440.

Rees, Jonathan. *Refrigeration Nation: A History of Ice, Appliances, and Enterprise in America*. Baltimore, MD: Johns Hopkins University Press, 2013.

"Reincarnationist." *Time Magazine* 12, no. 10 (September 3, 1928): 42.

"The Resplendent Ford Gift." *Detroit Free Press*, January 6, 1914.

Richards, William C. *The Last Billionaire: Henry Ford*. New York: Charles Scribner's Sons, 1948.

Rivett, Sarah. *The Science of the Soul in Colonial New England*. Chapel Hill: University of North Carolina Press, 2012.

Rivett, Sarah and Lerone Martin. "A Closing Conversation." Conversation. *MAVCOR Journal* 6, no. 3 (2022), doi: 10.22332/mav.convo.2022.6.

Roediger, David. "Americanism and Fordism—American Style: Kate Richards O'Hare's 'Has Henry Ford made good?'" *Labor History* 29.2 (1988): 241–252.

———. *The Wages of Whiteness: Race and the Making of the American Working Class*. New York: Verso, 1991.

———. *Working Toward Whiteness: How America's Immigrants Became White, The Strange Journey from Ellis Island to the Suburbs*. New York: Basic Books, 2005.

Roediger, David and Elizabeth D. Esch. *The Production of Difference: Race and the Management of Labor in U.S. History*. New York: Oxford University Press, 2012.

Rose, Sarah Frances. *No Right to Be Idle: The Invention of Disability, 1840s–1930s*. Chapel Hill: University of North Carolina Press, 2017.

Rosen, Christine. *Preaching Eugenics: Religious Leaders and the American Eugenics Movement*. New York: Oxford University Press, 2004.

Rotman, Andy. "Brandism vs. Bazaarism: Mediating Divinity in Banaras." In *Rethinking Markets in Modern India*, edited by Ajay Gandhi, Barbara Harriss-White, Douglas E. Haynes, and Sebastian Schwecke, 234–268. New York: Cambridge University Press, 2020.

Rudnyckyj, Daromir. *Spiritual Economies: Islam, Globalization, and the Afterlife of Development*. Ithaca, NY: Cornell University Press, 2010.

Russell, Jack. "The Coming of the Line: The Ford Highland Park Plant, 1910–1914." *Radical America* 12 (May–June 1978): 29–45.

"Sacrifices to the Modern Moloch." *St. Louis Star*, November 6, 1923.

Salvatore, Nick. *Eugene V. Debs: Citizen and Socialist*. Champaign, IL: Illini Books, 1984.

Sandage, Scott A. *Born Losers: A History of Failure in America*. Cambridge, MA: Harvard University Press, 2005.

Satter, Beryl. *Each Mind a Kingdom: American Women, Sexual Purity, and the New Thought Movement, 1875–1920*. Berkeley: University of California Press, 2001.

Schivelbusch, Wolfgang. *Disenchanted Night: The Industrialization of Light in the Nineteenth Century*. Berkeley: University of California Press, 1995.

Schmidt, Leigh E. *Consumer Rites: The Buying and Selling of American Holidays*. Princeton, NJ: Princeton University Press, 1995.

Schneider, Rebecca. *Performing Remains: Art and War in Times of Theatrical Reenactment*. New York: Routledge, 2011.

Schopen, Gregory. "Relic." In *Critical Terms for Religious Studies*, edited by Mark C. Taylor, 256–268. Chicago: University of Chicago Press, 1998.

Scott, David and Charles Hirschkind, eds. *Powers of the Secular Modern: Talal Asad and His Interlocutors*. Stanford, CA: Stanford University Press, 2006.

Seal, Andrew. "The Almost Century of the Common Man: Democracy, Heroism, and the United States, 1880–1960." PhD diss., Yale University, 2016.

Seales, Chad E. *Religion Around Bono: Evangelical Enchantment and Neoliberal Capitalism*. University Park: Pennsylvania State University Press, 2019.

"Second I.W.W. in Highland Park: Last Lot of Speakers Brand Matilda Rabinowitz Preacher of Anarchy." *Detroit Free Press*, May 2, 1913.

Sehat, David. *The Myth of American Religious Freedom*. New York: Oxford University Press, 2010.

Selden, Charles A. "Ford Renews the Past for a Machine Age." *New York Times*, September 16, 1928.

Sewell, William H., Jr. "The Temporalities of Capitalism." *Socio-Economic Review* (2008): 517–537.

Simonds, William. *Henry Ford and Greenfield Village*. New York: Frederick A. Stokes Company, 1938.

Sinclair, Upton. *The Flivver King: A Story of Ford-America*. Detroit, MI: United Automobile Workers of America, 1937.

Singh, Devin. "Debt Cancellation as Sovereign Crisis Management." *Cosmologics Magazine*, January 18, 2016. Accessed January 21, 2016, http://cosmologicsmagazine.com.

Skaff, Sheila. "Ambivalence and Cigarettes: Egon Erwin Kisch's 'At Ford's Place in Detroit,' with a Translation of the Text." *Michigan Historical Review* 29, no. 1 (2003): 119–131.

Slack, Jennifer Daryl and J. Macgregor Wise. *Culture and Technology: A Primer*. New York: Peter Lang, 2014.

Slomovitz, Philip. "Ford and Two Jewish Dailies." *Detroit Jewish Chronicle*, January 4, 1924.

Smith, A. M. "A Magnate and a Mystic Meet: Henry Ford and Inayat Khan Find Common Spiritual Ground." *Detroit News*, February 7, 1926.

Smith, Jonathan Z. *Imagining Religion*. Chicago: University of Chicago Press, 1982.

———. *To Take Place: Toward Theory in Ritual*. Chicago: University of Chicago Press, 1987.

————. *Things Said/Things Done: The Relations of Myth and Ritual*. Charlotte: University of North Carolina at Charlotte, 2009.

Smith, Orlando J. *A Short View of Great Questions*. New York: The Brandur Company, 1899.

Smith, Terry. *Making the Modern: Industry, Art, and Design in America*. Chicago: University of Chicago Press, 1993.

Smoodin, Eric Loren. *Disney Discourse: Producing the Magic Kingdom*. New York: Routledge, 1994.

Snow, Richard. *I Invented the Modern Age: The Rise of Henry Ford*. New York: Scribner, 2013.

"Socialism Urged by Woman in Auto: Highland Park Police Interrupt Noonday Address to Employes at Ford Plant." *Detroit Free Press*, April 25, 1913.

Sorensen, Charles, with Samuel T. Williamson. *My Forty Years with Ford*. 1956. Detroit, MI: Wayne State University Press, 2006.

Statement by Henry Ford: Regarding Charges Against Jews Made in His Publication, The Dearborn Independent, *and a Series of Pamphlets Entitled "The International Jew," Together with an Explanatory Statement by Louis Marshall, President of The American Jewish Committee, and His Reply to Mr. Ford*. New York: American Jewish Committee, 1927.

Staudenmaier, John M. "Two Technocrats, Two Rouges: Henry Ford and Diego Rivera as Contrasting Artists." *Polhem* 10 (1992): 2–28.

Stengs, Irene. "Sacred Waste." *Material Religion* 10, no. 2 (2014): 235–238.

Stewart, Phillip W. *Henry Ford's Moving Picture Show: An Investigator's Guide to the Films Produced by the Ford Motor Company, Volume One, 1914–1920*. Crestview, FL: PMS Press, 2011.

Stewart, Thomas A., Alex Taylor, III, Peter Petre, and Brent Schlender. "The Businessman of the Century." *Fortune*, November 22, 1999.

Stidger, William L. "Henry Ford Says: Put the Bible Back in School." *Good Housekeeping*, April 1924.

Stolow, Jeremy and Birgit Meyer. "Enlightening Religion: Light and Darkness in Religious Knowledge and Knowledge about Religion." *Critical Research on Religion* 9, no. 2 (2021): 119–125.

Stout, Harry S. *The Divine Dramatist: George Whitefield and the Rise of Modern Evangelicalism*. Grand Rapids, MI: William B. Eerdmans, 1991.

Stout, Lynn A. "Why We Should Stop Teaching *Dodge v. Ford*." *Virginia Law and Business Review* 3, no. 1 (2008): 163–176.

Street, Julian. *Abroad at Home: American Ramblings, Observations, and Adventures of Julian Street, with Pictorial Sidelights by Wallace Morgan*. New York: Century Co., 1914.

"Suburb, Goes on Record for Prohibition: Highland Park Council Favors 'Dry' Law in Resolution." *Detroit Free Press*, October 10, 1916.

Sullivan, Winnifred F. *The Impossibility of Religious Freedom*. Princeton, NJ: Princeton University Press, 2005.

———. *Church, State, Corporation: Construing Religion in U.S. Law.* Chicago: University of Chicago Press, 2020.

Supp-Montgomerie, Jenna. *When the Medium Was the Mission: The Atlantic Telegraph and the Religious Origins of Network Culture.* New York: New York University Press, 2021.

Susman, Warren. *Culture as History: The Transformation of American Society in the Twentieth Century.* New York: Pantheon Books, 1984.

Sutton, Matthew Avery. *Aimee Semple McPherson and the Resurrection of Christian America.* Cambridge, MA: Harvard University Press, 2007.

Swigger, Jessie. *"History Is Bunk": Assembling the Past at Henry Ford's Greenfield Village.* Amherst: University of Massachusetts Press, 2014.

Tarbell, Ida. *All in the Day's Work: An Autobiography.* New York: Macmillan, 1939.

———. "The Golden Rule in Business: Experiments in Justice." *American Magazine* 79, no. 3 (March 1915): 29–34, 79–83.

———. *New Ideals in Business.* New York: Macmillan, 1917.

Taussig, Michael. *Mimesis and Alterity: A Particular History of the Senses.* New York: Routledge, 1993.

Taves, Ann. *Fits, Trances, and Visions: Experiencing Religion and Explaining Experience from Wesley to James.* Princeton, NJ: Princeton University Press, 1999.

Taylor, Charles. *A Secular Age.* Cambridge, MA: Belknap Press, 2007.

Taylor, Diana. *The Archive and the Repertoire: Performing Cultural Memory in the Americas.* Durham, NC: Duke University Press, 2003.

Taylor, Frederick Winslow. *The Principles of Scientific Management*, 1911. New York: Harper and Brothers, 1913.

"Ten Thousand Men in Rush to Share Ford's Profit Plan." *Washington Times*, January 6, 1914.

Thompson, Clarence Bertrand, ed. *Scientific Management: A Collection of the More Significant Articles Describing the Taylor System of Management.* Cambridge, MA: Harvard University Press, 1914.

Thompson, E. P. "Time, Work-Discipline and Industrial Capitalism." *Past and Present* 38 (1967): 56–97.

Tomlin, T. J. *A Divinity for All Persuasions: Almanacs and Early American Religious Life.* New York: Oxford University Press, 2014.

Tone, Andrea. *The Business of Benevolence: Industrial Paternalism in Progressive America.* Ithaca, NY: Cornell University Press, 1997.

"Transcription of *Dodge v. Ford*: Cross-Examination of Henry Ford." *Dodge v. Ford Motor Co.: Primary Source Material, Chapman Law Review* 17, no. 2 (2014): 523–574.

Trine, Ralph Waldo. *The Power That Wins: Henry Ford and Ralph Waldo Trine in an Intimate Talk on Life—the Inner Things—the Things of the Mind and Spirit—and the Inner Powers and Forces that Make for Achievement.* Indianapolis, IN: Bobbs-Merrill, 1928.

Tye, Larry. *The Father of Spin: Edward L. Bernays and the Birth of Public Relations.* New York: Henry Holt, 1998.

Unkovic, Mary Caitlin. "When *Dodge v. Ford* Meets Ben & Jerry's: Reconciling 100 Years of Bad Precedent with the Reality of Modern Business." PhD diss., University of California, Berkeley, 2020.

"The Unveiling of Henry Ford." *The Nation* 109, no. 2821 (26 July 1919): 102.

Upward, Geoffrey C. *A Home for Our Heritage: The Building and Growth of Greenfield Village and Henry Ford Museum, 1929–1979*. Dearborn, MI: Henry Ford Museum Press, 1979.

Vaca, Daniel. *Evangelicals Incorporated: Books and the Business of Religion in America*. Cambridge, MA: Harvard University Press, 2019.

———. "Reimagining the Gospel of Efficiency." *American Religion* 5, no. 1 (2023): 33–65.

Valeri, Mark. *Heavenly Merchandize: How Religion Shaped Commerce in Puritan America*. Princeton, NJ: Princeton University Press, 2010.

Van de Water, Frederick F. *The Family Flivvers to Frisco*. New York: D. Appleton and Company, 1927.

Van Vlissingen, Arthur, Jr. "History Is Bunk." *American Legion Magazine*, October 1932.

———. "The Idea Behind Greenfield." *American Legion Magazine*, October 1932.

Vargas, Michael J. "*Dodge v. Ford Motor Co.* at 100: The Enduring Legacy of Corporate Law's Most Controversial Case." *Business Lawyer* 75, no. 3 (2020): 2103–2122.

Vargas, Zaragosa. "Life and Community in the 'Wonderful City of the Magic Motor': Mexican Immigrants in 1920s Detroit." *Michigan Historical Review* 15, no. 1 (1989): 45–68.

Viereck, George Sylvester. "Henry Ford Discusses Education, Food, and Other Things: Wizard of Motor Industry Foresees Aviation Progress." *Waco News-Tribune*, August 5, 1928.

———. "'I Have Lived Before'—Ford: 'And I Shall Live Again,' Says Car Magnate." *San Antonio Light*, September 6, 1928.

Wacker, Grant. *Heaven Below: Early Pentecostals and American Culture*. Cambridge, MA: Harvard University Press, 2001.

Walker, David. "The Humbug in American Religion: Ritual Theories of Nineteenth-Century Spiritualism." *Religion and American Culture* 23, no. 1 (2013): 30–74.

———. *Railroading Religion: Mormons, Tourists, and the Corporate Spirit of the West*. Chapel Hill: University of North Carolina Press, 2019.

Walton, Jonathan L. *Watch This! The Ethics and Aesthetics of Black Televangelism*. New York: New York University Press, 2009.

Warner, Michael. "Secularism." In *Keywords for American Cultural Studies*, edited by Bruce Burgett and Glenn Hendler, 220–224. New York: New York University Press, 2007.

———. *Varieties of Secularism in a Secular Age*. Cambridge, MA: Harvard University Press, 2010.

Watts, Steven. *The Magic Kingdom: Walt Disney and the American Way of Life*. Columbia: University of Missouri Press, 1997.

——. *The People's Tycoon: Henry Ford and the American Century*. New York: Alfred A. Knopf, 2005.

——. "Walt Disney: Art and Politics in the American Century." *Journal of American History* 82, no. 1 (1995): 84–110.

Weber, Max. *The Protestant Ethic and the Spirit of Capitalism*, 1930. New York: Routledge, 2007.

——. *The Sociology of Religion*, 1922. Boston, MA: Beacon Press, 1993.

Weiner, Isaac. "The Corporately Produced Conscience: Emergency Contraception and the Politics of Workplace Accommodations." *Journal of the American Academy of Religion* 85, no. 1 (2017): 31–63.

Weisenfeld, Judith. *New World A-Coming: Black Religion and Racial Identity during the Great Migration*. New York: New York University Press, 2017.

Weiss, Robert P. "Corporate Security at Ford Motor Company: From the Great War to the Cold War." In *Corporate Security in the Twenty-First Century: Theory and Practice in International Perspective*, edited by Kevin Walby and Randy Lippert, 17–38. New York: Palgrave Macmillan, 2014.

Wenger, Tisa. *Religious Freedom: The Contested History of an American Ideal*. Chapel Hill: University of North Carolina Press, 2017.

——. *We Have a Religion: The 1920s Pueblo Indian Dance Controversy and American Religious Freedom*. Chapel Hill: University of North Carolina Press, 2009.

"What Our Schools Are Doing." *Herald* 7, no. 7 (April 26, 1940).

Wheeler, Charles N. "Fight to Disarm His Life Work, Henry Ford Vows: Pacifist Sees Submarines as Powerful Agency to Destroy All Armament." *Chicago Tribune*, May 25, 1916.

White, Christopher G. *Unsettled Minds: Psychology and the American Search for Spiritual Assurance, 1830–1940*. Berkeley: University of California Press, 2008.

Wianecki, Shannon. "When America's Titans of Industry and Innovation Went Road-Tripping Together." *Smithsonian Magazine*, January 26, 2016.

Wiard, Jennifer. "The Gospel of Efficiency: Billy Sunday's Revival Bureaucracy and Evangelicalism in the Progressive Era." *Church History* 85, no. 3 (2016): 587–616.

Wik, Reynold M. *Henry Ford and Grass-Roots America*. Ann Arbor: University of Michigan Press, 1972.

Wilkins, Mira and Frank Ernest Hill. *American Business Abroad: Ford on Six Continents*. Detroit, MI: Wayne State University Press, 1964.

Winston, Diane. *Red Hot and Righteous: The Urban Religion of The Salvation Army*. Cambridge, MA: Harvard University Press, 1999.

Wisehart, M. K. "Henry Ford Talks to Young Men." *American Magazine*, August 1929.

Woeste, Victoria Saker. *Henry Ford's War on the Jews and the Legal Battle Against Hate Speech*. Stanford, CA: Stanford University Press, 2012.

Wolfe, Joel. *Autos and Progress: The Brazilian Search for Modernity*. New York: Oxford University Press, 2010.

Wood, Joseph S. "'Build, Therefore, Your Own World': The New England Village as Settlement Ideal." *Annals of the Association of American Geographers* 81, no. 1 (1991): 32–50.

———. *The New England Village*. Baltimore, MD: Johns Hopkins University Press, 1997.

Woolf, S. J. "Mr. Ford Shows His Museum: Amid Relics of the Past the Inventor Talks of Human Life Today and in the Future." *New York Times*, January 12, 1936.

"Workers Get $10,000,000 of Ford's Profits This Year—25,000 Employees Will Share." *Labor Journal*, January 16, 1914.

Wortham-Galvin, B. D. "The Fabrication of Place in America: The Fictions and Traditions of the New England Village." *Traditional Dwellings and Settlements Review* 21, no. 2 (2010): 21–34.

"Would Curb Foundation." *Baltimore Sun*, January 23, 1915.

Young, James C. "Ford Scans the Economic Scene." *New York Times*, May 24, 1931.

Zito, Angela. "Religion Is Media." *The Revealer: A Review of Religion and Media*. New York University, April 16, 2008. http://therevealer.org.

INDEX

abundance, 32, 38, 45–46, 49, 52, 66–67, 83, 151, 156–60, 165, 213n77

accumulation, x, 6, 71, 86, 89, 110, 143, 153, 165–67; and mass production, 36–41, 45, 50, 54. *See also* extraction; primitivism

Addams, Jane, 106, 144

Addison Ford Cemetery, 167

Adorno, Theodore, 169, 177, 202n46

advertising, 44, 75, 123, 125, 205n15, 220n10. *See also* Ford media; marketing; promotion; publicity; slogans

affiliation, 2, 5, 7, 9, 11–12, 59–60, 72

affinities, 13, 24, 107, 190n5, 201n39

Africa, 89, 141

Alanis, Juan P., 173

Albanese, Catherine, 43, 213n78

alcohol, 62, 70, 72, 75, 81, 90, 109, 168. *See also* Prohibition

Allen, James, 48

Amazon Awakens, The (film), 160

America First Committee, xi

American exceptionalism, 10, 102, 124, 143

American history, xv, 9–12, 129, 139, 142–43, 151–58, 160–68, 177–78. *See also* Edison Institute of Technology (Henry Ford Museum); past-making

American industry, 11, 15, 24, 57–58, 79, 145, 152, 168, 171–72

Americanization, 72, 89–94, 99–104, 125–30, 140, 150, 153–56, 195n25, 197n13, 211n66. *See also* assimilation

American Peace Society, 105–6, 108

American Railway Union, 27

American religious history, 3, 6, 25, 59, 95, 172, 192n10, 194n24, 207n34, 221n16. *See also* Catholicism; Christianity; Episcopalianism; evangelicalism

American Telegraph and Telephone Company, 144

Anglo-American heritage, 41, 98–100, 126, 161–62, 164–65, 211n66, 220n9

anthropology, 2–3, 39–40, 75, 141, 147–48

antisemitism, xii, 6, 9–10, 35, 42–43, 88–89, 99, 102, 153, 174–76, 214n7, 214n10, 216n30; and supersessionary secularism, 108–10, 116–18, 122–23, 130–38. *See also* Jewish communities; orientalism; racism

Arnold, Horace Lucien, 31, 103, 197n11

artifacts. *See* relics

Asad, Talal, 59–60, 192n10

assemblages, xii–xiii, xvii–xviii, 6, 21, 170, 174, 178, 190n5, 227n8; and mass production, 24, 26, 31, 41, 50, 52–53; and rite-to-work, 64, 75, 89, 95; and supersessionary secularism, 131, 136–37

assembly lines, x, xii, 18, 167, 176, 178, 197n11; and mass production, 24–26, 30–32, 34, 36, 45, 51–53; and rite-to-work, 61, 64, 90–91, 98; and supersessionary secularism, 103, 109, 125

assimilation, 73, 89–91, 100, 132, 178. *See also* Americanization

Atkinson, William Walker, 39, 48, 200n37

authority, 3–4, 6, 10–14, 28, 40, 113, 134, 148–49, 161, 174, 195n4, 198n31; and rite-to-work, 58, 96, 100–101. *See also* hegemony

ABOUT THE AUTHOR

KATI CURTS is Assistant Professor of Religious Studies at Sewanee: The University of the South.